Famous Gamblers, Poker History, and Texas Stories

Johnny Hughes

iUniverse, Inc.
Bloomington

Famous Gamblers, Poker History, and Texas Stories

iUniverse books may be ordered through booksellers or by contacting:

iUniverse
1663 Liberty Drive
Bloomington, IN 47403
www.iuniverse.com
1-800-Authors (1-800-288-4677)

ISBN: 978-1-4759-4215-6 (sc)
ISBN: 978-1-4759-4216-3 (hc)
ISBN: 978-1-4759-4217-0 (e)

Printed in the United States of America

iUniverse rev. date: 8/9/2012

This book is dedicated to Philip Conneller of London, my editor at *Bluff Europe Magazine*. Thanks Philip for your wisdom, skills, and great ideas. Thanks to all the fine people at *Bluff Magazine* and *Bluff Europe Magazine*, the two largest and most successful poker magazines in the world.

✻   ✻   ✻

This book is also dedicated to Sasha, Donna, and Cindy.

Cover Photo: Wyatt Earp
Web Site: www.JohnnyHughes.com
Previous Book: *Texas Poker Wisdom*

Reviews of this Book

This book should be required reading for all young players who have no knowledge of the history of poker. This is the true story of some of the men who laid the foundation for the phenomenon that poker has become worldwide. What a trip down memory lane for an old retired poker player. They say that history is written by the survivors. Thanks to Johnny Hughes for preserving the history of the beginnings of the phenomenon that poker has become.....**Crandell Addington**, Poker Hall of Fame. Record holder, most final table appearances at the main event of the World Series of Poker.

I remember most of the guys you talk about. You have a great writing style, very credible, and entertaining. Those were dangerous times. Sailor Roberts and I were living in San Angelo when Red Harris (who should have been a comedian) came to town to fade a dice game. We shot our way out of the Longhorn Motel when the hijackers tried to get us. Red was a little crazy, not at all like Curly who was always cool. Curly was the consummate gambler, probably the only one I ever knew. He had no leaks that me or anyone else knew of. Almost everyone has bad habits of some sort (including me) but as you said, Curly was always after the cash! Almost all of the guys are gone. A great book!......**Doyle Brunson**, Poker Hall of Fame. Winner of 11 World Series of Poker events, author of *The Godfather of Poker.*

He's known 'em all, and played with most of them. He's seen everything, and done most of it. He's as good a writer as he is a player. When it comes to poker tales of Texas and Vegas, old and new, Johnny Hughes is your man.... **Anthony Holden**, London, author of *Big Deal* and thirty-four other books, President of the International Federation of Poker.

I consider Johnny Hughes to be the William Manchester of poker historians. With Hughes, no task is too burdensome, and no detail is trivial. He flat out gets the story. His writings are a testament to an era of Americana that is as rich as the Old West. Scrolling the pages of a Hughes narrative is like lighting a lantern into the darkest recess of poker's subculture. He brings the legends of the past and present to life and often provides the very best portrait of these unique real-life characters of anyone on record.....**Nolan Dalla**, Las Vegas, Media Director. World Series of Poker. *Card Player* writer. Dalla co-authored the best-selling biography, *One of a Kind: The Rise and Fall of Stuey "the Kid" Ungar.*

Johnny Hughes is a historian of poker, and his tales are those from a wilder West, from the days before poker became a staple of Las Vegas' glittering casinos and was then homogenized into television programming for America's viewing public. His tales are as hard-scrabble as the West Texas Panhandle, filled with the romance of the game, the travels, and the ethics of Texas road gamblers a breed that was once prolific but is now fast receding. If you are a poker player, then this is your history. It was raw, even a bit dangerous, and a player needed to have his wits about him all the time. The early players, those Texas road gamblers, never realized they were the fathers of today's game, and they wouldn't have cared. They were poker players. But their story folds neatly into yours, a seamless journey from dusty West Texas to today's card rooms and casinos. Hughes tells these tales without adornment, in a simple, direct style. And that is just the way they should be told. There is no need to embellish; the characters and situations speak for themselves. And they are speaking directly to you. Pick up his book and read it....**Lou Krieger**, best selling author , radio host.

Johnny Hughes was embedded with hustlers, pimps, crooked sheriffs, and outlaws decades before most modern professional poker players were even born. Hughes is a captivating raconteur and avid historian of Texas gambling folklore. He seeks out characters cast off to the farthest fringes of society, then brings them to life with a unique flair and panache.

Johnny Hughes paints word pictures with witty, lush brush strokes reminiscent of Tom Wolfe, but with the bold brevity of Ernest Hemingway.

He is nonpareil when it comes to capturing the old-school, rough and tumble days of Texas road gamblers...**Paul "Dr. Pauly" McGuire**, *Bluff Magazine, Tao of Poker*, author of *Jack Tripper Stole My Dog.*

Reading through the deep history from Johnny Hughes is only paralleled by listening to him tell those stories in real time. His knowledge of poker and its key players both before and after anyone knew who they were is like putting yourself in the same room as it all unfolded. My favorite time in history that Johnny expertly portrays is when the mob ruled Las Vegas and Sinatra fooled around in it. We are ever excited to have Johnny visit us on air and count the days until he returns. If you want to know the real stories behind poker before it was on TV and the Internet, the works of Johnny Hughes are required course materials!....**Ryan Sayer**, Chief Operations Officer at *OnTilt Radio* LLC and Host of *The Ryan Sayer Show*

Johnny Hughes is not only a poker-history buff, as am I, but he lived much of it! I always glean something new from his stories and anecdotes. Keep 'em coming, Johnny!...**Blair Rodman**, WSOP bracelet winner and co-author of *Kill Phil.*

One of my all-time favorite poker writers. Johnny Hughes poker stories are a national treasure. As one of the few remaining genuine, old-school poker writers, Johnny's hilarious stories and colorful characters are timeless classics and deserve to be placed on the same shelf with all the classics of the genre. This is the stuff of history. Of where our beloved game came from. And it rightfully deserves to be shared...**Iggy a.k.a. Ignatius J. Reilly**, the Blogfather of Poker. *GuinnessandPoker.com*, Cincinnati, Ohio

A roller coaster ride of how road gamblers from Texas made their cash, played their game, along with the characters you would most likely meet along the way. This book is told with authenticity and the knowledge that only a true road gambler could possess. If you love poker, then you have just stumbled upon a book that you will love. If you don't play poker, you will surely have an enormous appetite for the great game after a few page turns. A highly enjoyable read. **Anthony Kelly**, Editor, *Player Europe Magazine*, Dublin, Ireland.

Johnny Hughes is a gifted writer from the Lone Star State. A Ph.D. A poker raconteur. Author of novels, short stories, essays and poems. The man is an enigma. Cryptic, dark. Irrefutably unique. Elliptical euphemism and metaphor are his tools. Gambling folklore and parables abound. All told with a twinkle in the eye and one finger on the trigger...**Tetusu**, *Bet-the-Pot.com*, London, England.

In a new-school industry full of new-school faces, an old-school voice reminds us of where we came from. I'm a Johnny Hughes fan; he has survived the wars of the felt and shared that experience with the world. Now, he gives us another gift; the benefits of his experience combined with a unique story-telling style that allows us to live that life through his narrative Hughes has a truly unique style there is no real substitute for actually having been there. Johnny has been there. Johnny's been everywhere. Johnny bore witness to a lot of the Texas road goings on that the rest of us only hear about Hughes' style is hard (like the man had to be. These men remember a time when poker wasn't so much glitz and glamour, when the cameras and lights were substituted for by cigars and guns. It feels a lot safer the way we do it now, but you have to admit there is a romance to what once was...**Gary Wise**, Toronto, Poker Historian. *Bluff Magazine*, ESPN.com.

Introduction

This book is written for everyone to read: men and women of all ages, all over the world.

Being too lazy to work, and too nervous to steal, I became a West Texas road gambler and have sixty years of personal gambling history. I've been robbed by shotguns, pistols, and a lawyer with a ball-point pen. I shot over the head of a robber, and walked three different people out of my gambling joint with my barking iron.

I was the original manager of the Joe Ely Band. One night while I was dancing at the legendary Cotton Club, I pulled my pistol out of my boot and fired a couple of rounds into the ceiling. Being West Texas, no one called the law. I'm old enough now to share the secrets.

These critically-acclaimed, humorous, revealing memories are added to decades of research in this collection of stories and articles previously published in magazines, mostly in Europe.

Benny Binion got me a job for Bill Boyd playing poker on house money at the Golden Nugget in Las Vegas when I was 21. I caught Titanic Thompson's son and a few more cheating, back in Texas. Both Johnny Moss and bridge-great, Oswald Jacoby have staked me to play bridge. We lost. I was arrested by the local police and the legendary Texas Rangers with some of the early gambling legends, and future World Series of Poker champions. I played poker half a century ago with Jack "Treetop" Straus, Bill Smith, Johnny Moss, Amarillo Slim, and Sailor Roberts, all world champs. Many of the outrageous characters in this book were people I knew very well.

This book tells a well-researched, history of America through the fascinating, larger-than-life, biographies of colorful gamblers, some famous, some not so famous: Wyatt Earp, Doc Holliday, Bat Masterson, Poker Alice, Lottie Deno, Nick the Greek, Johnny Moss, Benny Binion, Titanic Thompson, Arnold Rothstein, Minnesota Fats, Amarillo Slim, and so much more. The book has biography, cultural history, short stories, memoir, wisdom, philosophy, and psychology. This book is written to inform, but more importantly, to entertain! As Benny Binion said, "I'll tell you the truth, but I won't tell you everything."

Many of these articles and stories have appeared in *Bluff Magazine, Bluff Europe Magazine, Player Ireland, TexasMonthly.com, Pokerati.com, TwoPlusTwo Poker Forum,* and *The Texas Observer.* One of these stories won Honorable Mention in the 2012 *Texas Observer* short story contest. A second volume of these collected writings will be available on all Amazons in a few months.

Contents

I.
Famous Gamblers
in American History

When the Most Famous Gambler in the World was a Shill:
Nick the Greek versus Johnny Moss

*The next best thing to gambling and winning is gambling and losing...*Nick the Greek

*A wise gamester ought to take the dice even as they fall, and pay down quietly rather than grumble at his luck....*Sophocles

*The exhilaration of this form of economic existence is beyond my power to describe...*Nick the Greek

In 1949, Nicholas "Nick the Greek" Dandalos (often spelled Dandolos) had his worst poker year ever. It was to haunt him for life, and lead to one murder. First the Greek played Johnny Moss and *others,* off and on for five months and lost a lot of his bankroll. I'd guess two million.

Some poker writers question whether this match took place, whether it was for high stakes, but more importantly they decided that Johnny Moss was a broke and a liar, because they did not do their research homework. My Nick the Greek information comes from court records.

Poker writers use the same absolutely silly line: *Benny Binion put two million in the trunk and took his family to Las Vegas in 1946 because his sheriff lost.* Benny was worth tens of millions, and had all types of legal troubles, local, state, and federal, in Texas, where he said he spent thirty million on legal fees before going to prison for tax evasion.

Poker writers say Nick the Greek had won $50 million, and broke all the gamblers on the east coast, including the number one Mob boss, Arnold Rothstein. Rothstein usually seemed to beat Nick the Greek at everything, especially poker, but the enormous stakes there, and the Ray Ryan match would indicate Johnny and the Greek were playing as high as Johnny said they were.

Johnny Moss came to Las Vegas in 1949 to play the Greek heads up, and I think Benny Binion was staking Moss. Both Moss and the Greek were known for four and five day poker sessions, but I think they slept almost a normal amount after the first session. They played at the Las Vegas Club controlled by Benny. Moss called it the Horseshoe in his bio, wrongly. The Horseshoe came into being in 1951. I've played a lot of stake money, as did Johnny Moss. I believe Binion put up the bankroll to play the Greek on the halves. It Moss had of lost, he'd owe Benny half. At the end of the match, Nick the Greek uttered some of the most famous words in poker, "Mr. Moss. I have to let you go."

Nick the Greek, Johnny Moss, and I have all been arrested a few times for vagrancy with plenty of money on us, because that is the way they tagged gamblers. Benny Binion had been exiled to Las Vegas, a town of 18,000 people. He put bankroll in the Westerner, then the Las Vegas Club, and then the Eldorado, which became the Horseshoe. In a gambling license hearing for the Horseshoe, the front man was Dr. Monte Bernstein. Benny was listed as the restaurant manager. Dr. Bernstein said, "No person connected to the Eldorado Corporation has a criminal record." The mayor and the lieutenant governor spoke for Benny's man. The newspaper did not report Binion had been arrested a few times, including two homicides.

For certain, from *court records*. In 1949, the Greek played heads up low-ball and gin rummy outdoors at the Thunderbird five days off and on with high-roller, friend of movie stars, oil man, and big-time bookie, Ray Ryan. Ryan won $550,000 off the Greek, which would validate them playing that high. Benny Binion took the Greek to pay off the money. Benny said the Greek had in his hotel room closet under some old clothes. Nick the Greek had gambled with the biggest Mob bosses including Al Capone. The Greek was protected by Capone. It was said he could walk the streets of Chicago safely with $100,000 in his pocket. The Greek, from Chicago, and a Mob darling, went to the biggest Chicago bosses, Tony Accardo and Sam Giancana (Frank Sinatra's pal) and said he had been cheated. He did not think Benny Binion and Johnny Moss had cheated him, only Ray Ryan. Moss' win was a cool score. Ryan's win was a hot score.

They asked psychotic killer, Marshall Caifano, to get the money back. Initially, he asked for a $1,000,000 from Ray Ryan to avenge the poker cheating. Ryan had a confederate with binoculars signal the Greek's hand with a short-wave device. In low ball, a flash of a face card color will do it if you are "sending them over." This was depicted in the James Bond movie, *Goldfinger*, right before Ray Ryan was murdered for this long grudge in 1978. Along the way, Nick the Greek and Marshall Caifano tried to kidnap and extort Ray Ryan inside the Desert Inn in Las Vegas, and were arrested for it in 1963. Nick the Greek turned state's evidence, and was an un-indicted co-conspirator. Poker writers question why the Las Vegas newspaper didn't tell of this or the truth about Nick the Greek. A survey showed that Nick the Greek was a major tourist attraction in Las Vegas, ahead of the Hoover Dam. The myth was that he shot dice at the Strip casinos, read Mob casinos, each day. He was the most famous gambler in the world, and he was shilling, pretending to gamble, using house money to draw a crowd after 1949, and the loss of his last real bankroll to Binion, Moss, and Ray Ryan.

When crusading editor, Hank Greenspun, attacked Senator McCarran in the early fifties, the Strip casinos pulled all their advertising. Greenspun sued, but they worked it out. Sid Wyman and Moe Dalitz told him the Senator controlled casino licenses. The Las Vegas newspapers never told the truth about Nick the Greek or many things.

Benjamin "Bugsy" Siegel was the first of four legendary "Outside Men" sent to Las Vegas. This was the one person that scared everybody, and that could represent the Mafia back home, in all the casinos they controlled. He first came in 1941. In a top Mob meeting at the Hotel Nacional in 1946 in Havana, Cuba, it was voted Siegel had to be killed, but not in Las Vegas. An agreement was made not to do things to hurt the city's image. Meyer Lansky and Moe Dalitz owned a piece of the Cuban hotel, and were at the meeting along with Tony Accardo and others.

With Chicago the central control over Las Vegas, Tony Accardo and Gus Giancana, over the years, sent in three other "Outside Men." All were the *worst* possible choices. Johnny Roselli first, then Marshall Caifano in the 1950s and early 1960s, and Tony Spilotro in the late 1970s. All three made it into the Black List of excluded persons, meaning they were not supposed to enter a casino. James McManus wrote that Frank Sinatra was also on the blacklist of excluded persons, and that Johnny Moss was "banned" from Las Vegas for twenty years! Wrong again. Sinatra sang in casinos, often. McManus never heard of the Rat Pack.

All three later "Outside Men", Roselli, Caifano, and Spilotro were involved in card-cheating scandals. Roselli, was a very smooth operator, the CIA contact for attempts to kill Fidel Castro, and a roving Mafia charmer, and enforcer. He went to prison for the Friars Club gin rummy cheating scandals that bilked America's show business elite out of millions over many months. The Mob bosses killed Siegel, Roselli, and Spilotro. Caifano lived to be 92. Again, it was a peep hole, and short-wave, electronic signals that Roselli used at the Frairs Club. They were "sending them over."

If you described Caifano and Spilotro, the same adjectives apply, *chillingly*. Five foot five, volatile, morbidly sociopathic, sadistic killers with a long list of gruesome hits behind them, which included torture. They were totally self-centered, and generated great fear when they entered a room. They brought the worst publicity and law enforcement heat to Las Vegas.

When I went to Las Vegas in 1960, I played some auction bridge at Binion's Horseshoe, and was being cheated by three people. When I told them I could not pay, a booming voice behind me said I didn't have to. I had met Benny Binion. Curly Cavitt said I could use his name to "vouch" me in. Benny sent me across the street to the Golden Nugget. I went to work shilling in the poker room for Bill Boyd, another Poker Hall of Famer. I saw Nick the Greek shooting dice at the Sands, and was told he was just a shill for the Mob joints, which meant all the Strip hotels, and that he owed them a ton of money.

Big Sid Wyman, Poker Hall of Fame member, was an old-time bootlegger and dice man. He owned a very big piece of and ran casinos great. He dealt with the press, unions, celebrities, high rollers, movie stars, and junkets. He'd gone from having a piece of varied joints to a big piece of the Dunes in 1962. In 1968, Sid Wyman brought Johnny Moss to the Dunes to spread the poker in front of the main show room. According to Poker Hall of Fame member, Crandell Addington, "The early World Series of Poker was a minnow compared to the Dunes/Aladdin game. It was the biggest cash poker game of all time." One of the owner/partners, another big-time poker player, and the biggest sucker of all time, Major Riddle, was in the game. He was only one of the big producers in the poker game. He lost so much, he lost control of the Dunes. Doyle Brunson, an excellent authority on these matters, said that Major Riddle lost $40 million dollars over time playing poker.

Johnny Moss had won and lost $5 million dollars in Las Vegas in his first five years. His winnings came at poker and golf. His losses at dice and horses. He stayed away a few years, because as Doyle Brunson wrote, Gus Greenbaum thought he was cheated with a peep hole. But I wonder if it was Gus Greenbaum, but I always believe Doyle.

Also, Johnny Moss' mentor, backer, and protector, Benny Binion, was in prison. But maybe Moss just said Gus because Marshall Caifano had already murdered Gus Greenbaum and his wife in Phoenix in 1958. He nearly cut their heads off. If it wasn't for his admiration and long devotion to Nick the Greek, you would not have thought Caifano was a very sentimental guy.

Johnny Moss was not broke as some poker historians assume. The *most* reliable poker historians, bar none, are Poker Hall of Fame members Crandell Addington and Doyle Brunson, author of the classic, *The Godfather of Poker*. Crandell said the poker game that was Johnny Moss' and Sid Wyman's game at the Dunes, and later the Aladdin included Poker Hall of Fame members Johnny Moss, Sid Wyman, Crandell Addington, Doyle Brunson, Felton "Corky" McCorquodale, Joe Bernstein, Red Winn, Puggy Pearson, and Sarge Ferris. These nine Poker Hall of Famers had plenty of producers around. Edwin "Bud" Shrake, was at the Dunes in 1970 to interview Johnny Moss for *Sports Illustrated*, a real interview. Pots of $250,000 were common place, and they didn't make the poker history books. Sid Wyman did a whole lot of the talking in the earlier interview with Nick the Greek in a three-part series in *Collier's* in 1954. He did a lot of the talking in the interview with Johnny Moss. Moss was steadily shipping that money back to Texas when poker writers say he was broke, and before he won eight bracelets, and lots of other poker tournaments. Age, sleep, money, and gambling didn't mean the same to Johnny Moss as it does to guessing writers. Doyle Brunson said, "Johnny was more fearless, more dedicated and more consumed by poker than anyone I've ever known."

My cousin, Bill Stapp, worked the dice and blackjack at several Mob joints. He spent decades in Las Vegas and tells great stories. He was at the Sands when the Rat Pack was there. He was at the Dunes when the popular Sid Wyman was in charge. Everyone loved Sid: employees, the press, big time poker players, other casino bosses, movie stars, the whales he brought in on junkets, and the afternoon Minsky's follies girls, an early topless act.

The legendary poker player Joe Bernstein, who was playing in the game with Titanic Thompson and Arnold Rothstein that resulted in Rothstein's later death, bit one of the dealers that was my cousin's friend. Joe crapped out at the dice table. Bernstein always tried to cheat at gin. Puggy Pearson pissed on a dealer once. Can you imagine having all the living, early Poker Hall of Fame members around the Dunes? They played high! There was no cheating because they all knew all about cheating, and the Mob owned the joint.

When *Sports Illustrated* and one of Texas' best authors, Bud Shrake, interviewed Johnny Moss and several of the Hall of Famers in 1970, it was a Sid Wyman production that didn't even mention that Johnny Moss had been voted the champion down at Binion's Horseshoe. Johnny Moss didn't mention also that he built two luxury apartment houses in Odessa, Texas in 1967, which his family, whom I have talked with, operated until 2008. Moss was never broke after the late fifties. When Shrake interviewed Titanic Thompson, he told of the golf match with Johnny Moss in Lubbock in 1938, where he pulled the cups up, and Moss sent his caddy around to put them back down. Moss told the same identical story to Shrake. When I first met Johnny Moss in 1959, he was the most famous gambler in Texas. Titanic Thompson also told of traveling with Nick the Greek, and them cheating together in California, by signaling and with marked cards. Who knows?

The three-part *Collier's* series in 1954 about Nick the Greek was where much of the information, true, and erroneous, originated. The story was written by crusading newspaper publisher, Hank Greenspun. The story was managed by Sid Wyman, one of the most important men in the history of poker. Greenspun started out as Bugsy Siegel's publicity man, and had a piece of the Sands for awhile. The article was all one big pitch for the Mob joints, the Strip casinos, and it quoted Sid Wyman a lot. Of course the Greek didn't mention Benny Binion who was in prison, Ray Ryan, or Johnny Moss. He told old stories about his alleged triumphs back east. Most of it was malarkey trying to get folks to shoot dice. According to Benny Binion, the Greek lived in a little comped $10 a day room, and often took the bus. Benny tried and tried to get the Greek to tell him where he got his money. The Greek had been up and back broke seventy-three times. Most of that article was trying to get folks to believe that you could win at dice. No one has yet, but lots of folks are still trying. Its like slot machines. No slot has ever lost in the long run. No person has ever beat them in the long run. Keep trying, *you* may be the very first!

Some writers use Jon Bradshaw's *Fast Company,* and its interview with Johnny Moss to indicate he was a broke. I don't think the interview even took place. This was in 1974. It says Moss was old, tired, and broke, and had not played in the World Series of Poker main event in 1973. He was second. The publisher added an introduction to Bradshaw's book that said he was a liar, that he told whoppers, inserted himself into the story, and had zero credibility. He kept referring to Adrian Dolly Doyle. Bradshaw kept changing his own fictional biography. I think he was there at the World Series, but do not believe his dialog with Johnny Moss, or anyone else. The silly biography of Nick the Greek, written in child-like dialog has the Greek and John F. Kennedy riding around Las Vegas, and agreeing to eliminate the Mob. The Greek says all the joints had juice-dice and electro magnets. My cousin, Bill Stapp, said cheating at dice from either side of the table was extremely rare, since it is not needed, and the gaming agents could take away the gambling license. Any physical device, like the juice, would be evidence.

The biggest myth is that the biggest games had a lot of cheating. When you get the Hall of Fame talent at a poker table, everyone knows all about cheating. The reason Johnny Moss was selected to host the biggest poker game of all time was that the most famous road gamblers in America would gather, and they knew it would be a square game. He was known as a bird dog, skilled at catching the cheats. Who would cheat all these Hall of Famers in a Mob joint?

In 1960, the year I saw him shilling, the Greek was still very mad about the 1949 cheating, but obviously not mad at Benny Binion or Johnny Moss, just Ray Ryan. And Marshall Caifano was a lot madder. Again, he asked for money for the Greek from Ryan. In 1963, the now famous, high-roller Ray Ryan was staying at the Desert Inn in Las Vegas. Marshall Caifano had been put on the Black List in 1960, but he made a show of being seen in Mob joints. The Gaming Control Board sent in an army of agents to inspect the cards and dice at Strip casinos. Califano went to Ryan's room to talk with him about getting whole with the Greek. When Ryan saw the Greek and Charles Delmonico in the hall, he knew they were on the snatch, there to kidnap him. Ryan ran out through the casino. The FBI arrested Caifano and the Greek, but the Greek turned state's evidence and became an un-indicted co-conspirator. He testified against his long-term admirer, and sadistic killer, Marshall Caifano. So did Ray Ryan. Ray Ryan was a stubborn, vain man. Ryan was he major developer in Palm Springs. He also owned a safari club in Africa with actor William Holden. Several Mob figures, including Johnny Roselli, asked Ryan not to testify. Roselli predicted, correctly, that the IRS would use the trial evidence to hound Ryan the rest of his life, and they did. After he died, they hounded his estate.

In 1964, the Greek filed a $1.5 million lawsuit against Ray Ryan for that old poker game back in 1949, but it was dropped. Caifano went to prison. The Greek moved to California and played the cheap $5 limit games at Gardena. When asked about playing so cheat, Nick the Greek said, "Hey, its action." He died in 1966, or Caifano might have killed him. Five years after Caifano got out of prison, someone blew up Ray Ryan's car. Witness of protection stoolies told the FBI that Caifano had it done. Caifano lived to be 92.

Benny Binion and Johnny Moss were best friends, starting as teen-age paper boys in Dallas. Benny was bootlegging and selling papers at the same time. Moss ended up living his last years at Binion's Horseshoe in Las Vegas. I played poker with Moss in the big Odessa game in 1960, and the twenty dollar limit at Binion's when he was very old. Moe Dalitz and Sid Wyman had been high Mob figures, with Benny being the boss gambler of all Dallas. When they came to Las Vegas, it was a time of intense federal scrutiny, the Kefauver hearings on organized crime, and lots of heat. Right after World War ll, a move of anti-gambling reform swept America. Moe Dalitz told the hearings about his illegal gambling operations, "there were so many Judges and politicians shooting the dice, I thought it was all right." When asked about the bootlegging, Moe said, "Your granddaddy drank the whiskey we brought to them"

Wyman, Dalitz, and Binion spent their lives under FBI surveillance, and Internal Revenue Service, Gaming Control scrutiny. All had tens of millions and were not interested in illegal activities. All were philanthropists. Moe Dalitz built a hospital before he built the Desert Inn. He kept investing and had $100 millions. He started many entrepreneurs on their way. Both Dalitz and Binion won humanitarian awards for their philanthropy.

Benny Binion sought presidential pardons from every president from Eisenhower on, except Kennedy, because as Benny said, "his brother was so bad." Gamblers disliked Attorney General Robert Kennedy because of the "Bobby Law" that prohibited the transmission of gambling information across state lines. This hurt bookies needing horse race odds, sports lines, and layoff contacts.

In 1978, Benny dined in the White House with President Jimmy Carter's secretary. His advocates for a pardon included Robert Strauss, former cabinet member, middle east negotiator, and Democratic Party power broker. Both Nevada senators supported Benny. Benny also wanted them to name his and Sid Wyman's personal lawyer, Harry Claiborne, as a federal judge. Freedom of Information requests yielded the FBI records kept on Benny Binion from the early fifties until the time of his death. J. Edgar Hoover ordered them to "get something" on Binion every decade, and especially at this time.

Just then, Mafia biggie, and hit man, Jimmy "the Weasel" Fratianno went into the Witness Protection Program and told an outlandish, child-like story that Benny Binion promised to build a brand new casino and give the Mob 25 per cent ownership, a deal in the tens of millions, if they would kill Russian Louie Strauss, once Benny's bodyguard. Fratianno said that Benny traveled to the west and east coasts to meet with many Mafia leaders. Being seen with any of them could cost the Horseshoe its gambling license, even though Benny's name wasn't there. The aptly named "Weasel" said that eighteen months after he got the contract, he killed Russian Louie in front of several Mafia folks, half of whom went into Witness Protection. When a reporter contacted Benny, he was furious at such a crazy story. He said, "Tell them FBIs, I'm still capable of doing my own damn killing." Claiborne became a federal judge, but went to prison for tax evasion on a "gift" of a hundred large from Sid Wyman. It also looked bad that he banked at the cage at Binion's Horseshoe. When Claiborne got out of prison, the Nevada Supreme Court voted four to zero to give him back his law license, and he became Binion's lawyer again.

Several Mafia biggies went to prison over Fratianno's testimony, but Benny wasn't bothered or ever mentioned. The FBI's own records indicate there was no reason to tie Benny Binion to any hits, any business with the Mob, or anything illegal. If you had tens of millions, and the FBI taping you, and informants trying to trap you, and a tail in Las Vegas, and on the ranch, would you break the law?

In *Positively Fifth Street,* James Manus wrote, "With (Jimmy) Chagra on trial in Texas for heroin trafficking, Jack, Ted, and Benny Binion convened in Booth 1 of the Horseshoe with Oscar Goodman, the hyper-aggressive young Philadelphia lawyer representing the accused. The upshot of the meeting was a $50,000 contract for Charles Harrelson (actor Woody's father) to assassinate U.S. District Judge John Wood -- or so the lore goes."

That is as absurd a story as Fratianno's or Jon Bradshaw at his worst. Gary Cartwright had already written the definitive book on Jimmy Chagra, *Dirty Dealing,* and the whole true story was widely known. Goodman hired a lawyer. The publisher agreed to delete that paragraph, and take out a full page ad of apology in the *New York Times*. The financial settlement was undisclosed. Rumor said it was $50,000. Still, McManus refers to Benny Binion as a Meyer Lansky lieutenant, which is bottom of the barrel ludicrous! McManus has not researched Mob and Las Vegas history.

An interesting, but far-fetched book about Benny Binion by Gary Sleeper is taken from interviews with old policemen, and raw police files of what informants or snitches said. They blamed Benny for many of the killings and feuds that happened in Dallas and Ft. Worth with no real information, and long after he was gone.

When he first got to Las Vegas in 1946, Benny was locked in a feud with dice man, Herbert "Cat" Noble. Noble killed several of Benny's key employees. There were fourteen attempts on Cat Noble's life, and finally a bomb in his mailbox, detonated from across the road, killed him in August of 1951. It left a four-foot deep crater. Two playing cards, an ace of diamonds and a joker, were photographed near the hole.

This was in Time, Newsweek, and Life. Cat Noble, a pilot, had an airplane rigged with bombs. He planned to bomb Benny's family home in Las Vegas, but Texas authorities stopped him. They found a map with Benny's house marked on it. Several of the people trying to kill the Cat were acting independently, with hopes to go to Benny for a reward after the fact. They rigged the Cat's car, airplane, house, his wife's car, and finally his mail box with explosives. They shot him several times with shotguns, pistols, and rifles. His wife's car explosion killed her, and Cat went crazy with grief and a zeal for vengeance. Nine lives? Get it.

During several of these years, Curly Cavitt was fading with the Cat in the north Dallas area near current Love Field. They would divide up the bankroll each night because Herbert Noble might not see daylight.

Another reason I believe the big Johnny Moss/Nick the Greek poker duel took place in 1949, is that by 1951, Benny was getting too much publicity from the Mob bosses perspective. Many believe the match took place in 1951. However, gambling reform and the Kefauver hearings were sweeping America by then. They held hearings in 14 cities, including Las Vegas and Dallas. There were Texas gambling hearings, and indictments and attempted extradition of Benny back to Texas by then.

Curly Cavitt told me that Benny had some dispute with the Mob, and hired "sixty hop heads off the Jacksboro Highway" to sleep on the casino floor at some time or other. Davie Berman, known as "the toughest Jew in Las Vegas", and one of Sid Wyman's partners, allegedly talked with Benny about not getting so much bad press.

Although the government spent a fortune tailing, wire tapping, and for surveillance of Benny Binion, Sid Wyman, and Moe Dalitz, they did not need to do anything heavily illegal, since their legitimate investments made tens of millions of dollars. The FBI records demonstrate that they didn't do anything illegal.

When Jack Binion threw Benny an eighty-third birthday party at the University of Nevada, 19,000 people were there. Willie Nelson and Hank Williams, Jr. played music. Steve Wynn was the masters of ceremony. There were two and only two big chairs up on the stage, thrones really. One was for Benny Binion, and one was for Moe Dalitz. The Kings of Las Vegas.

BLUFF EUROPE MAGAZINE...THE IDEA OF BRILLIANT EDITOR, PHILIP CONNELLER, LONDON.

Titanic Thompson: The Gambler and Con Man, His Fantastic Proposition Bets and Amazing Eyes

*The race is not always to the swift, nor the battle to the strong, but that's the way to bet...*Damon Runyon

Titanic Thompson had the trained eyes of a skilled actor. His dark eyes could be gullible, child-like, confused, bemused, charming, magnetic, penetrating, predatory, all-knowing, and frightening when need be. Titanic Thompson, born Alvin C. Thomas, (1892-1974) grew up in rural Arkansas in a gambling family. As a child, he pitched pennies at the line, hunted small game with his .22 rifle, threw rocks at targets, and hunted birds by throwing rocks. He played poker, dominoes, and checkers. He invented his own proposition bet, where he threw pennies into a small box. As he would his whole life, Titanic was always practicing, and looking for a gaff, a gimmick, or a way to cheat.

He'd practice long hours cheating with a pair of dice or a deck of cards. He could do the standard mechanic's moves, but it was his supernatural vision that made him millions at poker and golf. Millions he lost on the horses and baseball bets to bookmakers.

With the sharpened nail on his little finger, Titanic could make marks, dents, and crimps on paper playing cards that only he could see with those amazing eyes. He could bend the cards where the slight wave would catch a glint of light. Titanic Thompson was able to play in the largest poker games all over the country and mark the old paper playing cards during the game against some top gamblers who were very alert to cheating and the standard mechanic's moves.

Titanic left home at age 16 to haunt the pool halls, domino games, bowling alleys, dice games and poker games. He learned to cheat at dice. He'd start with the aces or sixes or any combination of those touching, give a few false shakes that made a sound, and then roll stiff-wristed straight down the table to avoid craps. If you were accurate twice in a hundred times, you now had way the best of it. Titanic made most of his money from dice and poker before he took up golf, and he made millions. He was cheating top gamblers.

As a teen, Titanic got a job as a trick-shot artist with a traveling medicine show, which helped him learn the con. He won $2000 and a small river boat shooting dice, but killed a man in a fight on board in self-defense. In a few short years, Titanic made a large fortune. He'd travel in a huge, nickel-plated Pierce-Arrow automobile with the tools of his trade in the trunk: right and left-handed golf clubs, a pool cue, a bowling ball, a shotgun for skeet, and horseshoes. He was ambidextrous, and had many proposition bets to make all through any game. After winning at many changing props, he'd offer to bowl, play golf, shoot targets, or shoot pool left handed. He was a natural lefty.

Titanic wore loose, custom-tailored suits, made to partially conceal the .45 pistol he carried in a shoulder holster. There have been three poker robberies here in Lubbock, and gamblers are carrying guns inside gambling joints as they did back in Ty's day. Titanic hired a bodyguard to drive and carry an extra gun for 10 per cent of his winnings. When a dice game owner set Ty up for a robbery, Ty killed two more men, shooting the masked and armed robbers, even though he had a body guard. Later, an alarm bell at a poker game alerted them. Ty turned over the poker table to use as a shield. He and his bodyguard each shot a robber dead. Then he went to the police and pled self-defense. He was never charged for killing any of the five men he killed.

In 1932, in Tyler, Texas, Titanic killed his last man. When a man in a ski mask pointed a gun at him, Ty dropped to one knee, presenting a smaller target, and shot the man twice. It turned out to be his 16 year old caddy. The caddy lived long enough to tell the police he was a robber. Unlike the first four men he had killed, Titanic felt deep remorse for killing the young caddy. Having killed five men made Titanic most fearsome around the gambling halls of America.

In Missouri, he trapped two of the biggest gamblers on a proposition bet by moving a road sign that said 20 Miles to Joplin five miles closer to town, and betting the sign was wrong. These proposition bets became tales shared by gamblers who love to swap stories. He married five women, all of whom were teenagers on their wedding day, so the age gap between him and his wife kept getting bigger.

In the early twenties, Titanic went to Chicago where he met Nicholas "Nick the Greek" Dandalos, America's most famous gambler at the time. He asked the Greek to flip a coin for $15,000 at the first meeting. He sent his two-headed quarter into the air and grabbed it when the Greek called heads. Later, he tried to bet Nick Greek on the weight of a large rock they saw when out driving. The Greek pointed out that this rock looked very different than all the others, and Titanic admitted he had pre-weighed it and brought it there.

Al Capone was the absolute Mob boss of Chicago and a big admirer of Nick the Greek. This was during prohibition when the mobsters had tons of money. Capone got Nick the Greek and Titanic in some large poker games and they played partners. It was in these games that Titanic announced he could drive a golf ball five-hundred yards, when he "felt like it." After one poker game, Titanic bet Al Capone $500 he could throw an orange over a tall building. He palmed the orange and threw a lemon filled with lead, bird shot. This was one of Titanic's regular propositions. When winter came, Titanic took the gamblers out to a golf course next to frozen Lake Michigan when "he felt like" driving a golf ball 500 yards. He turned toward the lake and sent his golf ball flying unto the ice. Reportedly, he won $50,000. With Titanic, the myths, legends, and stories may or not be precisely true.

Nick the Greek and Titanic went to the lucrative poker games in San Francisco and Los Angeles, California. As partners, they made a fortune. It was here Ty took up golf, and he was terrific at it in a short time. He won $56,000 his first day to gamble at golf. The Greek could get them into the poker games, and Ty's eyes would beat them. However, Titanic lost millions on horses and sports bets. He followed the horses that followed the horses. In Tijuana, Mexico, Titanic attempted to fix a six-horse race. He bribed five of the jockeys, but one refused to go along. Titanic told him he had a man in the grandstands with a high-powered rifle and a scope. He would shoot any jockey whose horse got in front of Nellie. With Nellie nearing the finish line with a comfortable lead, she fell and broke her leg. That cost Titanic $1.5 million and broke him. He had bet with bookies around the country. Nick the Greek sent a fresh bankroll, and Titanic was playing poker that night. He bragged he never stayed broke over six hours.

Titanic would sit in a hotel lobby kicking his houseshoe up into the air and catching it on his foot. He had some props. He could throw the old hotel keys into the lock. Doyle Brunson said he saw him do it. He would bet on how many cards he could throw into a hat at twenty paces. Of course, he could always throw what he needed to win a bet, right or left-handed. Titanic would set the horseshoes stakes 41 feet apart, when regulation was 40 feet. The longer distance would fool champions at horseshoes. When future legendary gambler, Hubert Cokes, was 14 years old, he assisted Titanic by hiding in a hotel room next to his. Titanic would bet he could throw cards under the hotel room door and have them bounce into a hat. Hubert was hiding in the closet to place the cards in the hat. These two and Minnesota Fats became life-long friends.

Titanic, Nick the Greek, and Hubert "Daddy Warbucks" Cokes were all in New York at the end of the 1920s and a golden time. Titanic and Cokes were backing a teenage New York Fats, later to become Minnesota Fats, after the movie *The Hustler* came out in 1961. Cokes was called Daddy Warbucks after the character in *Little Orphan Annie*. He was tall, bald, very rich, and had an ever-present cigar. They taught Minnesota Fats "the conversation" and he became world class at it. The challenge, the proposition, the negotiation, the bragging, the con, the spots. They'd make the sucker really want to beat them and think he could. At pool, and later golf, they'd go after the best pool player in any town and hope he had the biggest gambler to back him. Ty would win a series of bets. First he'd get a spot and win by one stroke, then play even, then give spots, bet on several trick shots, and play left-handed or one-handed.

Tommy Thomas, Titanic's son, wrote me this:

Hubert Cokes was my God Father and I spent time with him when I was growing up and knew him very well... He was not a capable card man like Ty but used some of the gaffs. I still have a leather cup he gave me where you twist the bottom and the dice are switched. Used it playing backgammon, another cup just like it that was straight for your opponent... I would go down to the Elks in Evansville and watch Hubert play one pocket for hours. He would always get on Ty's case just like Ty would do when we were talking about him. Ty said Hubert was the most dangerous smart man he ever knew. He would carry two .45 pistols and walk into any pool hall and challenge anyone to a game of one pocket or a fist fight for any amount of money. Over the years, when I would call Hubert he would let me know he was following my career as a gambler and always seemed to know when I took off a big score. He did not teach me about cards but did teach me about life. Hubert told me a story about Ty you might like. He said they were in Kansas City and he bankrolled Ty to go to Evansville the first time where they were playing poker for high stakes because of all the oil money. Hubert had not heard from Ty for weeks and thought he would call him to see if he was winning any money. He talked to Ty and he told him things were so bad everyone was soaking watches just to get by. Hubert knew Ty well enough he caught the next train to Evansville. He walked into the poker game and saw that Ty was winning thousands of dollars. They both took their winnings and bought up oil leases and became wealthy in the oil business. Cokes kept his, Ty ended giving my mother all producing income and half of all mineral deeds when they divorced. That was about ten grand a month for mom in the forties. Ty and Hubert were always going to kill each other but really were good friends. The last serious beef they had was in the McCurdy Hotel. Ty was so angry at Hubert he waited in the hotel lobby for him to come down the elevator and was going to shoot him. Cokes figured Ty would be waiting for him and came down through the kitchen and walked up behind Ty and said, "Slim, are you ready to go to the golf course?" After that they managed to get along.

In New York, Titanic was courting the biggest Mob boss and gambler, Arnold Rothstein. The two became close friends. Damon Runyon, one of America's most famous writers was also there, hearing all the Titanic Thompson stories. His character, Sky Masterson, patterned on Titanic, was in a short story that became the hit play and movie *Guys and Dolls*. Arnold Rothstein was the model for the Nathan Detroit character. Like Ty, Sky was a fabulous dresser, very handsome, a lady's man, and a huge proposition bettor to whom the Sky was the limit. Marlon Brando played Sky in the movie. Frank Sinatra played Nathan Detroit.

Titanic won a bet from Rothstein throwing a heavy peanut across Times Square. He had packed the peanut with bird shot, lead. He did this with walnuts, pecans, oranges, and lemons. He was always ready. He won a bet on license plate poker when the car he had pre-arranged had 333 and drove by when Ty doffed his fedora. Ty hired an ex-math professor to teach him the odds on many dice, poker, and prop bets. He won a bet from Rothstein betting two of the next thirty people to walk by would have the same birthday. Ty learned a great many props from the professor. At any game, Titanic kept up a steady stream of challenges that he could keep in his head, but made other gamblers dizzy.

On a train ride to the track, the gamblers bet on how many white horses they would see. The next day, Rothstein had hired a man to plant extra white horses. Ty had hired a man to plant even more. Ty won the bet by guessing a number higher than Rothstein's. He then admitting what he had done.

Ty finally got Rothstein in a three-day poker game where everyone was cheating Rothstein, especially Nate Raymond, Ty, and Joe Bernstein, now in the Poker Hall of Fame. Rothstein lost $500,000 and was very slow to pay. The houseman for the game, George "Hump" McManus killed him.

The publicity for McManus' murder trial made Titanic Thompson a nationally-known name. The newspaper pictures showed a tall, rail-thin, handsome man, with thick, jet-black hair, fashionable clothing, and diamond rings. He hated that. Ty was immaculately dressed in expensive clothes, with big sparkling diamonds on several fingers. While testifying, Ty was asked if poker is a game of chance. "Not the way I play it," Ty said. The stock market crash and fame sent Titanic roaming all over America in the 1930s, often with Hubert Cokes or Minnesota Fats.

Titanic came here to Lubbock, Texas from the 1930s off and on until the early 1960s. Johnny Moss was living here in 1938, when Ty offered a proposition that Johnny could not shoot a 46 with only a four iron on nine holes at Meadowbrook, one of our local golf courses. Moss had his four iron welded down into a two iron. Moss couldn't sink putts because Titanic had paid a man to raise the lips on each cup. Moss snapped, and had a man go around and tap them back down. Moss had his whole bankroll bet, $8300, and won. At draw poker, Ty's prop was that Moss did all the dealing, but Ty could cut anytime. He had the Aces crimped and could cut to one as needed. In his biography, Moss said he won all his money back and a Cadillac after he figured it out.

When Ty would return to Meadowbrook when he was older, he'd have a top golfer as a partner, or do prop bets of throwing half dollars into the cup or a shot glass or pitching golf balls into a shot glass. He'd bet he could make two balls in three strokes from 25 feet. He'd hit both balls at the same time on the first stroke. At other golf courses, he'd bet he could chip into a row boat or bet he could shoot flying birds out of the air with his pistol. Like his peanuts, the pistol was loaded with bird shot.

I caddied at Meadowbrook as a teenager in the early fifties. One night on a full moon, called a Comanche Moon in Texas, the gamblers played by moonlight. One day, a rich-looking, tall man hired me to retrieve golf balls while he was trying to teach a Doberman Pinscher to catch balls he had lofted high into the air. The dog was trying, but usually would drop the golf ball. This guy would hit a hard, low line drive and hit the dog in the side. When I told people about this, they said it had to be Titanic Thompson, but I'll never know.

In 1939, there was an oil boom in Evansville, Indiana. The poker game at the McCurdy Hotel had $25,000 pots. Name gamblers playing included Titanic Thompson, Hubert Cokes, Minnesota Fats, and high-roller Ray Ryan. Ryan was a great card player, and he got very rich. Ten years later, he was to play and cheat Nick the Greek at gin and poker playing outdoors as a Las Vegas casino. He won $550,000, breaking the Greek, maybe for the last time. He cheated, having a confederate with binoculars watching the Greek's hand and sending Ryan a radio signal to a device he wore at his waist. Both Cokes and Ryan got very rich from oil royalties, but continued as road gamblers. Titanic made a lot of money on royalties but gave his mineral interest to his wife when they divorced. Neither Titanic nor Ryan could ever beat Minnesota Fats at one pocket and they lost a lot of money. In his delightful biography, Kevin Cook said Fats won a million from Titanic playing pool. Maybe, i seriously doubt it.

It was in Evansville that Titanic did a famous prop bet. He hired a farmer to count the watermelons on his truck and park near the McCurdy Hotel. He got the gamblers on the porch involved in "the conversation" and Ty bet he could guess very near the exact number of watermelons on the truck. As he did in golf, pool, or horseshoes, he only won by one. Just one, as always. When the big poker game there was robbed, Fats and Cokes were playing. The robbers got $150,000 cash.

Tommy Thomas, Titanic's son, was born in Evansville in 1944. Walter Winchell mentioned his birth in his national news column. After Titanic left his mother, Tommy read about him growing up and began to practice long hours with a deck of cards. He became a master cheater traveling the country.

Golf was Titanic's best game, and without cheating, he was one of the very best in the United States. He never entered golf tournaments, saying he could not afford the pay cut. He played for more on one hole than top pros made in a year. When Nick the Greek got him in the country clubs of California, he beat some of well-known golfers. He stayed one of the best for twenty years.

The "conversation" never stopped, a million props. The math props he'd learned. The eye-hand coordination props he'd practiced hours on end. He'd bring in a "ringer", a pro such as Ben Hogan, Raymond Floyd, or Lee Elder after he had worked up the bet.

Ty always put Vaseline, grease, or lip balm on the club face to improve distance and control. When Jack Binion had a professional gambler's golf tournament, they allowed "grease."

Titanic discovered and taught some top golfers. Ben Hogan, one of America's greatest golf legends said Ty was the best shot maker ever, best short game, and that he could beat anyone right or left-handed. Ty would join a country club, lose on the small, appear a braggart, and work up a really large bet. It might take weeks. When Lee Trevino refused his invitation to go on the road, Ty came back to El Paso with Raymond Floyd and he barely beat Trevino. This was when Ty was old and had $20,000 on the match. Ty played Byron Nelson, America's leading pro, in Dallas in 1933 for some big money with many people betting on Nelson, and Ty "moving in" to take all bets. The "conversation" had Ty getting three strokes. Nelson shot a 67. You know what Ty shot, exactly what he needed to win the bet, a 69. At times, he was near the course record if he got in a jam. His years of throwing and eyesight came in handy. He used slices and hooks as he needed them, and put a lot of English down when he needed it, be it pool, golf, or capturing another teenage bride.

When Ty was about to lose a big golf match to an obnoxious millionaire, his opponent's ball landed in a sand trap. Ty sent his caddy ahead to drop a $10 bill in the sand trap. His opponent picked it up and Ty called a one-stroke penalty. He'd bet on a long put over and over. He'd taken a garden hose to the green at night and watered over it to make an indentation or groove his ball would follow.

Titanic Thompson played partners with some of the most famous future pros. He'd try every kind of bet with Lee Elder, the first prominent African-American pro golfer, as his caddy. Elder would wear overalls and appear a little slow. Then Titanic would offer to take his caddy as partner and play the best two golfers in town, and Ty would play left-handed. To his credit, Titanic made Elder a full partner, and gave him an even split of the money.

As Ty became older and more famous, when he'd lay out a proposition, folks would ask if he was Titanic Thompson. Gamblers would make small bets against him just to see him do his throwing props. When plastic cards replaced paper cards, his big poker advantage vanished. Casinos, with their long dice tables, could prevent his control of the dice.

Tommy Thomas, Titanic's son, and I have exchanged several letters. Tommy practiced hours and hours and was a card mechanic better than Ty. Ty and I both said so. I caught Tommy cheating in a huge Hold 'em game in 1975. First night he showed, he cold-decked us from a deck inside a shirt jacket just above his naval. I didn't see it, but thought he was moving his hands in the way a cheater does to get you used to it. I did not see any "drippings", the edge of a card, or a flash of color. The next week, I just had the feeling he would cheat. I'd flopped two pair, Aces up, and bet them all the way, moving in finally. On Fifth Street, he studied a long time with his hand on his cheek, and the hand came down rapidly and now he had two Aces in the hole and could call. I knew he'd switched hole cards, but I didn't see any "drippings." I called the houseman outside and he said he was also Tommy's partner and to go on home. I'd had to give him half my action, and he owed me a lot of money. One week, he ran in Jack "Treetop" Straus to play me heads up. I pulled up a tiny bit loser.

When Benny Binion got together the first World Series of Poker at Binion's Horseshoe in Las Vegas in 1970, he paid for Titanic to come. They gave Titanic a trophy as a Living Legend.

When Tommy and an aging Titanic were reunited, they began to play against each other the rest of Ty's life, and to cheat each other. Ty helped his expert-cheater son to get in poker games, and he sent Tommy back to Evansville to be tutored by Hubert Cokes. Tommy wrote me this, about Ty's eye-hand coordination:

At twenty, I had just returned from six months in Hollywood where I had visions of being an actor. If it wasn't for the poker houses in Gardena I would have starved to death. Headed back to Texas and stopped off in El Paso to see Jack Lutz. Jack was a card cheater and we won about 20 grand each in a game he set up. I drove on to Texas where Dad was living. I made the mistake of letting dad see the money I had won. He was trying to figure a way to get that money from my pocket to his. I thought since I had been gone for six months he would be excited to see me but his excitement level shot up when he saw the money.

I said, "Dad, I am not going to let you win my money playing poker." Ty was the best in the world at playing a bend on paper cards along with a slight wave that only he could see. There is no defense unless you used plastic cards when you played him. We were sitting in the living room and I knew his brain was working overtime. He wanted to win my money. He finally got up and walked about 15 paces across the living room and put a quarter on the carpet. He then said how many throws for this half dollar to hit the quarter and make it pop up on top of the half dollar. I said 50 throws for fifty dollars. He did it the first time. I was loser and the game was on. I ended up losing a grand. Dad was excited but we both knew all he had to do was ask and I would have given him the money. It was all about winning.

In Arizona he won all gauges and all distances for trap and skeet shooting for several years. One of the best pistol shots in the world. He had a feel and a touch that made him one of the greatest short iron golfers in the world. He never got a callus from swinging golf clubs and used a baseball grip. He could play right and left handed....

Like so many of the great gamblers who had a lot of gamble in them: Johnny Moss, Nick the Greek, and Minnesota Fats, Ty didn't have much money at the end of his life. Jack "Treetop" Straus said, "If God wanted me to hold on the money, he would have put handles on it."

I asked Titanic's son Tommy about the end of Ty's life in the nursing home. He wrote me:

Yes, would love to write on the last chapter of Ty's life in the nursing home. Every week I was in town he would call every day saying, "What time will you be here?" I rarely missed a day being with my dad. Ty and I loved to gamble with each other. About 12 years earlier I met Ty, my dad, for the first time in San Antonio. He was 71 and I was 18. He taught me a lot about gambling over the years and I practiced 8 hours a day for years with a deck of cards becoming a top card mechanic in the business. He connected me with gamblers around the country who would set up games for me. I would come home with my share of the winnings and always give dad his part. We would always gamble with each other playing heads up poker. Whoever won the other's stack of chips got a hundred dollars. We both loved doing this and continued after he went into the nursing home. The only difference was dad didn't have much money and we played his best *game, Pitch. I reminded dad he had loaned me money to go to Tyler Junior College when we first met and after all the years of gambling with each other I felt like I still owed him five hundred dollars. Now dad had a bankroll and if he lost, I would take it off the five hundred. If he won, I would pay him. We played for $25.00 a game and he was very sharp and the best player. Make no mistake, dad and I took no prisoners, and would win at any cost. If we could cheat and get away with it, so be it. The final game and the last time I would see dad. I was riding my Harley to the nursing home and knew dad would be listening for the roar of the exhaust. Over the months the $500.00 I owed dad from college had been reduced to $200.00. Dad knew he was the best player and couldn't figure out how I was winning. That night I was on my way to Cincinnati to play poker for several weeks and knew dad would miss me. There was something different about today. I knew Ty had the cards on the bed waiting for me. I don't think he knew that weeks before I happened to look in the empty card box and saw that he had left two 10's in the box. This gave him a big advantage in the game of Pitch. As I walked into the nursing home he walked up and put his arms around me. He said, "Son, I think I am going to die here." then he said what I had been waiting my whole life to hear. "Son, I love you." We hugged each other and went to the bed for what would be our final game. While I was gone Ty had two strokes and died.*

Back to the final game. We are sitting on the bed and I dealt the cards for both of us. Knowing the advantage he had with the two 10's in the box he said "Son, something is not right. You should not be winning."

I said, "Dad, I have been cheating you." He said impossible, no way. I said if I can prove it can we call the debt I owe you after 12 years all even. We agreed and after showing him we were now even for the first time since he helped me go to college. What a day. Dad said he loved me and the debt was canceled. By the way, it easier to cheat the greatest gambler in the world when he is in his eighties with failing eye sight. Ty was the best hustler the world has ever known. He would win all your money and turn around and give you the shirt off his back. It was always about winning, not the money. For the last 16 years I have ministered in the maximum security prisons and know most of the men have never heard the words that I have come to cherish, "Son, I love you."

Thank you dad, I love you too..... Tommy Thomas

BLUFF EUROPE MAGAZINE THIS WAS A THREE-MONTH, THREE-PART ARTICLE.

Curly Cavitt: My Major Gambling Teacher

Whichever way your luck is running, it is bound to change...Curly Cavitt.

Curly Cavitt (1914-1996) was on the road more than any other Texas gambler, over sixty years. He never went broke. Of all the older men that I asked for advice and counsel, Curly was my most important gambling teacher. In measures of class, style, appearance, knowledge, and bankroll, he was way above the ordinary road gamblers. In my novel, *Texas Poker Wisdom*, I used Curly as the model for the major character, Moody O'Malley.

Crandell Addington, Poker Hall of Fame member, said this of his good friend, "Curly Cavitt was a will-of-the-wisp on the old road gamblers' circuit. Just appeared from what seemed as almost nowhere, didn't stay long in one place, got the money, and was gone again."

Curly was born on a farm south of Dallas, Texas. He met his first gambling partner and life-long friend, Pat Patton, in the fourth grade. Both became top poker and dice road gamblers. As teenagers in the great depression, both learned everything about gambling with dice and cards. They picked up expert cheating moves from the old timers. In the depression, gamblers cheated because, with no money around, losing was not an option. Few had a bankroll. Also living in nearby Ft. Worth was one of America's top dice men, Sealy Griffin. He taught Curly how to make loads, flats, and every type of gaffed dice. Curly learned all the switch and hand moves, which he'd practice for hours. He practiced with a deck of cards his whole life. Sealy took a gang of four to work the dice in a no-lose fashion all over the country. There is a book that lists all the Elk's stags, the Eagle's, Moose, and other lodge gambling nights.

Curly Cavitt attended college two years in San Marcos, Texas, but being the great depression, his father could only afford to send one son to college. Curly was the youngest of five children. He tried professional prize fighting at $10 a fight, but found road gambling with Pat around the little towns looking for poker games and dice games was a rough life, but it sure beat prize fighting. Once during the depression, Curly bet a man $100 he could beat him in a race hopping freight trains from Dallas to Kansas City. Curly won. Another time in Dallas, during the depression, he and Pat stole milk from richie's porches. When Curly won a "queer" (counterfeit) $10 bill, with off-color ink, he took it to an ice house, and bought a big block of ice, and got his change. Learning gambling in the towns around and on the streets of Dallas, Curly met life-long friends, Benny Binion and Johnny Moss. He played poker with both men, and thought Benny was as easy mark.

By his mid-twenties, during World War II, Curly had a good bankroll, and had perfected his cheating skills, and his poker play. He bought a 150 acre farm, a combine, and a tractor near Waxahachie, south of Dallas. This would keep him away from the Dallas gambling wars, and World War II. During the war, he started fading dice with Herbert Noble, later called the Cat. For decades, Curly would buy into a dice game for a percentage, putting up his share of the bankroll, providing protection as a strong ex-boxer, and with the pistol he always carried in the pocket of his loose, pleated slacks. He also provided the skills to switch in any kind of dice, and to keep from being cheated. The single most important thing that Curly Cavitt took with him on the road gambling in many states for sixty years was his word. A gambler is only as good as his word. He cut up square. Curly, and his long-term friend, Red Harris, had both lived in Oak Cliff. Red was also an expert dice man, knowing all the moves. Red ran a bar with a dice game in the area controlled by Benny Binion, and paid a percentage for political protection from police raids. Even with his profitable deal with Herbert Noble, Curly would still hit the road to conventions, and stags, sometimes traveling with Red Harris, or with Pat Patton, always fading that white line.

When Benny Binion went to Las Vegas to own a mere casino, he took a huge step down from his position as "Boss Gambler" of downtown Dallas, and secret partner in gambling houses in Ft. Worth, and other towns. He had five policy wheels, (the numbers racket), and a part of dice games everywhere, when that was the major form of gambling. As Curly said, "Benny didn't know a dice from a domino, but he had plenty of people that did." All the gambling in wide-open downtown Dallas paid Benny Binion twenty-five per cent street tax, including Red Harris' dice game. Benny had the laws and the politicians in his pocket, until his sheriff lost in 1946. Binion maintained a great deal of control of gambling in Dallas and Ft. Worth for a decade after moving to Las Vegas.

With all the heat in Dallas, gamblers were getting out. Several came here to Lubbock. Curly and Red Harris found the fast-growing, boomtown of Lubbock, Texas to be a strawberry patch. When Curly Cavitt arrived in Lubbock, he was thirty-seven years old. He had the biggest bankroll, and the most knowledge of gambling of anyone in town, before or since. A group he worked with had won over $100,000 in one day fading square dice in California. That is like $1,000,000 now.

He built a beautiful, spacious, natural-stone house south of Lubbock, and began his rounds of poker games, domino halls, pool halls, and golf courses. He faded dice with some of the less experienced dice men: Sherman Davis, Moody Young, and Reverend Ray Pruitt, all of whom I would work with a decade later. He beat everyone at gin rummy since he dealt himself eleven or twelve cards to start, and "cleaned up", putting the palmed cards on top when straightening the deck. Curly would play anyone heads up poker, and win many ways. Lubbock was becoming one of the biggest poker centers in Texas. Road gamblers came from all over. After Curly moved here, several professional gamblers, including Bill Smith, Red Harris, R.B. Grimes, Pat Patton, and James Roy a.k.a. Tennessee Longgoodie moved here. Pat Renfro, Curly's old friend, lived in Lubbock already.

Curly rented the top floor of a nice hotel in Ruidoso, New Mexico at the beginning of the horse race season to fade the craps, and book the ponies. Curly Cavitt was a walking gambling house. He played checkers, dominoes, pool, golf, poker, gin rummy, and faded the dice. You could bet a sports event or a horse, but in person, the old way. Curly was always there for the first count on a dice game unless he had a trusted partner there. There were few in his life. While working in Lubbock, Curly also roamed to Odessa in the oil country. He won $25,000 playing heads up Texas Hold 'em from Egghead Perry, only to be stiffed. The biggest poker games would move from town to town, and Curly would be there. Curly, Johnny Moss, and Pat Renfro were in a big game that was robbed in Beeville, Texas. The robbers had tear gas and shotguns. A joke was there were five things you could find at any Elk's Stag: Poker, Dice, Strippers, Alcohol, and Curly Cavitt.

When Curly was fading dice in Mexico, across from Laredo in Nuevo Laredo, with the fix in with the laws, he worked with Horsey Inman, whom I would work with in Lubbock a decade later. He was one of the best poker cheats, dealing bottoms and seconds after years of practice. While staying at a Holiday Inn, $10,000 that Curly left in the safe was stolen, in an obvious inside job. He sued, and later recovered half the money. The FBI questioned him, but let it go. Later, they questioned him again when he ordered some dice in the name of a dead gambler.

In 1952, Curly was arrested at the State Democratic Convention in Oklahoma City running a big dice game for delegates and politicians. The *Associated Press* released a wire service story to newspapers across the country mentioning crooked dice and marked cards. It showed pictures of Curly's 18-inch-square, wooden, dice case with small trays for every type of crooked dice in any color, to match what was down. This was also on all the television stations in Lubbock. After this, Curly was very careful about the heat the rest of his life. When his good friend, Benny Binion, told him the Internal Revenue Service and the Federal Bureau of Investigation would be on the rail at the World Series of Poker, Curly never attended, even though many of his old friends were there. Binion had a standing offer for Curly to come to Las Vegas and work as a floor boss or a pit boss, given his vast knowledge of cheating.

When I first went to Las Vegas, I told Benny Binion that Curly Cavitt said, "I was all right." That was outlaw talk, the same as a job reference. We talked about Curly a bit. Benny sent me across the street to see Bill Boyd at the Golden Nugget, and my pal and I went to work shilling in the poker room. Both Binion and Boyd were later inducted into the Poker Hall of Fame.

After that national press attention from the Democratic Party Convention raid, Red Harris and Curly Cavitt became partners for the first time. Red was magic around a gambling house, because he was so funny. Red knew Curly had the heat, but he needed a partner he could trust that had a big bankroll which Red did not have. The two were the best-dressed, highest-class gamblers anywhere. Their magnetic personalities drew the players. The dice game moved, but was always in a much nicer apartment, or office building than Lubbock was accustomed to. They put a big bowl of square, red dice on the table, and let the shooters select. Soon they had the ranchers, oil men, farmers, business owners, lawyers, and the socialites. Fading square dice high, they turned out some large winners. Their big store was the talk of the town. They would invite restaurant owners that shot dice, such as Chicken Box Johnny and Pete the Greek to bring over food. With a partner they could trust, Curly and Red did not both need to be at the dice game when it was open.

I asked Poker Hall of Fame member, Doyle Brunson, about Curly and Red. Doyle wrote me, "Sailor Roberts and I were living in San Angelo when Red Harris (who should have been a comedian) came to town to fade a dice game. We shot our way out of the Longhorn motel when the hijackers tried to get us. Red was a little crazy, not at all like Curly who was always cool. Curly was the consummate gambler, probably the only one I ever knew. He had no leaks that me or anyone else knew of. Almost everyone has bad habits of some sort (including me) but as you said, Curly was always after the cash!"

Gamblers are entertainers. They tell jokes. They want people to have a good time. Both Curly and Red were funny and charming. They joined Hillcrest Country Club. Curly and Red were still going on the road to Elk's Stags and conventions. They played on the square in Lubbock to protect their reputations, but anything goes on the road. The players are there for only a day or two and the rule was, "get the money before it walks." Curly and Red would "badge up", getting membership or credentials for gambling nights at Elks, Eagles, conventions, or golf tournaments. One time in Louisiana, Red gave Curly the "dust off" sign, the let us leave sign, rubbing the hands together. Red went outside, but Curly wanted to win their eye balls. Red heard a fight in progress, and went back to find three men had Curly down, and one was choking him by his tie. Curly rarely wore a tie after that.

Curly always drove big cars: Cadillacs, Buicks, and Pontiacs. Once when he and Red were coming off the road, Curly's Cadillac blew a tire, and rolled into a plowed field. Their clothes, dice, and cards were scattered everywhere. They grabbed the guns and gathered up everything else, and hitchhiked away. They did not report the accident. The next day, Curly bought a new Cadillac for cash.

As a teenager, I was intent on being a professional gambler. I traveled the bridge tournaments. My style was to go up to the most famous bridge players in the world: Charles Goren, Oswald Jacoby, and John Gerber, and ask questions. They'd answer. With Curly Cavitt, it was always, "Mr. Cavitt." and "Sir."

The most important thing Mr. Cavitt taught me was a combination of mathematics, self-discipline, and psychology. A professional never takes a percentage disadvantage on a bet. His mantra was always, "the best of it."

Gambling is never recreational for a professional. I never play any casino game except poker. Like my respected mentor, I have no gamble in me. I would not flip you for fifty cents.

Curly said a gambler's annual income is based on the volume of action he fades, multiplied by the percentage advantage. When he'd book a football game or a horse, he'd "go long", not booking nervous, and laying off the big bets to bigger bookies. In Dallas, the New Orleans Mob, Carlos "Little Man" Marcello, were requesting bookies lay off there. Jack Ruby was a bookie who laid off to Marcello. That was one reason Curly left Dallas.

Curly showed me all the cheating moves with cards and dice, and all the cheating devices, not where I could cheat, since I would never be that brave, but to protect myself from cheaters. Dealing off the bottom, seconds, holding out, cold decks, false cuts and shuffles, marked cards, crimped cards, flashing cards, peeking, and more. He had the funny colored sun glasses, and a hold out machine he paid $500 for, and only used once. It is worn under the coat, and was a collection of fishing line and plastic levers, and made a sound. He showed me "the light", a tiny mirror made from a piece of broken light bulb sprayed with a mirror substance. This is held, or placed under a bandage on the fingers.

Over the decades, I have caught cheating several times, always with what Curly taught me to constantly watch out for. I never, ever take my eyes off the deck of cards. The best two men with their hands that I ever witnessed were Curly and Titanic Thompson's son, Tommy Thomas a.k.a. Little Ty. I caught him holding out, and cold decking expertly. He was surprised that I knew several of his cheating methods, including a cold deck concealed in shirt jacket over the heart. He and his Dad knew Curly.

When I started winning a lot of money playing poker, I'd head downtown for the barber shops, hotel coffee shop, and to buy clothes. Curly and Red were fading in the Great Plains Life Building, Lubbock's only twenty-story building, and the premier location, at the time. When Curly was alone, I would walk right up and ask gambling questions, and questions about the varied poker players or plays.

In 1959, I rode with Curly on a trip to East Texas: Lufkin, Palestine, Gladewater, and Longview. He met up with Pat Patton in Lufkin. They played a big seven five low ball game, and faded dice. We went to a horse race, and a barn with many dice games. Curly pulled out a $1000 bill and asked a teenager for change. He'd carry $20,000 in one pocket, and a hammerless .38 revolver in the other. Gamblers carried these where the hammer would not stick coming out of the pocket. I carry one now. Best pocket pistol I ever owned. In Longview, at a big Elk's Stag, Curly was there to play, and to stake his long-term friend Johnny Moss, and also stake Pat Renfro in a big razz game with Sarge Ferris. Moss and Ferris were later inducted into the Poker Hall of Fame.

Being arrested on a gambling misdemeanor was just part it. We were all arrested several times. One night at Wilbank's Car Lot, the laws ran in. The lookout, a retired, San Antonio cop, tackled one. We always threw the Bee Brand decks in a hole in the wall when new decks came in. We played with all cash because chips were considered evidence of gambling. Curly threw his $20,000 bankroll, wrapped in rubber bands, in the trash can. He palmed a deck of cards in each hand. Not finding any gambling devices, chips, or cards, the police decided not to arrest us, but they could, and did often for vagrancy by association, a law later thrown out by the Supreme Court.

One night at Dolly's poker game, I was nearly broke when Curly came in. Mostly, we played Texas Hold 'em, but this was low ball. It was the only other game allowed, Kansas City, Seven-Five low ball. It always brought out the gamble, and the cheats. It was played higher. I asked Curly if he would throw in with me partners, and play the money. When it was time to register at Texas Tech University, four different gamblers cut up a critical winning with me over time that put me in college: Curly Cavitt, Red Harris, Moody Young, and Sherman Davis. Curly agreed, but put up enough money to cover every one. When the deck came to him, he caught the nuts, a seven five, and busted three men in a huge pot.

I was sitting on a bed behind him, and didn't see the move. What did he do? Cold deck them? Drop a whole hand off the bottom? Hold out a hand? Deal himself extra cards? Get lucky? He gave me my half of the money, and told me to go on home. When I caught up to him downtown and asked, he wouldn't tell me what he did or if he did anything.

Once Bill Smith was running a game at his house that attracted some real talent: Tennessee Longgoodie, Pat Renfro, Sherman Davis, Neal "Carney" Taylor, and I. Red Harris, who didn't play poker much, came over drunk. They hid his car in the garage because of the heat from the law that Red had from Deadbeat Davis, this rogue cop who followed gamblers around. I went broke, and Red staked me behind that college story. All the gamblers encouraged me to stay in school. The cards quickly hit me and I was $500 winner in a round. Red said let's cut out, and that I should quit the game. I did, of course. Then he decided he would leave, and wanted Bill Smith to open the garage door. Bill was busy playing in a hand, so Red crashed his car through the garage door.

Everyone challenged everyone to play heads up. I played Jack "Treetop" Straus and James "Tennessee Longgoodie" Roy each heads up the first night I met them. Bill Smith and I played often. Bill Smith and Red Harris played two days and nights drunk, and broke about even. There had to be some terrible play, and lots of gambling.

When a poker game was raided, the police were cheerful, friendly, and no one drew a gun or handcuffed anybody, except Detective Sergeant Deadbeat Davis. He was also assigned to state narcotics. He began to hassle all gamblers, and some young hippie girls, leaving notes on their cars, stalker like. He found one weak, young woman I knew and drove her a bit crazy. She dropped out of college, and left town. He asked the gamblers for bribes, but they were afraid he was wearing a wire, and trying to make a bribery case. Davis told folks he could arrest them at will. He showed up at Red's place by Buffalo Lake, fired his gun in the air, and asked for bribes. To keep the high class players that Red and Curly had attracted, you do not want any arrests or robberies. Davis was psycho, and he really had it in for Red Harris and vulnerable hippy girls.

I went down to police headquarters once to report a stolen diamond ring, that I had really lost. Deadbeat Davis put me in a little room and grilled me for an hour, asking the names of all the KGs, Known Gamblers. I denied knowing everyone I had been arrested with, saying they had those "funny names." I was very afraid of him. Later, Davis became head of the Department of Public Safety Narcotics in Dallas. He was fired, and sued a newspaper for saying he planted dope, and roughed up and robbed suspects. He sued and lost.

Curly and Red always had guns in their pockets, but they carried them like veteran police officers. Both men shot at robbers a few times. Red hit one robber in Lubbock, and it was ruled self-defense on the scene. Another time, Red and a dice game worker had a shootout with two robbers, and no one was hit. Guns are not for settling gambling disputes inside a joint. They are for defense from robbers. Robberies happen after you leave a poker game. In the East Texas woods, Curly encountered a robber while leaving a poker game, and he fired at him. He stayed out of that area for awhile. I shot over the head of someone at my back door in the middle of the night. Another time, I caught a guy coming in the second floor balcony, and walked him out at gun point.

This crazy guy pulled a gun, as if to rob Reverend Pruitt's dice game. Then he turned his back, and held the gun down by his side. The Rev grabbed the gun. Another time, the same guy held out the fat part of his side, and shot him self. He told all the characters that I had shot him. I didn't even know him.

By the mid-1960s, the heat from bad cop Davis, and other factors, meant the gambling was drying up in Lubbock, especially the biggest poker. Bill Smith, Longgoodie, and Curly moved on. Pat Renfro and Red Harris stayed.

Curly headquartered out of San Angelo, Texas in the oil and ranch country for some years, and later out of San Antonio, but his life after the lucrative Lubbock years was spent mostly on the road, right up until he was eighty-one years old. No gambler in the Southwest logged that many miles. He'd stay in a motel a while, and then he might go six hundred miles to the next poker or dice game. In his final years, he had some regular weekly spots around Dallas, where he had started out. He was healthy, and on the road until the last year of his life, when cancer claimed Curly Cavitt. I gambled around a university until I gained a Ph.D., and joined the Texas Tech faculty. Of all the professors I encountered, Curly Cavitt was my most important teacher.

BLUFF EUROPE MAGAZINE

Amarillo Slim and Johnny Hughes

Wyatt Earp, 1887 (also on the cover)

Wyatt Earp

Doc Holliday

Bat Masterson

Luke Short

Luke Short

Ben Thompson

Poker Alice

Lottie Deno

Wild Bill Hickok

Buffalo Bill Cody

Titanic Thompson

Arnold Rothstein

Benny "the Cowboy" Binion

Amarillo Slim, Johnny Moss, and Benny Binion

Johnny Moss

Sailor Roberts, Puggy Pearson, Doyle Brunson, and Crandell Addington
The last four images are used with the permission of the
University of Nevada, Las Vegas, Library Collection

Arnold Rothstein: America's Richest Gambler Murdered Over a Poker Game

*"I've loved baseball ever since Arnold Rothstein fixed the World Series in 1919...*Hyman Roth to Michael Corleone in *The Godfather.*

Arnold Rothstein, (1887 to 1928), was called the Brain and the Big Bankroll. He owned many gambling houses, was the biggest bookmaker in New York, and owned a fancy casino in Saratoga, New York, called the Brook. He financed many legit and underworld operations, especially bootlegging during prohibition. He also financed Broadway shows, stock market bucket shop operations, labor disputes, and heroin smuggling operations.

He fixed the 1919 World Series of Baseball. He could keep changing the odds on horse races until he had a tremendous advantage because he was the layoff man, the bookmaker's bookmaker.

Rothstein was the model for Meyer Wolfsheim in F. Scott Fitzgerald's *The Great Gatsby*. He was also the model for Nathan Detroit in Damon Runyon's *Guys and Dolls*. His close friend, Titanic Thompson, was the model for Sky Masterson in the same hit play and movie. The current HBO Series, *Boardwalk Empire*, has Arnold Rothstein as a historical character. A few years after his death, in 1934, Spencer Tracy starred in a movie entitled *Now I'll Tell*. It was based on Rothstein from a book by his wife.

Johnny Moss told his biographer that Nicholas "Nick the Greek" Dandalos "broke" Arnold Rothstein and all the gamblers on the east coast. Many poker historians parroted this silly statement. They gambled often. Rothstein's biographers agree that the Greek was Rothstein's pigeon. The

Greek was way up and back broke 73 times. Rothstein loaned him $25,000 when he was broke to bet on the fixed World Series.

Rothstein won the biggest pot in poker history at that time, $797,000, from the Greek playing five-card stud. The Greek started with back to back Kings. Rothstein started with the Ace and King of diamonds, the Ace in the hole. Both were raising all the way. With one card to come, all the money was in the pot. The Greek had the Kings, and Rothstein had a diamond flush draw, and could catch one of the three Aces or the last King if the Greek didn't help his hand. With the odds way against him, Rothstein built the pot and made the flush. I suspect cheating, maybe a cold deck. These early gambling giants coppered the odds anyway they could.

In a series of poker matches, Rothstein always beat the Greek, usually for sums over $100,000. He attributed his success to his superior bankroll. As the pots got bigger and bigger, the Greek had to play unlucky sooner or later.

Rothstein ran poker games. When three policemen were beating on the door of a poker game, he thought they were robbers. He fired three times through the door. In some miraculous shooting, he hit all three without any serious injuries. He was not charged, given his juice with the police and the politicians.

Arnold Rothstein was murdered because of one of the most famous poker games of all time. They started out playing high-stakes bridge and switched to poker. It started as all cash, no-limit, five-card stud. However, it was different from any poker game because Rothstein was using I.O.U.s or markers. As Rothstein got off big loser, the pots had lots of his small initialed chits. Titanic Thompson set up the game and was secret partners with everyone in the game, including Rothstein at the start. When he was $12,000 ahead, Titanic ended the partnership with Rothstein in the bathroom. His major confederate was another card sharp, Nate Raymond. Also in the game was future Poker Hall of Fame member Joe Bernstein. Doyle Brunson has written that Bernstein was "a likable and entertaining fellow, if something of a compulsive card cheat."

When the game ended after three days, Rothstein owed $475,000 in markers or I.O.U.s. Accounts vary. The "Houseman" or man running the game was George "Hump" McManus, who was responsible for collecting all debts.

Rothstein knew and said he had been cheated. Remember, he was also known as a swindler, cheater, and the fixer of the World Series. He said he would not pay and then said he would pay later. In those days, big gamblers paid off whether they had been cheated or not. During the game, Rothstein would take cash out of the pot and put in his markers. He'd also demand all the side bets he could get as to highest spade for $10,000. At the end of the match, Rothstein and Nate Raymond cut high card for $40,000 and Raymond won. Raymond, like Titanic Thompson, was an expert card mechanic. They could mark those old paper playing cards while the game was in progress. Basically, Thompson became partners with everyone in the poker game except Rothstein, so he was owed most of the Big Bankroll's markers. Those guys were close friends, but they would cheat each other.

Rothstein's friend, Nicky Arnstein, big gambler, and boyfriend of stage and screen star, Fannie Brice of the movie, *Funny Girl*, told Rothstein he must pay or his word would be bad on the street. Also, he would be labeled a sucker for being cheated. One reason that Rothstein gave for being slow to pay was the half-million dollars he had tied up in bets on President Hoover's election.

After many days, Rothstein, went to a meeting in a hotel room with a drunk McManus. The two men were shouting and cursing. Hump pulled his barking iron. Rothstein went for the gun, and there was a struggle. McManus shot him. True to the underworld code, Rothstein would not tell the police who shot him. He died a few days later. He would have won over half a million dollars the next day on the state and federal elections of 1928.

It took a year to put McManus on trial for first-degree murder, and it was a huge national newspaper story. Titanic was really owed half of the markers, almost a quarter of a million dollars. He promised to testify for the state and was released from jail as a material witness. At the trial, prosecutors expected Titanic to testify that he had seen McManus at the hotel shortly before the murder. Titanic said he didn't remember when he'd last seen McManus, citing his bad memory. He said he could bet $10,000 on a horse one day and not remember its name the next. To the judge's dismay, Titanic's testimony had the whole court room laughing. Newspaper photos of a dapper, handsome, perfectly-dressed Titanic with diamonds on several fingers coming and going from court were in newspapers across the country. This made Titanic nationally famous and hurt his cons and prop bets. Titanic said, "Publicity is not good for my business."

George "Hump" McManus was ruled innocent by the judge when the judge was asked for a directed verdict of acquittal. None of the poker players were good witnesses. The one eye witness changed her story saying McManus was not the man she saw leaving the hotel room. McManus had thrown the pistol out of the hotel room window. A witness had seen it and turned the pistol in to the police. There was a Chesterfield overcoat found in the hotel room monogrammed with McManus' initials, although the prosecution could not prove it was his. It had the hotel room key in the pocket. McManus had registered in a fake name, naturally. After he was acquitted, McManus asked for his coat back. He wore the prosecution's main exhibit as he left the court room. It's a wonder he didn't ask for the pistol back also.

BLUFF EUROPE MAGAZINE

Remembering Johnny Moss: The Grand Old Man of Poker

*I know about all those things because they were done to me. Being on the road is the best education in the world...*Johnny Moss

The first time I met Johnny Moss was in Longview, Texas in 1959. On the five hundred mile drive from Lubbock, Curly Cavitt taught me about gambling with his stories about Johnny Moss and Pat Renfro, who had been partners when they were only twenty-one years old, back in 1928. In his Cadillac, Curly had a high-powered rifle, a sawed-off shotgun, a .22 caliber semi-automatic pistol, and the .38 caliber revolver that he always carried inside gambling joints. Johnny Moss and Curly had known each other many years in Dallas. Both men wore the baggy, pleated, dark colored slacks that would help disguise the pistols they always carried. Being robbed or arrested was common place. Pat, Curly, and Johnny had just been robbed in a large poker game in Beeville, Texas, outside Corpus Christi.

The robbers were real pros out of Kansas City. They had shotguns and tear gas. Curly ran into the bathroom and hid most of his bankroll and his doorknob-size diamond ring. The robbers told him to come out or they would shoot through the door. As soon as Curly came out, the main masked bandit asked him, "Curly, where's that ring?"

The robbers made everyone line up and searched them. Then they announced that they were going to search again and if anyone was holding out they would be pistol whipped. The robbers took Curly's Cadillac but they told him they would leave it a couple of miles down the road.

Hijackers were a lot better class of people back in those days than they are now. When Curly went to his car, he was counting the Mexican money in boxes in the trunk. He had been fading dice in Mexico and had stacks of the much cheaper currency. The laws saw him and it was in the newspapers that the robbers had missed thousands of dollars which was not true.

We were often arrested at poker and dice games. Once when Johnny Moss was flying home from Alabama, he was having a pleasant conversation with a nice man. The gentleman asked, "Have we flown across the state line?" When Johnny said he thought they had, the FBI man arrested him for interstate gambling.

Curly told me that the poker game in Longview would be huge. He expected to play and to buy part of the action of Pat and Johnny. Johnny Moss had won millions of dollars at poker and golf. He lost millions shooting dice and betting sports and the horses. The big game was at the Elks Club in Longview. It was gambling night. There were five open dice tables down stairs. You could shoot or fade, throwing wads of cash on the table. Curly staked several faders. Upstairs there were two poker games. One was a five-dollar limit seven stud game. I jumped in there with. Curly watched as a very old man in bib overalls cheated me, using an overhand stack. Curly said he didn't pull me up because this was just part of my education.

Johnny Moss was the dominant force in the big poker game. He talked the most, verbally challenging people, "Come on. We drove a *long* way to gamble." He seemed to have the largest stack of currency. I climbed up in a shoe-shine chair in the corner of the room to watch. Back then we gambled with paper money. People usually kept twenties on the bottom, hundreds and larger in the middle, and fives on top. You couldn't look across the green felt and count a man down. You could not ask how much money an opponent had until it was all bet. The game was razz, seven stud, low ball to the wheel. The short stacks had a few thousand in front of them. When there were two or three cards showing, anyone with an advantage moved all in and the pot usually ended there. If Johnny Moss had an even gamble, he would move in on the short stacks. Moss would announce that he could cover them so no one knew how much money was in his five-inch high stack of bills. At the time, five hundred dollar bills and thousand dollar bills were in circulation. Curly taught me how to move money in and out of the game secretly. He had a pocket full of coarse notes, as the bigger bills were called. You could get in a pot with someone you thought was a short stack only to find they were on heavy money. If Johnny Moss doubled up a short stack, it was only then that there was a count. If he won, you couldn't even tell how big the pot was since he just swooped up the money. When a pot was being played, people who were not in the pot kept quiet. Moss ribbed and scolded and dared his opponents, making talk his weapon to tilt people. When a pot finished, there were zero celebration or gloating. When a man suffered a big loss or got knocked out, he showed no emotion. It was quiet at the end of a pot because you did not rib a loser. I was aware that many of the men in the room, including Curly and Johnny, had guns.

At first, Curly, Pat Renfro and Johnny Moss all played in the game. Pat played extremely tight as he did in all games all his life, regardless of what was going on around him. When a short stack got broke, there was always someone waiting to sit in. Late in the night it was apparent that Johnny Moss was losing and moaning about his luck. Curly quit the game about even. He gave more money to Johnny and Pat since the game was getting bigger as the night wore on. Finally, Johnny Moss went on a rush about daylight, breaking several players.

A few months later, Johnny Moss spent an afternoon sweating my partner and I in a bridge tournament in Oklahoma City. As always, I was mostly taken by his eyes and his poker face. His eyes were piercing, all-knowing, fearless, scary, bemused, cold, predatory, and conceited. It appeared as if he could see right through you and the backs of your cards. His eyes seemed to be permanently half opened. He scanned the room studying every detail.

Johnny Moss moved to Odessa, Texas in the mid-fifties to be near the oil boom, gambling, and the big-time gamblers including Paul Harvey and Tom "Pinkie" Roden. They had one of the biggest poker games in Texas for many years. Paul Harvey, a big-time bookmaker and gambler, catered to the oil-rich Texans in Midland and Odessa. One time, Paul and Johnny played heads-up poker for five days and nights. They took a two day break and played another five days and nights. Needless to say, Johnny won. Pinkie had been Texas' biggest bootlegger before he established the state's largest chain of retail liquor stores. Pinkie owned a small hotel in Odessa called the Inn of the Golden West. The poker games were in a private club in the hotel called the Golden Rooster. This was the home game of Johnny Moss and many of the future winners of the early World Series including Moss, Amarillo Slim, Doyle Brunson, Brian "Sailor" Roberts, Bill Smith, and Jack "Treetop" Straus. All of the famous road gamblers of the fifties and sixties went to Odessa to try Johnny Moss including Pat Renfro, Doc Ramsey, James "Longgoodie" Roy, Joe Floyd, and Charlie Hendrix.

My partner, Double Smart Jerry, and I rode down to Odessa to try the big game in 1961, when we were twenty-one. We rode down from Lubbock with our dear friend Bill Smith, who won the main event of the World Series in 1985. We knew our bankrolls of around four hundred each were laughable. We thought we could beat anyone at Texas Hold 'em. The very first pot Jerry played in the seven-five lowball game, he caught a pat ten and raised it on up. Paul Harvey drew two cards and moved Jerry all in. Jerry folded and Paul showed he had caught two face cards. Poker is hard on the low rollers.

Johnny Moss remembered me from the bridge tournament and from Longview. He told me to come early the next day and he would stake me in an auction bridge game. None of the gamblers were very good at bridge except Doyle Brunson and Sailor Roberts. A couple of months earlier, Bill Smith and I had played bridge all night long against Pat Renfro and Longgoodie and trounced them easily despite giving them a spot.

Later, Jerry got in a marathon gin rummy match. We went home with Tuffy Hufstedler and they played gin nearly all night. Jerry made enough money for us to try the big Hold 'em game again the next day.

The next afternoon, Johnny Moss and I played partners in three rubbers of auction bridge. He was betting a dollar a point. He also made some side bets. I never once had enough face cards to make a bid. We lost all three rubbers and the Hold 'em game started. Jerry was smart enough to get the seat right behind Johnny Moss but we were both clearly out bank rolled. This was the most talented gathering of poker players imaginable at the time. No wonder we got broke. The big producers in those days were the bookmakers, bootleggers, and the oil men. Famous gamblers from all over came to Pinkie's joint. They strutted up licking their chops and limped away licking their wounds.

Mickey Cohen, one of the biggest Mob bosses on the west coast, came to Odessa to gamble with Paul Harvey and his oil men. He was portrayed by Harvey Keitel in the movie *Bugsy*. He was Bugsy Siegel's right-hand man. The Texas Rangers heard Cohen had arrived and demanded he leave the state. When the Rangers telephoned Paul Harvey, he asked, "Well, what is he, an *outlaw*?" Paul Harvey provided Cohen a limo to Wichita Falls but the Rangers arrested him and drove him to Dallas where he flew back to Los Angeles.

Johnny Moss maintained his residence in Odessa and Las Vegas for the rest of his life. During the late seventies, eighties and nineties, I would always say hello to Johnny Moss at the World Series of Poker at Binion's Horseshoe in Las Vegas. He was very recognizable with his golf cap, cardigan sweater, and Buddy Holly glasses. He was extremely courteous to me but he had a reputation of being rather hard on the dealers. Moss won a total of eight bracelets at the World Series of Poker over the years. He won his last bracelet when he was 81 in 1988. Moss continued to play poker right up to his death at age 89 in 1997.

I was at the World Series most years after 1975. When he was pushing ninety, Johnny rode all around the Horseshoe in this electric cart. It had this little rubber horn he would squeeze like the one Harpo Marx always carried. He took great delight in honking the horn. He played twenty dollar limit and usually napped at the table. These naps might last a round. The dealers knew not to bother him. Around Binion's, Johnny Moss was treated like a king. He lived there free courtesy of Jack Binion. Johnny Moss rolled up beside me the last time I saw him and we played in the ten and twenty dollar limit Hold 'em game. The other players all knew who he was. He got out a small piece of paper from his wallet and said, "Johnny, read that. That's what I got." It said "gout". They called him the Grand Old Man of Poker and he really was a grand old man.

SOURCES:

JENKINS, DON. *JOHNNY MOSS: CHAMPION OF CHAMPIONS.* COPYRIGHT: JOHNNY MOSS.

NUGENT, JOHN. *MICKEY COHEN: IN MY OWN WORDS.* PRENTICE-HALL.

STOWERS, CARLTON. *THE UNSINKABLE TITANIC THOMPSON.* EAKIN PRESS.

Johnny Moss Timeline:
1907 - Born in Marshall, Texas.
1908 - Moved to Dallas.
1919 - Started playing poker.
1923 - Started working at a poker room watching for cheaters.
1927 - Married Virgie. They stayed together his whole life.
1926 - Daughter Eleoweese born.

1928 - Moved to Olney, Texas for the oil boom. First partnered with Pat Renfro.

1930 - They moved to Graham, Texas for the oil boom.

1938 - Moved to Lubbock, Texas and was promptly hijacked.

1938 - Celebrated golf match in Lubbock with Titanic Thompson. Ty bet Johnny he couldn't shoot a 46 on nine holes with a four iron. Johnny had his four iron welded into a two iron. Ty sent a man around to raise the cups on all the holes. Johnny caught on and sent his caddy around to put the cups back as they were. Johnny won the bet shooting a 41.

1939 - Moved back to Dallas and won $250,000 in one poker game. Lost it all on the horses.

1942 - Moved to Lake Charles, Louisiana.

1943 - Drafted into the Navy as a Seabee.

1945 - Honorable Discharge

1949 - Famous five month heads-up match at Binion's Las Vegas Club with Nick "the Greek" Dandalos. Moss and Benny Binion won nearly three million dollars from the Greek.

1950 - Met Amarillo Slim.

1953 - Met Doyle Brunson. Doyle has said that Johnny Moss was the best no-limit Hold 'em player in the world in his day.

1970 - Selected first World Series Champion by a vote of his peers.

1971 - Won the first World Series Championship

1974 - Won the World Series Championship.

1979 - The only living inductee into the Poker Hall of Fame.

1997 - Johnny Moss died at age 89. He won eight World Series bracelets and numerous other tournaments in his lifetime.

BLUFF MAGAZINE

Benny Binion: Texas Boss Gambler

It was 1960, and all the talk on the radio that summer was about John F. Kennedy versus Lyndon Johnson for the Democratic Party nomination for president. I've turned twenty-one and can get a police card to work in a casino, if need be. After misadventures traveling from our beloved West Texas, all along Route 66, the Mother Road, America's Highway, my poker and road partner and I are beating Las Vegas and Fremont Street hard on the free sandwiches, cigs, mixed drinks. He'd bet a buck on the pass line, and I'd bet a buck on the don't pass at the dice table. We'd get cigs, a sandwich, and a drink order in, and break even unless the dice hit boxcars, twelve. I tried a spin shot on the dice tables, where you kill a five on the bottom with spinning, centrifugal force. The gruff old box man told me, "go practice somewheres else, kid." There must have been some secret society, because all the old gamblers called you "kid."

I traveled bridge tournaments, big like poker now, and became a Life Master, the highest rank in my mid-twenties, so I thought I was unbeatable at all card games.

I found a money auction bridge game at the Horseshoe, owned by the legendary Benny Binion, the very man I had come to see. In no time, I was gambling at my road game, against three old men no smart person would trust. God could not have beaten them. I was getting cheated big time.

My bridge partner would bid really high, get doubled, and go down a bunch. Each hand, I owed more money. I told them I was pulling up, and we were a few hands into the first of three rubbers. Pleading dry pockets, I swore I would run to my flop house, and be back with the long green.

Then a booming voice behind me told me I did not have to pay them anything. I had met Benny Binion, the most legendary gambler Texas or

Las Vegas will ever produce. Benny sent my partner and I across the street to work for future Poker Hall of Fame member, Bill Boyd, shilling poker at the Golden Nugget. For decades, I would say hello at the World Series of Poker to the Poker Hall of Fame members that I met when I was 19 to 21: Johnny Moss, Bill Boyd, and Benny Binion. They'd pretend to remember me most graciously.

When Benny Binion went to Las Vegas to own a mere casino, he took a huge step down from his position as "Boss Gambler" of downtown Dallas, and secret partner in gambling houses in Ft. Worth, and other towns. He had five policy wheels, (the numbers racket), and a part of dice games everywhere, when that was the major form of gambling. All the gambling in wide-open downtown Dallas paid Benny Binion twenty-five per cent street tax. He had the laws and politicians in his pocket, until his sheriff lost in 1946 and a wave of reform swept America. Binion maintained a great deal of control in Dallas and Ft. Worth for a decade after moving to Las Vegas.

Benny Binion, though illiterate, was a marketing genius, a pure genius. He said he wanted to make the little people feel like big people. He invented food and booze comps for low rollers. Benny said folks want good food cheap, good whiskey cheap, and a square gamble. He invented the World Series of Poker with his five-month public match between Johnny Moss and Nick "the Greek" Dandalos, but they were taking off the Greek. Two or three million, probably.

When I first went to Vegas, Benny's joint had ten cent craps with a big neon sign. The dice table was at the front door, touching the sidewalk. Chips were a dime. The big dice table was elbow to elbow, and these system players stood at the edges, writing down each roll of the dice in the false belief that it mattered. (The Gambler's Fallacy) A big sign said to watch your own bets, because the whole dice spread was packed with stacks of ten cent chips, and folks would rob each other for a stack.

Benny Binion was a megalomaniac before he left Texas, wanting control of as much as possible. The Chicago and New Orleans Mobs had been in Dallas in a light way: pin balls, marble boards, slots, drugs, but Benny kept them out of his gambling operations, until he had to flee the state. He first opened up in Vegas as partners with an old-style, Sicilian Mob guy, but he didn't like Benny's take-any-size-bet philosophy. Benny pioneered high stakes; your first bet is your limit. He knew you could make more money off a square joint/rug joint in the long run, than you could from a bust-out/sawdust joint.

Davie Berman, the toughest Jew in Las Vegas, and a Mob spokesperson, supposedly called Benny to a sit down to say all the attention and national press about his running shoot out, and continual bombings of Herbert "the Cat" Noble had to stop. Some of those boys from Illinois don't need to threaten.

Benny brought in "sixty hop heads off the Jacksboro Highway" to sleep on the Horseshoe floor. These were gun toting, Ft. Worth and Dallas, thugs who played by no Mr. Nice Guy Mob rules. There was some very unseemly talk about going into Little Italy on Christmas Day to kill grandmothers. You know those Fort Worth folks. Mean.

The Texas Centennial in 1936 celebrated Texas' independence from Mexico. It was depression-era, hard times, and the political bosses of Dallas and Ft. Worth allowed wide-opening gambling. Benny flourished in hard times, first bootlegging, then dice, then the policy wheel.

Benny Binion had a dice joint in wide-open Ft. Worth over a Mexican-food restaurant, not at all a secret. They had a tame burro as the mascot of the joint. They put signs on the sides of the burro advertising the restaurant. Each morning, they would take the burro to another part of Ft. Worth, and let it out. It would head home by the side of the highway like a homing pigeon. And other pigeons would follow.

Benny would sit in his booth at the Sombrero Restaurant talking on the phone or telling stories. He wore a western shirt with signature, three-dollar gold piece buttons. Benny Binion died Christmas Day of 1989, at eighty-five years of age. He said, "I'll tell you the truth, but I won't tell you everything." I believe him.

In gathering material for this, a couple of quotes really stuck out. When law enforcement would ask Benny Binion if he knew a whole list of outlaws, including Mob guys, he would admit he did. Benny said the Mob had been into Dallas since the 1930s, but especially after 1946. When asked about a list of leading mobsters that were Binion friends and associates, Benny said, "They never told me they was in it."

Benny Binion controlled some of the numbers racket, and a great many gambling joints in Dallas and Ft. Worth. After spending $30 million on legal fees, he was convicted of income tax evasion. Benny told the federal judge, "I didn't intend to cheat the government. I'm kinda ignorant. I got to gambling and all, you know."

One year at the World Series, I was staying at the Mint, next door, which became part of Binion's Horseshoe. I always befriended those large Texas security guards. This was in the early eighties. I made a big winning, and while I cashed, the guard suggested he walk me to the Mint. My lock box was there. Neat, two armed guards to go next door.

During that World Series, a guy grabs a woman's purse and cuts out running. Those same two heavy guys gave chase. I ran along to see what happened. The guy runs into the Mint, knocks Dixie cups of quarters out of the hands of old ladies near the slots, knocks an old lady over, and then they tackled him, and led him back into Binion's. When other casinos had troubles, they would call the police. The Binion's allegedly "back roomed" cheats and thieves, which means took them to an office to beat the hell out of them.

Benny Binion used that same example in his later oral history. He said that beat folks up bad for stealing an old ladies purse, and folks cheer. He said it saved the woman from coming back to Las Vegas testify. Over the years, the casino has been in trouble several times for "back rooming", beating folks up.

I come from a few generations of gamblers, some con artists. We say, we are not "in the muscle end of it", meaning no violence. When you walk into another man's gambling joint, you follow their rules. You leave your gun in the car. As a poker player, I expected and got safety from the houseman.

Benny was being very careful all his life, and was under FBI surveillance in Las Vegas and at his ranch in Montana, and he knew it. At first he stopped them to explain he needed to know it was them, and not some enemy. Sometimes for kicks, he'd get to going very fast, and lose them, then go look for them. All lawmen and judges ate free at Benny's.

I interviewed Jack Binion in 1990. He said Benny Binion came to Las Vegas in 1946, and he did! There were lots of killings back in Dallas and Ft. Worth after he left, many over hijackings. My great uncle, a gambler, was beaten up badly , and died about this time, in what was called the "gambling wars."

J. Edgar Hoover had directed the FBI to get something on Benny Binion, and they tried from his release from prison in 1954 until his death. With tens of millions of dollars and several law enforcement agencies after him, Benny Binion didn't need to do anything illegal.

BLUFF EUROPE MAGAZINE, BLUFF MAGAZINE

Las Vegas, Show Business, and the Mob

*The gambling known as business looks with austere disfavor upon the business known as gambling...*Ambrose Bierce

Show business and gambling have always gone hand in hand. The recent poker scandal involving Ben Affleck, Leonardo DiCaprio, Matt Damon, and Tobey Maguire gained a lot of attention for high stakes, illegal poker. This is like the Friars Club cheating scandal in Los Angeles in the 1940s. It also gained world-wide press because of the stars involved: George Burns, George Jessel, George Raft, Chico Marx, Phil Silvers, and especially Mafia biggie Johnny Roselli. Roselli's application for Friars membership was promoted by Frank Sinatra and Dean Martin. The Mob was in the movie industry, and show business figures were used to dealing with them, and socializing with them. Roselli controlled the biggest talent booking agency in Las Vegas and helped his friends. He was also a loan shark to the famous in Los Angeles and Las Vegas.

From the 1930s on, the Mob show clubs in places like Atlantic City featured top entertainers, and had every game you'd see in a Las Vegas casino in the back. Dean Martin and Jerry Lewis, as well as Frank Sinatra, got their starts in these clubs and had long ties to the Mob. When Martin and Lewis were booked at the Flamingo in Las Vegas in the late 1940s, Lewis' gambling addiction quickly left him heavily in debt. The Mob set him up a budget and a payback plan and he paid them back. Frank Sinatra had played their clubs, paled around with them, and they promoted his career, as they did Martin and Lewis' career. The scene in the *Godfather,* where a horse's head is put in a producer's head to secure a movie part was about Sinatra. Johnny Roselli, the Mafia's go to guy on the West Coast and

Las Vegas, went to the movie producer and Sinatra got a career-mending, academy award-winning part in *From Here to Eternity*.

In Galveston, Texas, the Maceo brothers controlled gambling from the 1930s to the mid-fifties. They had a fancy casino featuring the Balinese Room, where performers included Guy Lombardo, Phil Harris, Bing Crosby, Bob Hope, Jack Teagarden, Duke Ellington, and Frank Sinatra.

In 1946, the Mafia held a conference in Havana to honor Lucky Luciano as the Boss of all Bosses. According to the FBI, Frank Sinatra transported $2 million to Havana for the Mob. He also sang for the big conference. It was here a vote was taken that meant that Benjamin Siegel would be murdered. The casinos in Havana had developed a reputation for cheating. Meyer Lansky was put in charge of cleaning them up and restoring "square gambling."

In the 1940s, 1950s and early 1960s, the Mob controlled the Las Vegas strip hotels and show rooms, and paid talent higher than anyone. Sinatra helped them by making the star-studded movie, *Ocean's Eleven*, and by having the Rat Pack: Sinatra, Martin, Sammy Davis, Jr., Peter Lawford and Joey Bishop play the Sands. These events really elevated the drop at the joint.

Frank Sinatra owned 9 per cent of the Sands at one time. He did have a very long association with, and promoted Las Vegas. His first Vegas movie was in 1941. Sinatra was a blackjack sucker, and the Mob may have torn up some of his markers. Howard Hughes had dated Ava Gardner, who became Sinatra's wife. The two men did not like each other. When Hughes bought the Sands, Sinatra still sang there and had a contract. However, he went kind of crazy, getting big drunk, cursing patrons, and dealers. Sinatra lost $50,000 at blackjack only to be told his credit was cut off. He really freaked. By some accounts, he broke a plate glass window with a golf cart. He finally got to see Carl Cohen, the casino manager. Sinatra cursed him, using racial epithets, and threw a chair. Cohen hit him in the mouth, knocking the caps off his two front teeth. Cohen had also owned part of the Sands before Hughes. Sinatra left the Sands, never to return. When Cohen walked through the casino, the employees all applauded. Later, Sinatra quipped, "Never fight a Jew in the desert."

Dean and Sammy were the opposite, always nice to the dealers. Dean had started out as a dealer in Mob joints back east and was good at it. When several of the celebrities would deal blackjack, they would show the players their hole card.

Sinatra did demand that Sammy Davis, Jr. be allowed to stay in the hotel, when blacks were still sent to their own area in Las Vegas. Sammy Davis did a lot for civil rights in Las Vegas. I was in Las Vegas when he died. They dimmed the lights on the strip and devoted the whole local television news to him. They ended with Sammy singing and dancing to Jerry Jeff Walker's tune, *Bojangles*.

Fats Domino was a rock and roll founder, legend, and gambling addict. He estimated he lost $2 million. He liked to watch those galloping dominoes jump across the green felt. Like Jerry Lewis, Fats got heavily indebted to the casinos, and paid them back as a performer, like so many others.

Col. Tom Parker, Elvis Presley's manager, was the worst gambling addict of them all. He had been a carnival barker, owner, and hustler. He had dancing chickens, chickens on a hot plate. With little experience and a checkered past of which little is known, Parker became the manager of Eddie Arnold, a country star, and then Elvis. The Colonel dominated Elvis, got the same income as Elvis, and kept them in Las Vegas eight years because he owed the Hilton a reputed $30 million when Elvis died. Elvis did 837 consecutive sold-out shows to 2.5 million people at the Hilton. With all that income, Col. Parker left only a $1 million estate. He would stand at a dice table hour after hour betting as high as they'd let him. He sometimes spent 12 to 14 hours a day gambling. Casinos used a system of getting show business people or key employees in debt as a golden handcuff, a way to keep them, a management strategy, and it worked.

There were fancy casinos in Texas, New York, L.A., and elsewhere in the 1920s and 1930s. With prohibition making bars illegal, they might as well add gambling. Same with bars and shows. The Mob was always there, but expanded. The late forties brought mobsters to Vegas. They already knew how to run casinos, and no one else did. If you were a dice man, pit boss, croupier, and even a poker player, you learned your trade in an illegal environment, and many early Vegas pioneers had records. However, these were not looked at heavily by the gaming board or authorities, at first. Show biz stars already worked with the Mob in their show rooms before they worked Vegas: Sinatra, Dean Martin/Jerry Lewis, and Sophie Tucker. A huge movie star and comedian, Jimmy Durante, owned a nightclub in Chicago and Al Capone, Lucky Luciano, and movie actor, pal of mobsters, George Raft shot dice there.

In 1940s, Los Angeles, mobsters and movie stars hung out together. Big movie star Lana Turner dated Johnny Stompanado, a lieutenant of gambling boss, Mickey Cohen. Turner's 14 year old daughter stabbed Stompanado to death.

Gladys Knight was another gambling addict and Las Vegas headliner, being a sucker for baccarat and blackjack. She ruined her career, gambling in the casino with her name on the marquee out front.

As for the question, did the Mob run things better? Yes and a big no. Yes on the floor, restaurant and show room. No on killing each other and no on too much skim, and short-term perspective.

My cousin, Bill Stapp, worked for the Mob casinos, Howard Hughes, and later the corporations over a 40 year period of time. He has a lot of personality and made big tips at the Sands when the Rat Pack were there, and later the Dunes with Big Sid Wyman. Each dealer could keep their tips rather than pooling, as they do now.

First casinos were a money laundering prop. Everyone came in for a piece. All those guys got their start working dice, poker, and smaller casinos. In gambling, as you know, customers go on tilt, huff around and calm down. A gambling manager needs a thick skin. The Mob guys were good at the hands on, walking around, friendly management. Benny Binion was not in the Mob, but he had a saying that sums this up, "Make the little man feel like a big man." In Las Vegas, when you saw the biggest stars, you could also see them or gamble with them on the floor. Sinatra or Martin would take over my cousin's blackjack table and just give house money away, and hustle him tips.

When celebrities were in the casino, the casino bosses might take the stick at the dice table. Big Sid Wyman, of the Poker Hall of Fame, is one of my favorites. He was known for great casino management and marketing innovations. He brought the first topless revue, the airplane junkets from New York, and the biggest cash poker game of all time right outside the showroom door at the Dunes, with nine other Poker Hall of Famers.

Cuban band leaders Desi Arnaz and Xavier Cugat got their start singing at Mob joints in Cuba. Desi was a long-term Vegas headliner, and married to the much, much bigger star, Lucille Ball or Lucy. He was a big, loud sucker, a skirt chaser, and an embarrassment to Lucy. One night he was off big loser at the craps and being obnoxious. Big Sid Wyman had taken the stick. This was at the Rivera, of which Sid was part owner. Desi got in a shouting feud with a lady at the table and Wyman told him to calm down. Desi threw a drink in his face. Hey, Wyman was a media guy too! He leaked the story to the columns, Walter Winchell, and the newspapers all across the United States. Perfect revenge. In the story, Wyman was referred to as "a croupier." Later, Lucy left Desi.

The people who brought you alcohol and gambling, also brought lots of show business. Movies, live shows, records. I managed Joe Ely on MCA Records. The early record business was seriously crooked with payola. It still was thirty years ago. The Mob founded MCA basically, and Mob money went into other movie and record companies. When they put up seed money, their hooks are in.

Martin and Sinatra had great talent, but they had the backing of an organization with power and influence coast to coast. MCA was big in television, movies, and records. They tap someone on the head, he is a star.

The gambling world creates great loyalties. You give accommodations to those who gave you accommodations starting out. The gambling world creates great courtesy from management. Their bosses are scary, don't forget that!

Bluff Europe Magazine

Amarillo Slim Remembered. A Great Hustler. An Even Greater Showman

*If you are going to be a sucker, be a quiet one...*Amarillo Slim

One of the most pivotal figures in poker history is Amarillo Slim Preston, the colorful Texan, who was just full of old sayings and gambling wisdom. When he won the World Series of Poker in 1972, he suddenly became a household name and the most famous gambler in the world. He made eleven *Tonight Show* appearances with Johnny Carson. Slim was on several TV game shows and had a part in a Robert Altman movie, *California Split*. Slim was just born for self-promotion. I watched the video of the 1973 World Series, again. At the final table were several men that would win the main event of the World Series later, some that would make the Poker Hall of Fame. Puggy Pearson defeated Johnny Moss that year. Treetop Straus and Sailor Roberts were there. Crandell Addington, my favorite, the flashy, good-looking fashionably dressed gambler they called "Dandy" was the guy I cheered for at the early World Series. With his Stetson, fine suit, and boots, Addington would be Hollywood's idea of what a Texas road gambler looked like. He still holds the record for the most final table appearances in the main event. But Amarillo Slim kept walking up to the table, wise-cracking, joking with the players, even though he was knocked out already.

I had played poker around here with Amarillo Slim in Lubbock as early as 1961. He was not all that great a player or winner. A little later, he began to travel with and share bankroll with Doyle Brunson and Sailor Roberts. They made a lot of money, and ended up busted in Las Vegas. I play a little poker now with Shaun Rice, Amarillo Slim's protege and traveling partner. He says Slim was the best hustler alive, and I believe that. He used his celebrity to play Doctors, Lawyers, and Square Johns heads up, easy marks. Slim was great at prop bets.

I first went to the World Series in 1975. Amarillo Slim and I sat together on the plane going out. As usual, we told funny stories about the West Texas gamblers we knew. We had our picture taken in front of the million dollars in ten-thousand dollar bills at Binion's. For many years after that time, if I saw someone with a press badge, I'd point them to Slim, and tell them truthfully, he was the best interview there. I didn't tell them that half of what he says is true, and I don't know which half. In the 1980s, Slim would reach millions of people in his interviews. I listened in a few times. I still have what he said in an interview with an Englishman: "You're an Englishman? Most Englishmen couldn't track an elephant in four feet of snow if the beast had a giant nose bleed."

Amarillo Slim was quoted repeatedly on his old sayings, "Sometimes the lamb slaughters the butcher." "I'd just as soon have my dick caught in a meat grinder as to bluff at him."

In the last years of the Shop, legendary Lubbock poker game, Slim came down and played a lot. He would wear shorts or golf clothes. In Las Vegas, he was always in costume. Finely tailored Western suits, a Stetson hat with a rattlesnake band with its mouth open as decor. He bought, at one time, ten pairs of boots in different colors. They had vents in the side, and he'd wear matching socks. He was skinny. One wag said he was "the advance man for a famine."

Slim would tell people, very truthfully, that he had done a whole lot for poker. For many years, he was the most famous gambler in America, not just poker player. I'd known Amarillo Slim since I was 21. Gamblers should be entertainers. The light players should be treated as customers, and he would be "on" in the show business sense. At the World Series, all the tourists wanted to see Amarillo Slim. He was most gracious, always laughing, always smiling and coming with the old sayings for everyone. Like Benny Binion, he treated the little man like a big man, talking to everyone.

The first day I met Slim was at Reverend Pruitt's poker game in 1961 in Lubbock. We were sitting around waiting for enough players to start and Slim was "on", entertaining and bull shitting. He was also going for a tough guy image. He said some guy pulled a gun at a poker game, and he already had his six-shooter pointed at him under the table. Then he went to his car and brought in this enormous, long-barreled six-shooter that would have been totally impractical for a gambler . When the tourists wanted autographs or to be photographed with him, he was very accessible, friendly, and represented Binion's and poker in a fabulous way everyone would remember.

Some years back, Slim's granddaughter accused him of inappropriately touching her. She has publicly recanted, and said she made it all up. All members of Amarillo Slim's family, including her parents, stand behind Slim. They have signed sworn, notarized documents backing Slim's total innocence of this bogus charge. On the advice of his attorney, and using common sense, Slim pled NO CONTEST to a misdemeanor assault charge on a plea bargain. This was not a sex charge in any way and did not require him to be listed as a sex offender. Some bargain! You would have to know how it works in West Texas. They told him this, Option One: Plead NO CONTEST to a lesser charge, pay a small fine, and leave the building. Option Two: Plead innocent and be charged with felony sexual assault. Face a jury and a possible sentence of life in prison. Life? or a fine? Choose. Amarillo Slim had pled guilty or NO CONTEST to gambling and vagrancy charges several times, as had I. When we pled guilty to vagrancy by association, it didn't mean we were broke, didn't have a residence, or anything much. It was the cost of doing business for a gambler. NO CONTEST is not a plea of guilty, but saying it is better not to fight these charges.

In Tulia, Texas, one lying rogue undercover narcotics officer framed scores of black people. Many pled guilty when they were innocent on plea bargains to get a lighter sentence. Later this was all discovered, and the governor gave pardons. None of Amarillo Slim's friends ever believed that he had become a child molester after age seventy. Doyle Brunson, one of the most respected men in poker, and one of Slim's best friends and old road partners, spoke out on Slim's behalf early on, as did any Texan I know of. Shawn Rice had known Slim for twenty-five years. They traveled together, and shared a bankroll. Like Doyle and myself, Shawn is very outspoken in defense of Slim's total innocence. Nolan Dalla, Media Director for the World Series of Poker, did an interview with Slim pointing to his innocence. Nolan himself has maintained journalistic neutrality. It is illogical to believe that Amarillo Slim was guilty of this when his whole family and his Texas friends agree that he was innocent.

BLUFF EUROPE MAGAZINE

Minnesota Fats: The World's Greatest Pool Hustler

I am the most intelligent man I know. I know everything that anybody else knows, and nobody knows what I know...Minnesota Fats.

When I played pool, I was like a good psychiatrist. I cured 'em all of their day dreams and delusions...Minnesota Fats.

Minnesota Fats, a.k.a. Rudolf Wanderone, (1913-1996) was one of America's best known gamblers for decades. In many television appearances and pool exhibitions, the public knew a rotund, jovial, lovable scamp, proud of being a professional gambler who had never worked, whose long monologues about himself were a combination of outrageous, part truthful boasts and some obvious lies. Fats said he learned pool and poker at age five, played cards and pool for money by age ten, had traveled around the world, beating *everyone* who put up cash money. He said he could whistle in five languages, had survived two ship wrecks, and knew kings, queens, and movie stars. Fats said he was the greatest pool hustler of all time. I think he was. At five feet and ten inches and nearing three hundred pounds, he was a natural-born comedian. Minnesota Fats is the most famous name associated with pool.

Early on, he was called New York Fats or Broadway Fats. His father encouraged him and staked him to gamble from an early age. When he was thirteen, the automobile dealers in New York promoted a big pool match between Fats and a world-champion nine-ball player and pool celebrity, Cowboy Weston. Weston wore a massive white hat, boots, and had matching pearl-handled pistols. Fats beat him.

Fats arrived on Broadway, the heart of New York, in the roaring 1920s. Gambling and pool were very big across America. Ralph Greenleaf made $2000 a week from his vaudeville act at the Palace, shooting trick shots and bank shots. There were mirrors on the ceiling. Fats practiced and practiced all these shots.

While still a teenager, Fats became a friend and protege of Titanic Thompson, one of America's best known gamblers. Ty became famous as a witness in the sensational trial of George McManus for the murder of Arnold Rothstein. Titanic was also famous for his proposition bets and his large wagers. Titanic introduced New York Fats to Nick the Greek, Damon Runyon, Milton Berle, Bing Crosby, Nicky Arnstein, Babe Ruth, and his best friend, Hubert "the Giant" Cokes. Cokes backed a teenaged Fats to play pool games for $1000 a game. Tommy Thomas, Titanic's son, wrote me, "Ty said Hubert was the most dangerous smart man he ever knew. He would carry two .45 pistols and walk into any pool hall and challenge anyone to a game of one pocket or a fist fight for any amount of money."

More than anything else Fats learned from his mentors, he learned the art of "the conversation", the taunts, brags, challenges, and negotiations over the game or the spot, and finally the bet. Fats also learned not to have backers.

In one epic match, Fats played a top pool player, Coney Island Al, backed by a big-bookmaker named Smart Henry. After Titanic and Cokes made many side bets and increasing bets, Fats beat him. This led Titanic Thompson to lay a new road name on Fats, Double-Smart Fats.

During the depression of the 1930s, Fats went on the road in his brand new Cadillac, coast to coast, playing the "lemon proposition", shooting under his skill level and hustling everyone. Not only did Fats have "the conversation" to set up the match, he talked all the time, whenever he shot or you shot or any time. Fats made them want to beat him, and believe they could as the stakes increased. His motto was: "I'll give you an out and take out after you."

When Fats arrived in Oklahoma City, the big gambling game was one pocket, where you had to sink any eight balls in one corner pocket. Jack Hill invented the game and Cokes had already been there. Fats stayed six months and came away the best one pocket player in gambling except for Cokes.

As a road gambler, Fats played all card games: poker, gin rummy, knock rummy, and clabber. He said, "What if you are the best gin rummy player in the world and they don't play gin rummy?" In his tours through the country in the 1930s, he wasn't well known. Although he often bragged he beat everyone, he did go broke in some poker games, and his wife, more credible, said he had a weakness for dice. She said they "lived like kings." When you found the big pool hall in a town, you found gamblers for dominos, gin, a bookie for sports or horses, and access to a poker game. The pool hall was the men's gathering place. In the late thirties, Fats ran into Wimpy Lassiter, a top road hustler and tournament champion, in Washington, D.C. They played all night, and Fats left him scratching a broke man's ass.

Fats would go to billiard and pool tournaments, but rarely enter. He was there for the gambling on the side. At the 1941 World Championships in Chicago, Willie Mosconi won, but Fats set up a booking operation with a line on all the matches. He booked 156 bets and won 154 of them. Flush with cash, he headed his new LaSalle to the Little Egypt part of Southern Illinois known for its wide-open gambling. The high-roller poker game in tiny Du Quoin, Illinois was run by Muzz Riggio and Joe Scoffic. Fats became a regular. Fats stayed at their St. Nicholas Hotel. Titanic and Hubert Cokes both played in the poker game. As he often did, Fats challenged the pool hall owner or houseman to play any game heads up. Fats played Muzz pool for several days and beat him badly. They would play varied pool propositions for hours, then gin and clabber for hours, then poker, and return to the pool table.

In 1941, Fats met his wife of forty-four years there working at the Evening Star, a night club and gambling joint owned by Riggio and Scoffic. His beloved Evelyn did all the driving, carried the bags, fixed the flats, and dealt with the hotels. Evelyn said, "The heaviest thing Fats ever lifted was a silver dollar." She had a house in nearby Dowell, Illinois, which became Fats headquarters during most of their long marriage.

One night, the big poker game at the St. Nicholas was robbed by men with machine guns. Hubert Cokes, Muff Riggio, and Fats were among those playing. The robbers told them to take off their clothes and lay on the floor. Fats started "the conversation" saying he was too fat to lay on the floor and citing health problems. They told him to stand against the wall and shut up or they'd kill him. He kept talking. The robbers got $150,000 in cash. The poker game went on with markers.

Nearby Evansville, Indiana had experienced an oil boom and also had wide-open gambling. Legendary gamblers Titanic Thompson, Ray Ryan, and Hubert Cokes were playing in a large poker game at the McCurdy Hotel. They were joined by mobsters and oil men. Fats made frequent trips to Evansville. Ray Ryan won $250,000 from oil man H. L. Hunt playing gin rummy. He won $550,000 from Nick the Greek in heads up poker in Las Vegas in 1949, but he cheated. Fats played a series of pool matches over several days with high-roller Ryan. They changed the bet many ways, but Fats always won.

Titanic Thompson was known for his eye-hand coordination. He traveled with right and left-handed golf clubs, pool cues, a bowling ball, horse shoes, and a shotgun for skeet shooting. However, he never beat Fats on the pool table! Fats won $25,000 from Titanic in Evansville playing one pocket. According to Carlton Stowers, Ty Thompson's biographer, Ty told Hubert Cokes, "I got to figure the guy's about half crazy in addition to being a helluva pool player. God, he never shut up....Not making much sense, just talking to hear his damn head rattle. Like to drove me crazy." Ty played all games right and left-handed, as did Fats. Ty admitted that Fats also beat him one handed.

It was at the McCurdy Hotel that Titanic Thompson made his big prop bets that he could guess the nearest and then the exact amount of watermelons on a truck. He had paid the farmer to count the watermelons in advance.

During World War II, the biggest gambling action was in Norfolk, Virginia, home of the fleet, and a great deal of war-related industry. Titanic and his new bride relocated there, as did Fats and his new bride. Ty rented an old mansion and had frequent parties. Pool hustler Wimpy Lassiter showed up. Fats refused to play him again, but took him on as a partner and they toured country clubs and pool halls in nearby states working the "lemon proposition."

Tommy Thomas, Ty Thompson's son, wrote me that Ty was playing one pocket against Fats the night he was born in 1944. Ty said Fats was the very best at playing his own money. Many pool hustlers were staked. When Tommy Thomas came of age and was on the road hustling poker, Ty sent him to Evansville, Indiana to stay at the McCurdy Hotel and learn from his Godfather, Hubert "Daddy Warbucks" Cokes. Cokes had the new name because of his bald head, cigar, and massive bankroll.

After World War II, Fats and Evelyn returned to Dowell, Illinois. Big gambling was under assault from the Kefauver Hearings and a wave of post-war, anti-gambling reform. Pool was out of favor, with pool halls closing. Fats spent the 1950s in semi-retirement, playing pool and poker around Little Egypt.

In 1961, *The Hustler*, one of the best gambling movies of all time, was released. It starred Paul Newman as Fast Eddie, a pool hustler, Jackie Gleason as Minnesota Fats, and George C. Scott as a cold-hearted, professional gambler. These three and Piper Laurie received Academy Award nominations. Willie Mosconi, long-time world champion of billiards, was a technical advisor for the film. He did many of the trick shots. He told a reporter that the Fats character "was patterned after a real live pool hustler known as New York Fats." The author of the novel, Walter Tevis, said it was not. This big hit movie started a real revival in pool rooms and pool products.

In the film, Minnesota Fats is elegantly groomed and very taciturn, a man of few words. New York Fats, Broadway Fats, Double-Smart Fats looked like an unmade bed and never shut up. However, Fats took the name Minnesota Fats and swore until his dying day the film was about him. In the novel, but not the movie, Fats has a facial tick. He jerks his head up every ten seconds of so. The new Minnesota Fats did that sometimes, and used it in his comic delivery of a constant monologue. I think the novel was largely patterned after him.

From 1961 until 1972, the Jansco brothers held a Hustler's Pool Tournament in Johnston City, Illinois, a short drive from Fats' home. The new Minnesota Fats was the press spokesperson. He told *Sports Illustrated* that he would sue the movie people for stealing his life. Titanic Thompson and Hubert Cokes were there. Ty said, "There ain't a fine, worthwhile hustler in the world who is not here."

Fats always made fun of tournaments. He told the press the winner would get $20,000 and he'd play him for that. Typical of Fats' performance at the Hustler's convention tourney was 1970. Richie Florence, 25, was considered the best pool shooter in America, touring the country and never losing in money matches. Fats played him off and on for two weeks and won $20,000 from him. Fats would wait until Richie was tired or drinking to play. He'd quit if Richie was shooting good. He wouldn't show up when scheduled. In other years, Fats won almost $100,000 from some of the young champions using the same strategy, including Ronnie Allen and Ed Kelly. Like his mentor, Titanic Thompson, Fats never drank or smoked. He'd show up in the middle of the night ready to play all night. He was a buffoon on purpose, but Fats won big money. The biggest winner at the pool tournaments was Minnesota Fats, and he did not enter the tournament, just dusted out the champions in cash games. If you lined up famous gamblers like Ray Ryan, Wimpy Lassiter, and Titanic Thompson, it would be hard to believe the rumpled clown beat them all consistently. His bragging about the huge gambling on television and in magazines probably led to the FBI gambling raid in 1972 that ended the Hustler's Tourneys.

After six pool hustlers had testified before the grand jury, Minnesota Fats went in. "The conversation" won the day. The grand jurors followed him out in the hall for autographs. The charges were dropped.

In interviews, Fats would ridicule billiard tournaments and Willie Mosconi, who was world champ fifteen times. Fats would say, "Putting a tuxedo on a pool player is like putting ice cream on a hot dog. What if they played golf or tennis or baseball in tuxedos? If I wanted a trophy, I'd buy a trophy."

In 1978, Howard Cosell and *ABC Wide World of Sports* featured a pool match between Fats and Willie Mosconi. It was the second highest rated sports show that year behind the Ali-Spinks championship boxing match. Mosconi set the rules: no one pocket, and Fats could *not* talk while Mosconi was shooting. The audience saw mostly that Mosconi stayed furious the whole time. He hated Fats. Both were 65 years old. Fats kept up the chatter and the needle, "the conversation." The studio audience laughed throughout. Once when Mosconi was shooting, Fats walked over and addressed the audience at length. He said, "I am an expert, world champion card player... beat everybody living playing cards. I'm a high-rolling gambler."

He offered to play one pocket for $20,000, and threw a big wad of money, maybe $35,000 in $1000 and $500 bills, on the pool table from his fat boodle. Those denominations were not in circulation any longer. Cosell and his helpers pushed him toward his seat. Mosconi won the match. Minnesota Fats won the hearts of the television audience.

Minnesota Fats was at Tom Moore's invitation-only gambler's convention in Reno in 1969. This was a forerunner to the World Series of Poker. He was at the 1979 World Series when the Poker Hall of Fame started. In a televised interview, Fats said he had played poker with most of the greats, mentioning Red Winn and saying he'd known Johnny Moss all his life. Fats said poker players are "one hundred to one over any other kind of people on earth...bet 'em $5000 with your finger, you'll get paid."

As pool and Fats became very popular, he appeared on many television shows including the *Tonight Show, Joey Bishop*, and *What's My Line?* There was an autobiography, and magazine profiles in *Sports Illustrated* and *Esquire*. He played himself in some television series and one flop movie. He had his own television series, *Celebrity Billiards,* with guests such as Zsa Zsa Gabor, Milton Berle, and James Garner. Garner, who played *Maverick,* beat Fats at pool. Garner had started out as a gambler and pool hustler.

With Minnesota Fats the best known name in pool, he was hired by a billiards equipment manufacturer to tour and do exhibits. After 44 years of marriage, his beloved Evelyn divorced him. She said she was tired of the, "talk, talk, talk."

In 1984, Fats moved to Nashville, Tennessee. The elegant, old Hermitage Hotel gave him a $100 a day suite for $13 a day. He lived there eight years. Fats would sit in the lobby and ask folks if they wanted his autograph. He had a silver stamp pad with a rubber stamp of his name. At nights, he'd go to a night club in Music City and have the band introduce him. He'd dance and stamp out a few autographs. Fats married a woman half his age and lived with her his last years. He died at age 82.

Thanks to *Bluff Magazine* Editor Lance Bradley. This was his idea. This also appeared in *Bluff Europe Magazine.*

Oswald Jacoby: The Smartest
Card Player of All Time.

O swald Jacoby (1902-1984) was one of America's best all-around card players. He wrote books on poker, gin rummy, contract bridge, backgammon, canasta, gambling, and probability. Ozzie started winning at poker at age eight, playing with older boys. He lied about his age at 15 to join the Army in World War One for the last two months of the war. He spent all his time playing poker and saved $2,000 in winnings. Jacoby dropped out of Columbia University at 21 when he became the youngest licensed actuary in New York history, calculating probabilities for insurance companies. As Jacoby pointed out, insurance was gambling and started out illegal. Jacoby could make seemingly impossible calculations in his head, such as multiplying five numbers by five numbers (32,493 times 97,735). He could look through a deck of cards and quickly memorize the location of all 52 cards.

Jacoby became a regular gambler by age 23 at New York's legendary Cavendish Club where the best card players in the country gambled with millionaires. Another regular gambler at the Cavendish was Harold Vanderbilt, from America's richest family. As a yachtsman, he won the World Cup three times. The Cavendish was located in the Mayfair Hotel, where Vanderbilt had a suite of 15 rooms. Vanderbilt invented contract bridge in 1925 which, along with poker, became one of America's favorite card games.

Jacoby, called affectionately Ozzie, quit work at 28 to spend his life playing games, gambling on games, and writing about games. Jacoby first gained international fame in a celebrated bridge match with partner

Sidney Lenz against the most famous couple in bridge, Ely and Josephine Culbertson. This match was written up in newspapers across the country. Jacoby's legendary temper led him to quit after many days. It was contract bridge that made Jacoby famous. From the 1930s to the late 1960s, bridge tournaments were massive in America. They were held in the fanciest hotel ballrooms. The eccentric, brainy, quirky, conceited stars like Jacoby were written up often in major magazines such as *Time, Life*, and *Sports Illustrated.* Bridge is played in partnerships. Each player has 13 cards and they bid on the tricks they can take. Now, bridge tournaments are for an older crowd. Their senior's event is open to people seventy and over. In poker, it is fifty and over.

At the Cavendish and other New York gambling spots, Jacoby played his four big games: poker, gin rummy, bridge, and backgammon for high stakes, and he won. Those would be his best games the rest of his life.

Jacoby formed a bridge team from the young gamblers at the Cavendish, the Four Aces, that dominated bridge tournaments in the 1930s. They won the world championship from France playing in Madison Square Garden. Jacoby wrote over 10,000 articles on bridge for his syndicated column carried in newspapers all over the country.

Jacoby moved to Dallas, Texas, a big gambling town, in 1937. He played in the largest poker games with oil millionaires and expert players even though it was above his bankroll. He won. In 1940, he wrote his first book on poker. Directed at home games, it covered the rules, ethics, etiquette, stakes, strategy, probability, deception, and tells. He wrote about high and low draw, five and seven-card stud, and high-low split, but not Texas Hold 'em. His best advice was to limit the range of games in a dealer's choice game to the major games to avoid wild-card games.

When one of America's richest men, Dallasite H.L. Hunt, lost $250,000 to gambler Ray Ryan playing gin rummy, Hunt hired Jacoby to teach him expert play. This friendship helped Jacoby enter some of the largest, and most secret, Texas poker games.

When World War Two started with Pearl Harbor, Jacoby got a substitute to finish a national bridge tournament and joined Naval intelligence where he became a lieutenant commander. His group broke the Japanese and German codes. When the Korean War started, Jacoby went back to the Navy for the duration. They called to say, "We need a computer." They meant his amazing trick brain. He was a true patriot and served in three wars.

When I was 20, I began to travel the bridge tournament circuit and became a Life Master, the highest rank at that time. Like poker now, one of the attractions of bridge was that the common man can compete with the best and most famous players in the world. I played against and watched Jacoby often. He was always the most famous person in the room, with tufts of gray hair, a childish grin of warm enthusiasm, and restless energy. Playing against him was intimidating because there was a small group of kibitzers and he was the fastest card player in the world. Jacoby would open his hand and glance at his 13 cards without sorting them into suits like everyone else. Then he would bid or play at break-neck speed never looking back, but pulling the correct card from his hand. He always seemed to be rushing his opponents. He estimated that he spent six years of his life waiting for other people to play in card games. People described Jacoby often as a genius, child-like, and the most impatient man of all time.

When Jacoby was the dummy or the round was over, he would bound from the table to walk all around the room talking with everyone, doing a crossword puzzle rapidly, making prop bets, checking sports scores, and appearing to be having great fun. He was very friendly and approachable and would answer all of my questions. People would come up to Jacoby and ask him to remember a tournament hand from 40 years back and he'd remember all the cards and the outcome. I've never known of anyone who could match his mental tricks.

I once saw Jacoby go behind the scoring table right after a bridge tournament while the scores were being added up. He glanced over the sheet and announced correctly the 1st, 2nd, and 3rd place winners, adding all those numbers in his head.

My mother and I appeared on Jacoby's TV show which was a bidding contest against another pair . We would bid the hands which were shown on the screen and Jacoby would give a critique. Then, my feisty mother would tell him in an angry voice that he was really wrong! Jacoby was known for his mercurial temper but it did not come into play. I never witnessed it personally.

Once in Dallas. there was a Calcutta pool with cash prizes. The entering pairs are auctioned off with the bids making up the prize pool. I was traveling with bridge great Butch Adams. Jacoby bought us for the minimum bid of $40. I was embarrassed no one else bid. By custom, you have half your action. The prize pool became large due to ego bids, friendship bids, and Dallas money. We played poorly.

I watched Jacoby shoot dice. He was betting the front side, hard ways, and having a blast. I also watched him play gin rummy. His first discard was his lowest card. If you discarded first, he would discard a card that touched yours. If you threw an eight, he'd throw a seven or nine. As he did in other games, he played rapidly never seeming to think. His book on gin rummy is still the classic.

In the fifties there was a gin rummy cheating scandal at the Friars Club in Los Angeles. Many show business celebrities lost millions. A man in the ceiling with a peep hole would send radio signals to a device worn on the cheater's waist. This is called, "sending them over" when someone sees your hand and signals. One of their victims was Oswald Jacoby who testified at the trial, "They seemed like good players. No wonder I couldn't beat them." It seems to me the giant brain would have caught them.

When he was in college, Jacoby won a chess match against the world champion. Forty years later, he played the Russian world champion to a draw at lightening chess, however chess was just too slow for him.

It was for tournament bridge that he was most famous, authoring six major bridge books. I still play his most famous bidding conventions: the Jacoby Two No Trump, the Jacoby Transfer, weak jump overcalls, and limit raises.

All bridge tournaments award Master Points for winning and placing. While away at two wars, Jacoby fell far behind his fellow experts in the race for the most Master Points of all time. Each year, the McKenney trophy is given to the player who wins the most Master Points that year. Even though no one over fifty had ever won it, Jacoby won the most Master Points the years he was 57, 59, 60, and 61. The McKenney race requires constant travel to bridge tournaments and is a test of stamina. He swam each day a pool was available to stay in shape. He often selected very young partners. This made him the all-time Master Point leader for awhile. He had won more national and international championships than anyone except his old Cavendish buddies and first team mates, John Crawford and Howard Shenken.

Oswald Jacoby retired from the Master Point race, but he never stopped gambling. He won national backgammon titles three years in a row: 1966, 1967, and 1968. He then wrote the first scientific book on backgammon in 1970. The Jacoby Rule is named for him. A player can challenge to double the bet. His opponent must accept or concede the match. Of course, it speeds up the game and increases the action. Jacoby won the World Backgammon championship in 1972, when he was 69.

Expert backgammon players have included poker greats Stu Ungar, Paul Magriel, Dan Harrington, Erik Seidel, and Gus Hansen. Ozzie said a fast backgammon player can beat a good backgammon player 40 per cent of the time. Harrington and Seidel are recent inductees into the Poker Hall of Fame.

When Jacoby was 74, *Sports Illustrated* profiled him as an all-around gambler. He was still playing high stakes gin rummy and poker at the Dallas Country Club. Never known to be modest, Jacoby said, "I am the best seventy-four year old player of any game. Bridge, backgammon, poker, gin rummy, any of them. I play bridge better today than I did forty years ago." When asked who won or lost gambling or the stakes, Oswald Jacoby, with the greatest memory of all time, would always say he did not remember, and flash his child-like grin.

Author's Note: The two nicest, most-respected men, in poker history are Doyle Brunson and Crandell Addington. Doyle's book, *The Godfather of Poker*, is one of the best poker book ever. Doyle and Crandell have been kind enough to give me comments on my articles and poker history. Here is what Doyle wrote about bridge after reading this article:

> *I read this and it is very good and accurate. One thing....Sailor and me were the best bridge players in that time. We beat Oswald Jacoby and a man named Goodman in Waco. I beat all the gamblers, including Jacoby in "double dummy" bridge. I never got beat, nobody ever snapped about the position. You always wanted your opponent to your right where you would have position when you both had big hands..... Nice read and good luck!*

BLUFF EUROPE MAGAZINE

The Mysterious Death of Austin Squatty

John Jenkins (1949-1989) a.k.a. Austin Squatty was a flashy and well-known poker player around the cash games and tournaments of the World Series of Poker in the 1980s. I played with Squatty in the cash games. He wore a Binion's World Series hat and coat. He introduced himself to everyone at the table by his road name. He was very talkative and charming. Squatty had three cashes in the World Series. In 1983, he made the final table and placed seventh. Tom McEvoy knocked him out on his way to a bracelet. A seventh place finish only paid $21,600, a little over double the $10,000 entry fee. The hand Jack-Seven is named for him. Jenkins was a high-stakes gambler at poker and golf. After his death, there were rumors of large gambling losses and debts.

In real life, John Jenkins was an author, publisher, coin dealer, and one of America's best known rare book and document dealers. He made millions, much of in on Texas rare books and documents. The 1970s and 1980s were perfect for him. A huge interest grew in all documents from the Texas Revolution from Mexico, circa 1836. John Jenkins procured many of his books and documents from Dorman David of Houston. Before Jenkins and David teamed up, there were five known copies of the Texas Declaration of Independence. A few years later there were twenty in museums, libraries, and held by private collectors all over Texas.

There was also a brisk trade in letters written by the noble Alamo defenders while under siege and facing death from overwhelming Mexican forces. Davy Crockett wrote a few valuable letters. However, a rather suspicious number of those letters began to come on the market. During this renewed interest in rare books and documents, a team of sophisticated thieves were raiding archives, county courthouses, and libraries all over Texas and down into Mexico. They knew what they were looking for.

Dorman David and John Jenkins were on the top of the world. Jenkins name and reputation were enough to provide provenance for old documents and books. Then it began to fall apart. A team of experts discovered many forged documents. A thief was caught leaving a library with a list of what to steal. He fingered Dorman David as the leader of the ring of thieves. Dorman also turned out to be a master forger on paper he baked in the oven. But did Austin Squatty know? He said until his death that David's skillfully forged documents fooled him, just like they fooled experts, museums, historical libraries, and collectors. No one could forge a document better than Dorman David. Nobody could talk smoother than Austin Squatty. They even sold a forged Texas Declaration of Independence to the Governor of Texas.

Larry McMurtry, arguably America's best novelist, is also a large-scale rare book dealer. He says that Jenkins and David knew exactly what they were doing and enjoyed the con and fooling the whole rare book and document world. Jenkins said he was innocent and bought back many of the fakes he had sold. McMurtry thinks the whole idea that Jenkins could be innocent is absurd. When I worked at McGraw-Hill Book Company, I met McMurtry and we had a long talk. He had three books out then and the movie, *Hud,* starring Paul Newman. I sent his three books and letters to the proper McGraw-Hill editor trying to get them to sign him. After a long wait, a letter came saying Larry McMurty was a "regional novelist." McMurtry had a sweat shirt made that said that.

A bitter Dorman David has said Jenkins was an informer who made a deal. Jenkins had debts, lawsuits, and was facing a possible indictment. There were three mysterious fires at Jenkins' well-insured warehouse. The last fire, on Christmas Eve of 1985, destroyed 500,000 rare books and documents. The District Attorney has said it was arson. It is difficult for me to believe Jenkins torched his own collection.

On April 16, 1989, John Jenkins was found floating in a shallow part of the river near Bastrop, Texas with a gun-shot wound to the back of his head. His wallet was on the ground with credit cards missing and five-hundred dollars missing. His Mercedes was parked a few feet away with the door open. No gun was found. Originally, the coroner ruled it a homicide. The sheriff, all powerful in Texas, ruled it a suicide. He thought the con-man Austin Squatty shot himself and painted this last scene to get insurance money for his family. The sheriff thought Squatty had some flotation device that would float the gun on down the river. We will never know for sure.

Bluff Europe Magazine

E.W. Chapman a.k.a. Ol' 186

When Johnny Chan first went to Las Vegas, he discovered poker and jumped off big winner. Then he ran into E.W. "Ol' 186" Chapman, a Texas road gambler that moved his chips as fast as any man you have ever seen. E.W. busted Johnny and he busted many a good poker player. E.W. made his living playing poker but he had more leaks than the levees in New Orleans. I met E.W. when I was twenty and he was forty in 1960. We often discussed poker strategy. E.W. never helped get a game started in the afternoon. He would plunge into the game after a few hours and become the most frequent raiser and re-raiser. He waited until the losers were trapped in the Gambler's Fallacy of believing they "were due" and were playing double up and catch up. At the start of the game, everyone plays real tight and E.W. didn't want any part of that. All the games in Texas were no limit, even the small games.

The dealer anted a dollar and the blind was two dollars in Texas Hold 'em. Often there was a straddle. The standard raise was twenty dollars, ten times the blind. I asked E.W. one time why he raised so often. He said he raised because the other players didn't want him to. "If they had wanted it raised, they would have raised it themselves," he said. E.W. was very hard to play against. He told me you have to play flush draws like they are already made. He just kept firing at it. He was ready to move in regardless of the next board card. We were always engaged in that argument about whether it is better to play tight or loose but E.W. didn't really have but one gear. He had no choice. E.W. said, "I really have too much gamble in me to leather ass the proposition. I like to draw."

Back then, we played with paper currency. E.W. was a nut about money, especially twenty-dollar bills. He'd play with his whole stack in neat twenties all facing up. He taught me to repair the corners and smooth out all the bills. He was constantly doing this to all the money in the game. All of us were pretty slick with paper money, counting our bets incredibly fast. The word would spread around West Texas when E.W. was striking, on a winning run. We played a lot of heads-up challenge matches. When E.W. was striking, he would go visit gamblers in their homes in the mornings and break them.

E.W. could play a rush better than anyone but he could also simulate a rush. He'd semi-bluff really high and hit some miracle hands. He was the hero of countless bad beat stories. It was common to try to win all the money on the table. E.W. tried to bust players like it was a tournament. He took pills, uppers and downers at the same time, and could get really wild. He was always well mannered and gentlemanly except the time he shot Morgan in the foot.

E.W.'s real road game was seven-five, Kansas City lowball draw. E.W. didn't mind going broke on any given day because it was easy to get a backer and become a stake horse. He'd put all the money he had on the table. The dealer anted ten dollars and everyone else anted five. We played seven-five higher than we played Hold 'em. When E.W. drew one card, he would act like he looked, but he would move in without looking. He'd always show his bluffs. In no time he had the table steaming. E.W. and I would stake each other and loan to each other. Several people were willing to stake a broke just to fill up the game. It was a friendly thing to do.

One time when I was flat broke, I went by a big low ball game to eat the home-made stew which was the day's specialty. Big poker and dice games had a single menu item each day. They used food as a draw and called all the players for steak, catfish, chili, stew, and barbecue. E.W. was big winner and had everyone gambling. A pal staked me and a few hours later I was $1800 winner. I wanted to take $35 off the table to pay my rent and pick up my laundry. At first they wouldn't let me, but finally they let me run the three blocks to my pad and pay the overdue rent and get the laundry. I came back and went broke.

E.W. and I were in Ruidoso one time in a big low ball game and we suspected there would be some wolfing going on. One guy had some bandages on his hands and E.W. reached out and felt of the bandages to see if he had "the light", a tiny mirror under the bandage. This would allow him to see your hole cards befoe you do. He was a little fellow, quite and well mannered but he was fearless. We both made good winnings.

I would stake E.W. but I usually wanted to cut out when I went home. A couple of times I stayed in with him and he went on this pilling run. E.W. took uppers and downers, chain smoked menthol cigarettes, and sometimes didn't sleep for days. E.W. was such a character that the other poker players told stories about him often. A favorite was the time he bought a large quantity of black mollies, a long black pill of speed, and engraved his initials on the sides of the pills in gold leaf. When E.W. was on a pilling run, he would go all around town playing heads-up or getting in games until he got broke or robbed.

Twice when I had him staked, he ran off on one of these runs. I would hear about him and occasionally catch him on the phone, but I couldn't catch up with him to cut out. Finally, I caught him and he had the whole front room of his apartment full of the junk he had won. He had one old bookmaker's clothes and lawn mower and implements, rake and hoe. He had won one of my college pal's overcoat and Texas Tech ring. There was this enormous mirror. E.W. was higher than a kite. He would ask me if I wanted the item and then set a price on it, more than it was worth, and give me the cash. I was silent during this, but I ended up with all the money.

Another time when I had him staked, he ran off and I finally found him in the middle of the night at his apartment playing heads up against the Mule. They were both pilling. They both had high piles of currency in front of them, mostly ones and twenties. I told E.W. I wanted to cut out but the Mule strongly objected. Then they began to straddle it. It was four, eight, sixteen, until they had put all of the Mule's money in the pot before the cards were dealt. I ran on out of there before the deal. I can smell a hot score brewing better than any man that ever walked in shoe leather. Later, I heard the Mule won the pot. Probably, he put the hat on E.W.

We played at a woman named Dolly's six days and nights a week. On Tuesdays, she closed and the game moved to Morgan's whore house. Bill Smith and E.W. raised each other back and forth. It came as natural as fighting chickens . I have noticed that some of the great aggressive players like Stu Ungar and Jack "Treetop" Straus were suckers for the sports bets. E.W. was like that. He was addicted to the action. One night Bill Smith put on this ridiculous women's hat of Dolly's. Then he went on a rush, raising every pot. One of the players was a little bit slow and he paid Bill ten bucks for the hat. He won a pot and E.W. paid him ten bucks for the hat.

At the outlaw whisper joints you didn't ask a man his last name, how he made his living, where he lived, where he came from or where he was going. E.W. got robbed a lot on his nocturnal gambling rounds. He would go over to the black area and be the only white guy in an after-hours joint playing low ball. I've done that but I would not recommend it. If someone asked anyone where they lived, the answer was always, "Next door to E.W."

"Where's that?" they'd ask.

"Well, E.W. doesn't want anyone to know where he lives. " was the answer.

When I first started playing at Morgan's whore house, there had been a fight and his wife, Bell, shot another fellow once and Morgan twice by accident. Morgan was huge, about three hundred pounds. Sometimes the young working girls would be there when we played. They traveled to several cities on a circuit called "the wheel." One night Morgan was drinking and E.W. was pilling and they were beginning to argue . I hit the road out of there. Later, E.W. pulled his pistol and fired across the table at Morgan. His first shot blew the air conditioner out of the window. His second went into the wall. His third shot hit Morgan in the foot. Then E.W. ran and Morgan limped after him. E.W. left his car there and ran down the street. Morgan fired a couple of shots his way. The next week we were all back playing as if nothing happened.

One Christmas, several of the gamblers were going to El Paso for the horse races. Buddy the Beat and I took the bus there and stayed on the main drag in Juarez, Mexico in a cheap hotel. E.W. advised me to bet the favorites to show and that worked until the last race. We met E.W. back in Juarez and he was incredibly wild. He had a big bankroll. He would buy things from the street vendors and then trade it and some money for other things, a sombrero, a huge ceramic bull. When we'd go in a bar, he would buy drinks for the largest whore and give her the crap he had bought. He was really going out of his way to be nice to the bigger ones. Finally, a cop arrested E.W. and I. I wasn't sure what for. Maybe being drunk like everyone else. They hustled us into the back of a car and drove us a long way from the bridge. By this time, we really didn't have much money left on us. E. W. said to let him do all the talking. When he was pilling, he talked really slow as if he were in an echo chamber.

We had this trial in this little court room with a judge in a tie who looked to be all of fourteen. E.W. explained that we didn't have any relatives that would send us money. In the Juarez jail, prisoners had to arrange for their own food. Finally, the judge ordered us to empty our pockets on this little table. He came over and took what he wanted: a few dollars, my silver-dollar money clip, and my comb. Then the cops took my cigarettes and change and they let us go.

I rode back from Juarez with E.W. My friend, Buddy the Beat, had hitchhiked all over the United States riding with whatever stranger pulled over in the dark of night, but he wouldn't ride with E.W. It was a three hundred and thirty mile drive home and it took us twelve hours in E. W.'s old Chevy, which he called "Old Smokey." He kept calling his dear friend Morgan and telling him to hold the poker game together because we were nearly there. He said to tell them he would play anyone there heads-up for his case dough.

You ask how did "Ol' 186" get his road name? Road names were common. *Two by Two Poker Forum* would be called, Little Joe the Hard Way. Bookies had a code number. E.W. asked for the same number with all the bookies. The bookies had pagers. You would call and give your number and they would call you back on a pay phone or a safe phone. That way no names were used over the phone.

The Shop was this wonderful outlaw hangout in Lubbock, Texas for thirty-five years. Road gamblers came from all over to play there. There was a no-limit Hold 'em game in the afternoons and sometimes all night. E.W. would call and you would hear him on one of the bookmaker's pagers. He'd always say, "Its Ol' 186." This would start people telling E.W. stories. Some of the bigger bookmakers worked front office--back office . They could hear the incoming pager calls as could the front office phone man. They would know who was betting but would not return the call unless it was a big special player like a judge or something. Once while Tooter was being arrested, a judge did call and the cops told him they were in the middle of a raid. The judge said he didn't care and told them to tell Tooter he would take $500 on the Dallas Cowboys.

The Shop and outlaw gambling in general had more rules than the post office. You didn't use any real names over the phone. E.W. was a real loner. He didn't hang out with the other gamblers. The Shop had this schedule. It would open up in the early mornings for coffee and old stories, the best part. Several of the big bookmakers went there every day. They were competitors, not partners. In the mornings, there was a very cheap domino game. They would play for $1 or $5 and yell and get very emotional and angry. They would slam the dominoes down with great force and insult each other freely.

The same guys who yelled at dominoes showed no emotion at poker. If someone trash talked or celebrated as they do today, one of the old guys would have shot them and all anybody would have said would have been, "seat open." E.W. would skip the old stories and the early part of the game to walk around the South Plains Mall. He'd read the *Thrifty Nickel,* the free shopping guide. He seemed to have no concept of time, never having to show up any place at a specific time. We were "Outside Men," someone who made our whole living from poker. The "Inside Men" ran poker games, dice games, loaned money, and were bookies. They didn't go broke, no romance to it. We Outside Men exchanged information when we met away from the poker game. E.W. and I would talk about how the other guys played, who had a temper, when there was heat from the law, what road gamblers were in town, and who had been on a winning or losing streak. The houseman or lady would not tell you how everyone was doing as a matter of professionalism. You were not supposed to wake up the suckers giving poker lessons at the table. You just did not discuss how to play a hand. The one thing that did teach people about the math of poker was laying insurance. When there was a draw about to happen, the players would show both hands and the various bookmakers would quote a price or the odds on the draw. They did this in Las Vegas also.

As money management, E.W. would often take the insurance bets when he had his case money on the table. You could bet on the insurance bets even if you weren't in the pot. When he was striking and pilling, E.W. would bet on every hand he had a chance to. Because we had staked each other and loaned each other, we became friends. E.W. was broke more times than the Ten Commandments but he always ironed it out. He would go to Big Ed Bradford, who ran the game, for loans at 5% interest or juice per week if his pockets were dry. Once E.W. soaked his small portable T.V. to me. I loaned him $200 on it. When an Outside Man borrowed money, there usually wasn't a specific deadline for repayment. You'd always say truthfully, "I'll pay you when I win." I didn't hear from E.W. for awhile. I gave the TV to this young couple who were getting married. We'd win all kinds of things: rings, watches, clothes, car titles, rubber checks, and guns. E.W. got back on his feet and he wanted the TV back. He was really insistent that I had broken a rule moving a soaked TV. I had to go get it back, Indian-giver style.

E.W. and I rarely discussed anything but poker and poker players. He did tell me he had been 4-F during World War Two, and therefore exempt from service. He said he drove a bus and the soldiers harassed him. He was a little guy about 140 pounds. He always wore slacks, a nice shirt, and a hat with a full brim. Never trust a man in a narrow-brimmed hat. He's sit up at the table with his coffee, menthol cigarettes, and a big stack of money. One night he went broke and Bill Smith said, "Turn your hat around E.W." If you were going to sit at the poker table broke, you had to turn your hat around backwards where the dealer would know not to deal to you.

Someone might say, "I saw E.W. downtown and his hat was on backwards." That meant he was broke. E.W. would sometimes slip speed into his coffee while we played. You would never see him doing this but his speech would change and he'd get pretty crazy . If someone else did something weird, they might say, "I musta got a holt of E.W.'s coffee." One night when we were playing higher than usual and E.W. was high also, he was dealt a blank card. We played with diamond-back Bee's. He freaked out. He just sat there staring at the blank card. He called the first bet and then stopped the action to ask for another card . He thought it was some sort of trick. He jumped up and ran out of there like his horse was tied in a red ant bed.

When I first met E.W., we played in the back of a car lot at Wilbanks' place. Wilbanks was the primary producer and he would stake two or more players. In the fall in West Texas there is a ton of money around. The farmer's have the cotton harvest and the college students come back which perks up all business. However, the big factor for the poker economy was the football betting. The bookies were knee deep in money in the fall.

By summer, guys like me and E.W. might be checking the couch for spare change. We'd play in poker games where Wilbanks had three of us staked and we'd still try to break each other.

Shortly after I met E.W., he was at a late night game with the tough crowd of other honky-tonk pill heads when he got robbed, again. I avoided those places. A robber ran in with a bowling pin in one hand and a pistol in the other. He hit E.W. in the head and shot out the light. Neither was called for. Pill heads make terrible hijackers. This same guy came over to my little poker game. We just quit rather than deal with him. He told one of the college boys, "Ol' Bennie won't let me sleep.", meaning benzedrine.

The Shop was the safest place I ever went in America. In the whole thirty-five years I went there, I never saw a robbery, a fight, or an arrest, which makes you wonder. The Shop had been an auto repair shop on east 50th street. It set on an acre of land surrounded by a chain link fence topped by three strands of barbed wire a.k.a. the Devil's Rope. There were two big bay doors that were left open in the warm weather. Gene, Ed Bradford's brother, worked the phones and loaned a little money but mostly he was the lookout. There were a couple of shotguns hidden which I was told about after fifteen years. The poker was in a room in the back.

Once this one bad detective I call Deadbeat Davis came walking up and everyone ran. It was hot, hot summer and I dove into some tall careless weeds. House Mover followed me. There were millions of bugs. Later we found out that Big Ed had this mysterious friendship with the big detectives.

The only time they closed the game early was because this bad outlaw sat down to play. I never knew who he was. He kept asking about drugs which were not allowed at the Shop. He commented on several of his traveling companions. Finally, Gene came in and said the game is over. I asked if it was the law. We all cashed in very fast and did the old heel and toe. Later that night, I was "riding around and counting the cars." This meant you would go by various gambling joints to see how many and who was there. You tried to learn the cars of the other players, especially the all day suckers.

I was surprised to see that several of the old timers were at the Shop. I went in the poker room and took a seat. There were two shotguns and two rifles leaning against the wall behind the players. A couple of them had pistols showing in their belts. As was the iron-clad custom, I didn't ask any questions. We were playing pretty high. I tipped over a nice little score. The next day, I read in the newspaper that one of the top ten most wanted criminals had passed through town. I wasn't sure that was him. A long time later, I asked Ed about it. I said, "Were y'all afraid of that guy?"

He replied, "We're not afraid of anybody." I could tell the discussion was over.

E.W. loved the actual paper money itself more than what it might buy. He would sit there riffling though and counting and playing with his money all through the game. I once asked him what he really wanted in life. This seemed to puzzle him and he pondered it awhile. He said, "I'd like to have one room of my house filled all the way up with twenty dollars bills. From the floor to the ceiling, with twenty dollar bills." E.W. taught me to always respect the houseman. If it wasn't for the houseman, we could not play. E.W. always brought these weird presents for Ed and Gene Bradford from those trinket shops on Fremont Street when he went to Las Vegas. Who wouldn't want a clock made out of dice?

BLUFF EUROPE MAGAZINE

II.
Famous Gamblers
of the Old West

Wyatt Earp: A Leader Among Gambling Men

*The good Lord owes me an explanation for the things
that have happened in my life...Wyatt Earp.*

*I have always found him a quiet, unassuming man, not given
to brag or bluster...under all circumstances a loyal friend...
absolutely destitute of physical fear...Bat Masterson.*

I am not ashamed of anything I ever did...Wyatt Earp.

Wyatt Earp (1847-1929) was a professional gambler who played poker, dealt and banked faro, and had gambling joints most of his long life. The gunfight near the O.K. Corral in 1881 has spawned countless books and fifty-five movies that make Wyatt a town-taming sheriff, the very symbol of law and order. Wyatt only served as a lawman for brief periods and was a deputy marshal or deputy sheriff, and never in charge officially, but Wyatt was the leader, always wielding political power behind the scenes.

Wyatt was the middle brother of five brothers. He married early and his pregnant wife and unborn child died of yellow fever. Wyatt left Illinois where he had been a bouncer in his brother's brothels for Arkansas. Wyatt Earp was a tough man with his fists, six feet tall, about 170 pounds of all muscle. During the civil war period, men wore beards. In this time after the war, men wore handlebar mustaches, and Wyatt's was the champ. About five inches with a swoop upward.

In Illinois, he had three charges against him for the family business of prostitution. In Arkansas, he was arrested and jailed for stealing horses, but he broke jail. In Kansas, Wyatt joined the buffalo slaughter and met Bat Masterson, who became his life-long friend, and one of his loyal followers. They were "saddle-blanket" gamblers, playing poker by campfire or candle light and dreaming of being the fancily dressed gamblers they had seen in boomtown after boomtown. In the Old West, being a professional gambler was not just respectable, it was one of the most respectable professions of all. Wyatt and Bat both had TV series made about them much later.

In April of 1875, Wyatt Earp was hired as a city policeman in Wichita, Kansas. Huge herds of Texas longhorn cattle were driven to Kansas to ship on the railroads. The rowdy Texas cowboys were the natural enemy of the Kansas lawmen. They would get big drunk, called a "jollification" and go shoot out lights and signs, and occasionally shoot into buildings. This was called "hurrahing the town" and it was common. In Wichita, Wyatt was praised in a few newspaper articles. He arrested a drunk man who had $500 on him, and the man woke up with his money. That Wyatt didn't roll the drunk was news. Over his lifetime, Wyatt was the center of national newspaper controversies several times. His pride was severely wounded at times. Wyatt Earp remained a vain man all his life. In Wichita, Wyatt was playing poker in the backroom of a saloon when his pistol fell from his holster and discharged. This made the newspaper. Wyatt beat up a city alderman and was fired. The City Council gave him the choice of leaving town, or being charged with vagrancy. He moved on to Dodge City, Kansas.

In 1877, Bat Masterson, only 23 years old, was elected sheriff of Ford county, including Dodge City. Wyatt went to Deadwood, South Dakota and on to Fort Worth, Texas on gambling trips. In Fort Worth, he found a long-term companion, Mattie Blaylock. They went to the wild gambling town of Fort Griffin Flat, Texas. It was here that Wyatt met Doc Holliday. Doc already had a reputation as a gunfighter and killer. The two became more than friends. The loyalty that was to exist between the two defines them. Wyatt Earp, the persuasive leader, convinced people to move where he was going. He told Doc about the gambling riches in the boomtown of Dodge City, Kansas. Maybe he wanted Doc for the muscle and his scary reputation. He always had Wyatt's back and followed Wyatt. I have written about Doc in the Flat killing a man in a poker game in another article.

In 1878, Wyatt became an assistant marshal in Dodge City, Kansas. This was a glorious time. The famous gambler/gunfighters that lived there also included Doc Holliday, Luke Short, Bat Masterson, and Ben Thompson. The Celebrity Five. As lawmen, Wyatt Earp and Bat Masterson could be found in a fancy gambling joint at the poker or faro table. Wyatt spent his life as a gambler in gambling joints. Kate Elder, Doc Holliday's woman, said that, "Most of the time, Wyatt could be seen at a table in a saloon playing a hand of cribbage...or taking a hand in a poker game." Wyatt only arrested about one person a week.

It was here that Wyatt further developed his style in dealing with armed cowboys. There was a city ordinance against cowboys wearing guns or riding horses into a saloon. A drunk cowboy rode a horse into a saloon where Johnny Ringo and others were playing poker. They shot him dead and took up a collection for his funeral. Ringo robbed a poker game when he was drunk. The next morning, he gave the money back. My pal, Bill Smith, World Series of Poker champ of 1985, did exactly that in Roswell, New Mexico.

Wyatt would approach cowboys in the calmest manner, speaking softly. He usually had one of his brothers or Bat standing nearby with a Wells Fargo shotgun. He'd put his hand on the cowboy's pistol. If there was any resistance, Wyatt would pistol whip them with a long barreled pistol.

Wyatt, and at times, Ben Thompson, dealt faro at the famed Long Branch Saloon, managed by Luke Short. Doc Holliday also worked there. These gamblers loved jokes. When a preacher wrote requesting to lecture on sexually transmitted diseases, Bat and Wyatt set it up and sat on either side of him. The crowd was in on the joke. After his talk started, men would shout out and disrupt. Finally, Bat and Wyatt started firing pistols with blanks. When the Lady's Aid Society had a beautiful baby contest, Luke Short donated $100 in gold coins as first prize. People could buy votes, the money going to the church. The gamblers rigged it, and a black dance hall girl's baby won. Everyone was there for the vote count, and Wyatt and Bat escorted the dance hall girl in at the last minute with her baby.

Famous actor and comedian, Eddie Foy, spent a time in Dodge performing. When he first got there, Bat staged a mock hanging and they even had the rope around Foy's neck. He saw Bat laughing. Later, while Foy was performing, a few cowboys were "hurrahing the town." They fired bullets into the gambling joint while Foy was reciting a poem. He thought at first it was another joke. Bat had been dealing Spanish monte to Doc. Foy saw them hit the floor fast, and followed suit. Wyatt had been walking right outside. He and a couple of others fired at the cowboys. George Hoy, who'd been shooting at Foy, was hit and later died. This was the first man Wyatt Earp killed. This was written up in the *National Police Gazette*, with

1,000,000 weekly readers. It credited Wyatt with Hoy's death, and called Wyatt, "a good fellow and brave officer." Wyatt was thirty.

Well-known Texas gunfighter, Clay Allison, came to town to avenge his friend Hoy's death. He had coined the term "shootist" when he listed it as his occupation. Wyatt Earp walked right up to him on the street, and explained quietly that he was the one who had killed the cowboy. When Allison looked to the side, he could see Bat Masterson holding a shotgun. That was Wyatt's style. Allison "stared Wyatt in the eye and backed down" which is in a song.

When Wyatt was trying to disarm a Texas cowboy outside the Long Branch saloon, Doc was inside at a poker table. He saw one of the cowboys draw a gun through the window. Doc ran out yelling, "Throw up your hands" and pointed a gun at the terrified cowboys Doc held up to twenty-five cowboys at gunpoint, may have shot one, and saved Wyatt's life. Doc Holliday's reputation was just plain frightening! Wyatt would speak and write of that often over the years. He wrote, "It was because of that episode that I became the friend of Doc Holliday ever after." Although, Doc was a liability to Wyatt's increasing political ambitions, Wyatt would stand behind him whenever Doc messed up. Doc was on his best behavior in Dodge. Ben Thompson, another gunfighter with a reputation equal to Doc's, had saved Bat Masterson's life. They were loyal to each other. Neither Ben nor his troublesome brother, Billy, caused much trouble in Dodge. Bat's friendship with Doc and Ben Thompson probably cost him the election when he ran again for sheriff. The story of these Old West gamblers is the story of their incredible loyalty to each other, and the personal risks that loyalty would demand.

All of Wyatt's candidates lost in Dodge, and the bloom was off the rose of the boom. Wyatt and his brother, James, and their common law wives, left for Tombstone, Arizona by wagon. Wyatt had fifteen head of fine horses along, including race horses, which he'd be involved with for many years. Virgil Earp was living in Prescott, Arizona. He and brother Morgan would join Wyatt in Tombstone, making four Earp brothers there. On the way, Wyatt stopped in Las Vegas, New Mexico to persuade Doc Holliday to come with him to Tombstone. Doc owned a saloon, and had been doing well but had already killed a man, which was his signal to move on. Doc went with them. Kate didn't want to follow Wyatt, but she did. When they hooked up with Virgil, in Prescott, Arizona, Doc found a juicy poker game and stayed eight months, beating it for $40,000. Then, at Wyatt's urging, Doc went to Tombstone.

Tombstone had a giant silver strike. It was 25 miles from the Mexican border, and known nationally as a lawless region. A loose confederation called "the Cowboys" numbered around 100 men. They raided into Mexico stealing cattle and killing people. They stole cattle in the U.S. also. Some robbed stagecoaches which made them enemies of the powerful Wells Fargo. The Earp family had a strong connection to Wells Fargo. Wyatt and Morgan were stagecoach guards. Wyatt was a secret Wells Fargo detective, called a "private man." No stagecoach with an Earp aboard was ever robbed. The businessmen and silver miners were mostly Republican, as was Wyatt. The ranchers and cowboys were mostly Democrats. There were two opposing newspapers in Tombstone, one who favored Wyatt's side, one against.

Wyatt had said he did not want to be a lawman any more. Virgil was a deputy U.S. marshal. The Oriental Saloon was a fancy gambling joint, with thick carpet, a long, mirrored, mahogany bar, live music, and a big poker game. Their success had the opposition trying to disrupt business by sending some tough guys to scare folks off. Milt Joyce, one of the owners, cut a deal with Wyatt. He would give Wyatt 25 per cent of the gambling profits if he would provide security. He really did that. Wyatt hired Doc Holliday as a dealer. He sent to Dodge for Luke Short and Bat Masterson, and hired them as dealers. The fame of the dealers packed the joint.

As a leader, Wyatt Earp was at his finest. He had recruited three of his brothers, as well as Doc, Bat, and Luke to join him in Tombstone. Most of his living came from gambling. Wyatt took a job for awhile as a Pima county deputy sheriff, as he thought it might be a political stepping stone. Virgil Earp became Tombstone Chief of Police, and still had a part-time appointment as a deputy U.S. marshal.

Ever political, Wyatt wanted to be county sheriff because he could make up to $40,000 a year as his part of fines and taxes. Johnny Behan was to become the chief rival of Wyatt's life. He got the governor's appointment for sheriff that Wyatt wanted. Behan lied to Wyatt, saying that he would make him deputy and they became life-long enemies. Behan was a Democrat and a crook. He was in league with the Cowboys. Behan and Wyatt both loved race horses. Behan brought a beautiful, Jewish actress, Josephine Marcus, from a rich San Francisco family, to Tombstone as his fiancee. Wyatt was to later spend the last 46 years of his life with her.

The team Wyatt gathered around him were men whose lives were frequently altered by the pungent aroma of gun smoke. Doc got very drunk and in a dispute at the Oriental Saloon. When they would not return the pistol he checked in, he went to his rooming house and got one. He shot Milt Joyce, the main owner, in the hand, and another owner in the big toe, probably by accident. Joyce beat up Doc in the melee. Wyatt came forth to stand behind Doc. No witnesses showed up at the hearing and Doc paid a $31 fine, thanks to Wyatt's growing political influence. However, Joyce became a powerful personal and political enemy, but the lucrative gambling business went on at the Oriental Saloon.

Luke Short was dealing faro at the Oriental when a known gunfighter made accusations and threats. He was also a friend of Bat Masterson's who separated them temporarily. Later, the man called him out, and Luke killed him right outside the Oriental door.

Bat Masterson's brothers were lawmen back in Dodge. When Ed Masterson was killed, Bat went back to Dodge. When another man was killed at the Oriental a week after Luke killed a man, Joyce shut down gambling temporarily.

The Earp's troubles with the Clantons and McLaurys, the leaders of the Cowboys, were all mixed up with Wells Fargo. These men had large ranches where they fenced the stolen cattle. The confederation of the Cowboys was never as well defined or organized as their enemies thought. This included the Governor of Arizona and the President of the United States. They both appealed for troops to combat the Cowboys. The president appealed to congress to suspend the *Posse Comitatus Act* to allow the Army to pursue the Cowboys, but the congress refused. The Mexican Army invaded southern Arizona and killed five Cowboys, including Old Man Clanton, the father of Ike, Billy, and Phin Clanton. Some American newspapers cheered that action.

Wyatt, Virgil, his brother Morgan, and even Johnny Behan went out on posse rides together chasing those who had held up Wells Fargo shipments on stagecoaches. When the Benson stage was robbed with two men killed, the robbers names were known shortly. Wyatt went to the Cowboy leader, Ike Clanton, offering him the $3600 Wells Fargo reward in secret in exchange for the location of the three stagecoach robbers. Wyatt Earp spoke for Wells Fargo. Ike had him wire Wells Fargo's home office in San Francisco to ask if the reward was dead or alive, and Wells Fargo said "dead or alive." Here is a private corporation putting a death bounty on the heads of named men who had not been charged yet with any crime. Ike agreed. Later, the three robbers were killed in another incident but Ike remained totally worried that Wyatt or Doc would tell the outlaws he was an informant. This fear caused the gunfight near the O.K. Corral.

When Ike Clanton came into Tombstone very drunk, he and Doc had a verbal altercation about this. Later that night, there was a big all-night poker game at the Occidental Saloon. Doc Holliday played, and left early after he and Ike traded barbs. Deputy U.S. Marshal Virgil Earp, who was also chief of police, Sheriff Johnny Behan, Ike Clanton, and Tom McLaury played poker until six a.m. Ike made threats and challenges to the Earps and Doc. Four of the people in the upcoming gunfight were in the poker game. The gunfight left three dead, Billy Clanton, and the two McLaurys. Morgan and Virgil were wounded. Doc was carrying a Wells Fargo shotgun, borrowed from the local office.

After the gunfight, Doc and Wyatt had a twenty-eight day hearing to see if they'd be charged with murder. Wyatt did all the talking, since Doc's reputation and record kept him off the witness stand. They were cleared. However, after that, Cowboys ambushed Virgil Earp as he left the Oriental Saloon, hitting his arm with a shotgun, and crippling him for life. A little later, Morgan Earp was assassinated while shooting pool. Wyatt was there.

The big gunfight near the O.K. Corral was national news in America, and the drama played out for days in newspapers. For most, Wyatt and his crew were seen as the true representatives of law and order. They were just upholding the law. Actually, Virgil, a deputy U.S. marshal deputized Wyatt, Morgan, and Doc right before they started walking to the corral. Anybody could deputize anybody for a posse back then.

After Morgan's death, everyone's life changed suddenly. Wyatt sold out of the Oriental and sent all the Earp family to California where his parents lived. Then he formed a posse known as the "Vendetta Ride." Wyatt secured financial backing from Wells Fargo and a mine company owner. Wells Fargo would supply financial support all through the Vendetta Ride, but it was highly secret. Wyatt had the posse all named U.S. deputy marshals. His posse had up to eight men, including Doc Holliday, and the youngest brother, Warren Earp. They were all armed with pistols, rifles, and Wells Fargo shotguns. In about a week, they killed three and maybe four more men. Wyatt probably killed them all. They didn't try to arrest anybody. At one point, Curly Bill, a Cowboy leader, set up an ambush for Wyatt's posse. Wyatt survived an initial burst of gunfire to face Curly Bill. They both had Wells Fargo shotguns. Bill, who died, had a stolen one.

In the past, if a Cowboy was put in the Tombstone jail, either Johnny Behan would let them escape or six Cowboys would come forward to provide alibis. As Wyatt's group caught and killed the men on their hit list, many newspapers across the country began to condemn him, but some still supported him. Wells Fargo's home office in San Francisco issued an unusual, long statement of support for Wyatt and Doc, calling Doc dissipated.

Johnny Behan formed another posse to chase Wyatt and Doc, who had been charged with murder and were fugitives in Arizona. His posse included Wyatt's enemies: Ike and Phin Clanton and Johnny Ringo. It grew to thirty members. Everybody in both posses were deputies and lawmen. Some were also killers and bad outlaws. Wyatt and his group fled to Trinidad, Colorado, where Bat Masterson was city marshal and banked a faro game. Wyatt announced to the press he sought a pardon from the Arizona governor and that he planned to return to Tombstone and run for sheriff, but no pardon came. Doc and his brother Warren spread the faro in nearby Gunnison, Colorado. Doc moved on to gamble in Leadville and Denver. Warren, who always had a drinking problem, killed two men in the years to come and was later killed in a gunfight.

Three of Wyatt's brothers got shot and two died. Three men died near the O.K. Corral, and three more on the vendetta ride. Wyatt was never wounded. In the Curly Bill ambush, bullets went through his coat tails. The rifle shots that hit Morgan may have been meant for him. Wyatt Earp began to believe he had this mystical protection. He was amazingly lucky when lead was flying through the air. Wells Fargo funded the vengeance ride at first, but even they pulled up. They aided and funded Wyatt's travel to Colorado for the whole group. It didn't take Wyatt long to get that Wells Fargo money in action at a faro table. Wyatt was 34 when he left Tombstone. After 28 months, he was to say it was the worst time of his life.

In Gunnison, Colorado, the toughest guy in town accused Wyatt's faro dealer of cheating when Wyatt was gone. He demanded his money back. The dealer said we have to wait for Wyatt. When Wyatt returned, he calmly told the man he may have been cheated, but he would not give the money back because it would look like he backed down. The man left town.

Wyatt went to San Francisco to court and win the heart of Josephine "Josie" Marcus, who had been the most beautiful woman in Tombstone and Sheriff Johnny Behan's fiancee. Wyatt and his beloved, Josie, were both adventuresome spirits ready to head off to the next boomtown, silver strike, gold strike, or gambling opportunity. They both loved gambling and horse racing. The forty-six years they spent together were full of dreams, love, and chasing the pot of gold at the end of the next rainbow. When Wyatt's made big winnings, he'd buy Josie diamonds. She hocked them later to play poker herself, poorly.

In Dodge City, the mayor had a gambling joint that competed with Luke Short's Long Branch Saloon. He started having Luke's employees arrested, and forced Luke to leave town. Luke sent a wire to Bat Masterson and Wyatt Earp. Each went to Dodge with a handful of men. Luke came back. The rumors were that Doc Holliday would be there any day. This was called the Dodge City War, and the forces lined up against Luke gave up without a shot being fired. Luke Short got his gambling joint back. The boom was over in Dodge, and reform elements were a threat to gambling. Luke sold out and moved to Fort Worth, Texas.

Wyatt and Josie went on the road. When they got to Fort Worth, Texas, Luke Short owned the fanciest gambling joint there, the White Elephant. Bat Masterson said it was, "one of the largest and costliest establishments of its kind in the whole Southwest." In one celebrity poker game, Wyatt Earp, Luke Short, Bat Masterson, and Long Haired Jim Courtright played. Bat sat in for $9000. Later, Luke outdrew the famed gunman, Courtright, and killed him right outside the door of the White Elephant. That was the second time Luke killed a man right outside the door of the fanciest gambling joint in a boomtown with Bat Masterson nearby.

Wyatt had an emotional last meeting with Doc Holliday in a Denver hotel lobby. Josephine has written about it. Both men wept.

In 1896. Wyatt was selected to be the referee of the heavy-weight fight between Sharkey and Fitzsimmons in San Francisco. The winner would take on the champ for the title. There was controversy. It was a huge bout, followed and bet on nationally. Wyatt was selected on the last day when the two sides could not agree. Rumors of a fixed fight were flooding the nation. Wyatt had referred a few bare-knuckle fights but never one with Marquis of Queensbury rules.

When Wyatt Earp entered the ring and removed his jacket, he had forgotten a big six-gun in his back pocket. A police officer confiscated it. Wyatt later paid a $50 fine. The arena with 10,000 people exploded with sustained laughter. Given Wyatt's nation-wide celebrity as a gunfighter, this gained laughs and was to continue in the press for the next month.

Sharkey was the underdog and losing. He hit the mat in the eighth round holding his groin and moaning in pain. Wyatt ruled there was a low blow from Fitzsimmons and awarded the match to Sharkey on the foul.

What happened? Did Sharkey fool Wyatt? No one could see the exact blow in question, but could Wyatt?

This was a nation-wide controversy with many accusations against Wyatt. He was a professional gambler. Bat Masterson made big wagers on the fight, and he had lost a ton of money. Bat did newspaper interviews standing by Wyatt and attesting to his honesty. What must have hurt the always vain Wyatt the most were the editorial cartoons. This was in their glory time, and the image of the gunfighter with an actual gun in the ring brought laughs coast to coast. Wyatt's reputation in San Francisco was tarnished and he wanted out of there.

There was gold in Alaska so the gamblers headed there. In Nome, in 1887, Wyatt owned a gambling joint with Josie's brother, The Dexter House. It was prosperous. Next door was Wyatt's dear friend, Tex Richard's, gambling house. He was to become America's premier boxing promoter, associated with heavy-weight champ, Jack Dempsey. I met Dempsey as a kid when he came to Big Spring, Texas to referee the wrestling matches for my uncle, Rowdy Pat O'Dowdy. After the match, Dempsey cooked a big spaghetti dinner for a crowd of people at Pat and Ruth's house.

Wyatt and Josie left Alaska in 1901 with $80,000 in winnings. There was another gold strike in Goldfield, Nevada, so Wyatt opened one more gambling house.

Back in Los Angeles, Wyatt won a trotting horse in a poker game. He got in that business, managing a string of race horses. He had saloons and faro games and things were as usual. In 1911, Wyatt was arrested in what was said to be a rigged faro game used as a confidence game against one rich player. He gave a fake name. He got off. The newspaper said Wyatt Earp was a professional gambler known for "fleecing the unwary in card games."

When a man had robbed a bank and caught a train to near where Wyatt was living, the sheriff called Wyatt. He stuck a pistol in his pocket and went to the train station. He was told the man was in a nearby store holding hostages at gunpoint. Wyatt walked in with his hand on the gun in his pocket and ordered the man to give up. When he was asked why the man should give up, he said, "I'm Wyatt Earp." The man surrendered and said he was so happy to be arrested by such a famous man.

In the 1920s, Wyatt Earp had one of his most interesting and certainly influential time periods. In his seventies, Wyatt was handsome, with an erect, military bearing, steel gray, close-cropped hair, and a much shorter mustache. It was obvious he still had a charismatic, magnetic power over others, and a very special fame. The next big boom was the movies. Wyatt had met the famous writer, Jack London, in Alaska. London drove Wyatt to the movie studio. Charlie Chaplin came up pretending to be the waiter, doing a comedy routine, to meet Wyatt Earp. This was at the time of the big western movies, and Wyatt became close friends with the biggest stars of all, Tom Mix and William S. Hart. Mix starred in 335 films. They would both serve as pall bearers at his funeral. Wyatt was a consultant for the movies, coaching them on the fast draw and being authentic. They were all friends and all the big wheels in Hollywood played poker, and Wyatt played with them. Poker was a major networking vehicle in Hollywood. Poker introduced Wyatt to many famous people. He needed the money. Historian R. J. Reidhead has written, "He could always find a good poker game where the stakes were fairly high. He rarely lost."

Wyatt had a poorly written biography he was trying to peddle to the movies. William S. Hart helped but his effort failed. Wyatt felt he had been wronged often by the press and he wanted his real story told, or his version of real. He wrote to William S. Hart, saying, "Many wrong impressions of the early days of Tombstone and myself have been created by writers... Any wrong impression, I want made right before I go away. The screen could do all this."

One of the men most impressed with Wyatt Earp was famed movie director, John Ford. Wyatt was the perfect consultant for Ford, and he was awed by Wyatt. Ford and Tom Mix hired a young football player to be a prop boy and extra, John Wayne. Wayne would later say he got his walk, talk, and persona from Wyatt Earp. Wayne said, "I knew him..I often thought of Wyatt Earp when I played a film character. There's a guy that actually did what I'm trying to do."

John Ford kept a poker game going on movie sets for years. Ford said, "We didn't talk film at night. We played poker and dominoes." They were also a hard-drinking crew. Ford got John Wayne, Henry Fonda, and Ward Bond out of jail in Mexico twice in the same day. His regular actors like John Wayne, Ward Bond, Ben Johnson, and Henry Fonda played poker for decades.

In Wyatt's final years, Wyatt and Josie lived in a one-room apartment and stayed broke because of her poker habit. She sold everything her family gave her to pump money for the backroom poker games of L.A.

Wyatt Earp died in 1929. He was eighty. Josephine said his last words were, "Suppose. Suppose." Wyatt Earp remained a dreamer until his very last breath.

In his last two years, he had been working on an authorized biography with Stuart Lake. Lake had been the press secretary to President Theodore Roosevelt when he heard Bat Masterson tell the President that the true story of the Old West was Wyatt Earp. Josephine had editorial control over Lake's book, and some stories are false. Wyatt said he killed Johnny Ringo, who committed suicide in Arizona when Wyatt could not go there. This book did not portray Wyatt as a gambler.

After Wyatt died, the movies started coming and he was portrayed by many famous actors. When the TV western craze began in the 1950s, there were six series based on Wyatt Earp and his pals on television at one time. Some ran for years. John Ford made *My Darling Clementine* with Henry Fonda about Wyatt Earp, using Stuart Lake's book in 1946. There were already several movies about Wyatt but this was the classic, painting him as an iconic Old West hero, symbolic of an era. Much later, John Ford directed another movie about Wyatt, *Cheyenne Autumn*, and Wyatt's character was less heroic, more ambitious and motivated by financial success.

Wyatt had been a close friend of actor Joel McCrea. Wyatt had wanted McCrea to play him in a movie. He did, and so did over fifty actors, including Walter Huston, Henry Fonda, Burt Lancaster, Randolph Scott, Errol Flynn, James Stewart, Hugh O'Brien, James Garner, Will Geer, Ronald Reagan, Kurt Russell, and Kevin Costner.

Tombstone is said to have been born in the silver boom and kept from dying by Wyatt Earp. There is a huge tourist industry, with seminars, books, staged fake gun fights, and local business places with a period design, like the Oriental Saloon. Nearly a half million tourists go there each year. This is mostly about gun fighting. They stage fake gun fights. Wyatt was a professional gambler all his life. The gunfight near the O.K. Corral lasted thirty seconds.

A new movie is in the works starring Harrison Ford as an older Wyatt Earp. He goes to New York to join Bat Masterson in saving Doc Holliday's son from Al Capone.

BLUFF EUROPE MAGAZINE, PART 1 AND 2

Doc Holliday:
A Gunfight Waiting to Happen

*He was the most skillful gambler, and the nerviest, fastest,
deadliest man with a six-gun I ever saw...*Wyatt Earp

*Holliday had a mean disposition and an ungovernable temper,
and under the influence of liquor was a most dangerous
man...hot-headed and impetuous...*Bat Masterson

John H. "Doc" Holliday, (1851-1887). was a skilled professional gambler, making his living playing poker and dealing and banking faro in boomtowns across the Old West. He was one of the best poker players. Born in Griffin, Georgia to an aristocratic, affluent, upper-class family, Doc learned to gamble at cards at an early age. The family servant, Sophie Walton, taught Doc and his two cousins the old slave game of skin, which was adapted from faro, and poker. They played with buttons as chips. Doc learned to remember what cards had been played, calculate percentages, and to detect a little sleight of hand. They played for years.

Doc was graduated from dental college at age 20. He was diagnosed with consumption or tuberculosis. Doc moved west for the drier climate, first starting a dental practice in Dallas, Texas in 1875 near Dealey Plaza and the red light district, called Scream Town. Doc's coughing and disease cost him dental patients. At that time, tuberculosis was not thought of as contagious. Doc started spending more and more time at the poker tables, and could make more money there right off. He bought more expensive, tailor-made clothes, and had them designed with the weapons he would always carry in mind. Doc and another man had a brief shootout, but both missed their target. Doc was fined for gambling and carrying a pistol. This made the newspaper, as Doc's exploits would do for all of his life. By the time he was thirty, Doc Holliday was nationally famous, being written up coast to coast in newspapers, dime novels, and magazines. In my view, the fame and constant publicity shaped Wyatt's and Doc's actions. Both were overly proud men.

Doc was six feet tall, and a thin, 140 pounds, with ash blond hair and a handlebar mustache. Doc had eyes that three newspapers described as "piercing blue." Being frail from his illness, he knew his battles must be waged with a weapon. He often practiced his fast draw with his two guns, one from his left shoulder holster and one on his right hip, and the large, sharp knife in his breast pocket. Bat Masterson said, "..as desperate a man in a tight place as the West ever knew." Doc had a fatalistic view, living under a death sentence from consumption. As his reputation grew, he was a bit of a bully, challenging men to shoot it out if he was offended, and he was easily offended. He also enhanced his own reputation as the "Deadly Dentist." The number of men he killed was not known, but never as many as the newspapers reported.

Myth and fact are hard to separate but new books by Tefertiller, Tanner, and Roberts are fantastically researched and accurate. Myth says Doc shot a prominent citizen in Dallas over a $500 poker pot and had to flee. He shot another or maybe two in Jacksboro over poker disputes. In Denver, he cut a man up bad in the face and neck over a poker squabble. In Breckenridge, Texas, he beat a man severely with his cane over a poker dispute. Later that day, the man shot him, injuring Doc seriously.

Ft. Griffin Flat, here in West Texas, was the hell hole of all Texas, and why Doc was even there mystifies this humble scribe. It was called "the Sodom of the West." It was near an Army fort, the buffalo hunters, and the trail drives. Famous gamblers to pass through there included John Wesley Hardin, Wyatt Earp, Lottie Deno, and Pat Garrett, the man who killed Billy the Kid. Ft. Griffin was known for the Tin Hat Brigade, a vigilante group that had shot or hung more men than any such group in Texas. If that wasn't bad enough, a group of Tonkawa Indians lived there. They were hated by all the other tribes because they were U.S. Army scouts and cannibals. When the tribes were settled in Oklahoma, five other tribes banded together and attacked the Tonkawas, killing a great many. The sheriff and head of the Tin Hats was John Larn, himself a rustler, later killed by the Tin Hats. His deputy was a rustler, John Selman, who killed John Wesley Hardin, years later.

Doc first came to the Flat in 1875 and was fined for gambling. In the Flat, in 1877, Doc first met Big Nose Kate Elder, a prostitute who would become his off and on companion for many turbulent years. Doc called her his intellectual equal. Like Doc, she came from an upper class family. She was called Big Nose because she was nosy, always into everyone else's business. Kate had been arrested with Wyatt Earp's sister-in-law as whores. She disliked the whole Earp family, especially Wyatt. Kate thought the influence he was to have over Doc was sinister. Wyatt had three pimping charges on his record in Illinois. Pimping was the family business.

In the Flat, the most famous gambler was Lottie Deno, a red-headed beauty that always wore the latest fashions. She was the model for Miss Kitty on the TV series, *Gunsmoke* and the lead character in a series of novels by Alfred Henry Lewis, who became one of America's most famous writers. He was also in the Flat. The name Lottie Deno comes from the Spanish word for money, lots of *dinero*. She got the name when she won all the money on the table in a poker game. In different towns she was called, Faro Nell, the Poker Queen, Mystic Maude, The Angel of San Antonio, and other names. Kate and Doc had become a couple. One night, Kate, being jealous of Lottie, started a fuss and pulled her gun. Lottie pulled her gun and they cursed each other, but Doc stepped between them.

Another time in Fort Griffin, two poker players stood up and shot each other dead across the table. The room emptied out, except for Lottie, who kept her chair at the faro table. The sheriff ran in and told Lottie he could not see why she didn't run like everyone else. Lottie said, "You have never been a desperate woman."

One night, Doc won $3000 and broke the faro bank. Lottie took over and won all of Doc's money for herself. The very next night, Doc won $500 in a poker game. The big name gamblers of the Old West were drawn there for the action. Lottie left the Flat with a small trunk filled with money. She moved to Deming, New Mexico and married gambler, Frank Thurmond. Her investments in mining, real estates, and ranching made her very rich.

It was there Doc met his life-long friend and fellow professional gambler, Wyatt Earp. Earp was a natural-born leader of men, gaining loyalty with his quiet persuasion and the dreams that would take him to most historic Old West boomtowns. He told Doc all about a bigger boom-town, Dodge City, Kansas, where the Texas cowboys ended the long trail drives with pockets full of money and an urge to gamble. Rich Texas ranchers were there in the poker games, after selling their herds.

Wyatt told the story of how Doc left Fort Griffin Flat, as he did from more than a few towns, fast, very fast! He was in a big poker game with a man named Ed Bailey. Bailey kept looking at the deadwood, the discards. Doc told him not to, saying, "Play Poker!" This meant stop cheating in the Old West. When Bailey did it again, Doc pulled down the pot without showing his hand which was correct under the rules. Bailey made a move for his pistol, but Doc was faster with his knife, stabbing Bailey in the stomach and killing him. The crowd disarmed Doc. He was held in his hotel room under heavy guard. Kate heard that the Tin Hat Brigade was getting up a lynch party. She knew Doc would be one of a couple of dozen men that had been left swinging from pecan trees near the banks of the Brazos River.

Kate procured, maybe stole, two horses, and borrowed another pistol. She set a shed on fire as a diversion, and it worked. Fire in those tinderbox, wooden towns was a huge threat. All of the guards watching Doc, except one, left to fight the fire. Kate came in with guns in both hands and rescued Doc. They rode off across the wilds of the Texas panhandle to Dodge City. The very deep loyalty that Doc felt to Kate, and later to Wyatt Earp, were to shape the major events of his life.

Several of Wyatt's brothers had worked in law enforcement. Wyatt was the clear leader of his family and a political faction in Dodge City and later, Tombstone. Wyatt had met fellow gamblers Bat Masterson, and Luke Short as buffalo hunters. This group became a strong coalition behind Wyatt's latest plans, and Doc was part of it. In Dodge, Kate and Doc pretended to be man and wife at first. Doc hung out another dental shingle. After a few months, Kate said she liked the whore's life and was going back. She and Doc fought often and loudly. In Dodge, Doc dealt faro at the Long Branch Saloon for Luke Short. At times, Ben Thompson did also.

In Dodge, Wyatt was attempting to disarm a Texas cowboy, with twenty-five of his armed friends watching. Doc was playing poker. One of the cowboys behind Wyatt started to pull a pistol when Doc came yelling fiercely with his gun on the cowboys. So scary was Doc's reputation, that the whole group backed down. Wyatt would say or write many times, that Doc saved his life that night. Their bond and mutual loyalty was a legend after that. The *National Police Gazette* wrote of this incident. Doc was still more famous than Wyatt, and that drew attention to Wyatt.

Doc Holliday had ridden into a new town and was getting a drink at the bar. A group of cowboys began to hurrah him over his fancy clothes. Being frail and weak looking, and walking with a cane, Doc attracted bullies. Doc turned to face the whole group and caught them with the famous "piercing blue eyes." He told them it would be wise to leave him alone. When asked why, he said, "I'm Doc Holliday." They emptied the room. That same scene came up over and over in history. "I'm Wyatt Earp." "I'm Bat Masterson." "I'm Ben Thompson." The gambler/gun fighters in the Old West were celebrities, and they knew it.

Wyatt Earp was a tough guy, fist fighter. He'd started out as a bouncer in his brother's brothels in Illinois and Wichita, Kansas. As a lawman, he was quiet and calm, but he would hit people over the head often with long the barrel of his pistol. If Wyatt had a dispute, Doc might escalate, threatening to kill any enemy of Wyatt's. The two men were opposites. Wyatt was soft spoken, unexcitable, always sober, charismatic, and admired. Doc was a volatile hot-head, with a mercurial temper fueled by alcohol. One minute Doc was charming and funny, quoting Latin, and in an instant he became the scariest man in the Old West. Doc played no limit at poker, life, and death.

All of these gamblers dealt and banked faro whether they were lawmen or not. Faro and poker were the most popular gambling games played in nearly all saloons. They were lawmen for brief periods, but professional gamblers for life. As lawmen, Wyatt, Bat, and Ben Thompson operated from a fancy gambling house poker or faro table. In faro, the house has a three per cent edge, which goes up on sucker bets. Did they cheat? I do not know. There was a professionally prepared crooked faro dealing box available mail order. However, all these name players went up against the house at faro, called "bucking the tiger." I certainly doubt there was much sleight of hand cheating at poker or faro, since folks knew that Doc and guys like him would kill folks for cheating. In most writing of poker history, cheating is wrongly considered more common than it was in the high-stakes, professional gambler card games. Too much about cheating was known.

In Dodge, Doc developed a friendship with Eddie Foy, the actor and comedian who would become very famous. While Doc and Bat Masterson were playing Spanish monte and Foy was reciting a poem, a group of cowboys rode by shooting into the bar. This ritual was common for the Texas cowboys. They called getting drunk and shooting out the lights, a "jollification" and "hurrahing the town." Foy thought it was a joke until the crowd hit the floor. Wyatt was outside, and he shot a cowboy who later died. It was George Hoy shooting at Eddie Foy. Somebody should have written a song.

Doc and Kate left Dodge for Las Vegas, New Mexico, a drier climate and a gambling boomtown. Las Vegas had hot springs, thought good for Doc's health. Doc did well there ending up with his own saloon. One day a drunken cowboy came into the saloon and harassed one of the women. Then he went into the street and shot back into the saloon. Doc went outside and killed him. This was probably needless. He was tried and acquitted.

Shortly after that, Wyatt Earp, and his current woman, Mattie, came to Las Vegas to persuade Doc to join them in the next dream town, boomtown, Tombstone, Arizona. Doc loaded up and went with them by wagon. Kate didn't like them, but she went along. They stopped in Prescott, Arizona, another boomtown with a silver strike. Virgil Earp, Wyatt's brother lived there. Doc found a most wonderful poker game. Wyatt went on to Tombstone, but Doc stayed several months, by some versions, winning $40,000. Wyatt wrote letters urging him to come on to Tombstone. With this bankroll, Kate was happy to go on to Tombstone. and they finally rode into town in style. Again, Doc took newspaper ads as a dentist. He and Wyatt made investments in silver mines.

The Oriental Saloon was one of the fanciest gambling joints in the Old West with one of the biggest poker games. It had lush carpet, a chandelier, a mirrored bar, the latest gambling equipment, and live violin and piano music. Troublemakers sent by their competitors were disrupting play and driving off customers. Milt Joyce, one of the owners, was a powerful man. He gave Wyatt Earp a fourth of the gambling concession to provide security. Wyatt hired Doc Holliday, Bat Masterson, and Luke Short as dealers. With these celebrities on the floor, it quickly became the most successful gambling house in the town. With these gun fighters around, only a mad man would disrupt it, so Doc did.

One night when he was very drunk, Doc had been in a dispute, and later in an argument about his guns. He shot Joyce in the hand and another owner in the big toe. It was probably an accident. Wyatt stood up for Doc and he got off with a small fine when no witnesses showed up. However, Joyce became Wyatt's serious enemy, but the gambling went on. Doc paid a small fine and continued in the Oriental poker game.

When the Benson stage was robbed, Wyatt's enemy, Sheriff Johnny Behan and Milt Joyce got Kate Elder very drunk. She signed a false statement that Doc had admitted he helped rob the stage. She later recanted. Doc asked Wyatt if he wanted him to leave town. Wyatt asked him to get Kate to leave. The events leading up to the gunfight near the O.K. Corral were most complicated. This thirty-second shootout left three dead and led to nation-wide news for weeks. After a long hearing, Wyatt and Doc were cleared. Virgil Earp was shot from ambush and lost use of one hand. Morgan Earp was murdered from ambush.

At this point, Wyatt formed a posse of deputy federal marshals funded also by Wells Fargo, and some mine owners. They carried Wells Fargo shotguns, and conferred with Wells Fargo agents and executives all the way. This included his brother Warren, Doc, and four or five others. Over a period of time, they tracked down and executed three or four men. When Curly Bill arranged an ambush, he and Wyatt faced each other with Wells Fargo shotguns, Bill's stolen. The national newspapers were covering this on a daily basis, and some were for and some were against Wyatt's famed "Vendetta Ride." At the end of this, Wyatt's group fled to Colorado, as fugitives indicted for murder. Bat Masterson was the city marshal and had a faro bank in Trinidad, Colorado so they headed there. Wyatt appealed to the governor of Arizona for a pardon and announced he planned to return to Tombstone and run for sheriff, but no pardon ever came. During the "Vendetta Ride", Wyatt and his posse had funding from Wells Fargo, the Santa Fe Railroad, the Tombstone vigilantes, and the U.S. government. Wyatt and Warren opened right up with faro banks in another boomtown, Gunnison, Colorado.

Doc went on to Denver where a confidence man named Mallon, posing as a detective, arrested him. He was jailed awaiting extradition to Arizona for murder. This was in the *National Police Gazette*. The *Gazette* had an article saying Ben Thompson was a more deadly gunfighter than Doc Holliday or Bat Masterson. Wyatt asked Bat Masterson to help Doc and the miracle man swung into action. He saved Billy Thompson, Ben's brother. He helped save Wyatt and Luke Short, and now Doc. Bat went to Denver and got up a pro-Doc press campaign with the three newspapers. Doc did interviews. Bat got in to see the governor, and saved the day. Wyatt had made sure that Wells Fargo, the Santa Fe Railroad, and his allies were in Doc's corner. At one point in all this, the San Francisco home office of Wells Fargo issued a long statement of support for Wyatt Earp and Doc Holliday. This was all a follow-up story to the gunfight and vendetta ride, so it was national news and seemed to drag out. Doc Holliday and Bat

Masterson convinced the nation, truthfully, that Doc Holliday would be killed if he was returned to Arizona.

Bat had fabricated a warrant saying Doc was wanted in his jurisdiction for a minor bunko, or fraud charge. The governor refused to extradite. Doc made bond on the lesser charge. In Colorado legal circles, bonding out on a lesser charge is still called, "Hollidaying."

Doc Holliday was now the most famous gambler in Colorado, a state he could not leave. The West's most troublesome man had to stay out of trouble. Doc was getting old enough to mature some, so he was charming and well liked in Colorado. Doc moved on to the biggest boomtown of them all, Leadville, Colorado. Soon he was playing in the famed stud and draw poker games at the Board of Trade Saloon, and making powerful friends. Doc got a job dealing faro. He was an ideal employee, drawing customers who pointed at him in awe and whispered to each other. Things were swell, but his health was growing progressively worse, and soon he could not work. Doc had to be on his best behavior to avoid extradition. A few of his old enemies bullied him, and he was broke. Doc borrowed $5 from a bartender and could not pay. The man went around town making threats. Finally, Doc told a friend, "I'm just going to wing him." He hid a pistol at the end of the bar in a place he had worked and waited. When his adversary entered with his hands in his pockets, Doc shot him in the arm, just as he'd said he would. He was tried and acquitted. At trial, Doc said he weighed 122 pounds and his opponent over 170. Doc was probably broke and too proud to ask for handouts. A number of prominent citizens helped with his bond and legal defense.

Doc Holliday and Wyatt Earp met one last, emotional time in the lobby of the Windsor Hotel in Denver in 1885 or 1886. Wyatt's common-law wife, Josephine Earp, was with him and has written about it. Josephine said she had never seen anyone as happy as Doc at this meeting. The old friends laughed and cried alone in a long conversation. Wyatt thanked Doc again for saving his life. Doc had a persistent cough and was unsteady on his feet as he gamely walked away, frail, gray, and gaunt.

Doc died in 1887 at age 36. Laying in bed, he looked at his feet and said, "This is funny." The *Denver Evening Times* reported, "Doc Holliday died with his boots off." On his tombstone it says only, "He died in bed."

William "Bat" Masterson:
The Most Loyal Friend in the Old West

I have been connected nearly all the time...in the gambling business and have experienced the vicissitudes which have always characterized the business. Some days -- plenty, and more days -- nothing...Bat Masterson.

B at Masterson (1851-1921) was born in Canada. His family migrated to Kansas. Bat and his two brothers, Ed and Jim, became buffalo hunters as teenagers. At 20, Bat went with a group of hunters to the Texas panhandle to establish a trading post at Adobe Walls. They built three sod houses with two-foot thick walls. There were twenty-three men and one woman there when Comanche Chief Quanah Parker attacked with 250 Indians from four tribes. The half-breed Quanah was the son of Cynthia Ann Parker, the most famous Comanche captive. Quanah would go on to be America's richest and one of the most famous Indians. He and Bat Masterson would both be friends with the President of the United States, Theodore Roosevelt.

At Adobe Walls, the hunters were equally split between three buildings. They were firing the .50 caliber Sharp's rifles, called the Big Fifties. They could pick the Indians off at will. At one point, Quanah's horse was shot out from under him and he was wounded at 500 yards. Billy Dixon, later a Medal of Honor winner, shot an Indian off his horse at 1500 yards, nearly a mile.

Quanah had a bugler, a black Army deserter. Finally, someone shot the annoying bugler.

After the Indian's retreat, several of their bodies were decapitated, and their heads were hung on poles out front.

Bat Masterson was in the gambling town of Mobeetie, also in the Texas panhandle, when he met famed gambler and gunman Ben Thompson. He also killed the only man he ever killed in a gunfight. An Army bad man, Sgt. Melvin King, rushed into a crowded saloon and gambling hall and shot the woman Bat was talking to, Mollie Brennen, killing her. He also shot Bat in the groin. Bat got off a single shot right though King's heart. Accounts vary but the squabble was over either the woman or poker. With Bat on the floor, some of the soldiers went for their guns. Ben Thompson jumped on the top of his faro table with both guns drawn. His fierce reputation controlled the room, as it did often. Bat would always remember Ben saved his life.

When Bat recovered from his gunshot wound, he went to Cheyenne, Wyoming on his way to the big gold strike in Deadwood, South Dakota. By now a professional gambler, Bat had a five-week lucky winning streak at faro and poker and just stayed there.

When Bat returned to Dodge City, Kansas, he joined a political group called "the Dodge City Gang" which favored wide open gambling and saloons. The town people knew Bat from the time a confidence man had fleeced the Masterson brothers out of $300. When he found out the man was coming through on a train, Bat went aboard, marched him off at gunpoint and made him pay up. A crowd watched. Later a 300 pound sheriff's deputy was abusing a prisoner he was escorting to jail. Bat jumped in to fight for the little guy and ended up beaten up and in jail

At age 23, Bat was elected sheriff of the county. He ran against the same 300 pound man he fought with and won by three votes. Bat and his friends dealt faro and worked in gambling joints, and the whole crew was there: Wyatt Earp and his brothers, Doc Holliday, Bat Masterson, Luke Short, and Ben and Billy Thompson. As sheriff, Bat would take off on the gambling circuit to Colorado and the big poker games. Bat played poker with the biggest names. Bat and Luke Short hit the gambling circuit in Colorado together. Luke won $10,000 in one all-night poker game in Leadville.

Bat also ran the Lone Star Dance Hall which had a dance floor, dancing girls, faro, poker, roulette, monte, and chuck-a-luck. His friendship and association with known killers like Doc Holliday and Ben Thompson looked bad. However, with Bat as sheriff, and Wyatt as a police officer, these men who were known for making trouble all across the Old West were on their best behavior because of friendship and loyalty.

As sheriff, Bat spent his time running the Lone Star gambling concession. Early in his term, Bat had some success with posses made up of his gambler friends. These gambler's posses made several notable arrests. Bat would carry his Sharp's Big Fifty. He brought down a noted train robber named Dave Rudabaugh from a great distance. Rudabaugh was a leader of a gang. He testified against his own gang for immunity. The newspaper said, "He was given a chance to squeal and he squole." Rather than reform as promised, he joined Billy the Kid's gang.

In 1878, Bat's brother, Ed, was killed by two drunk cowboys. Bat came fast and shot them both, but only wounded them.

Jim Kenedy was the son of one of the very richest Texans and a partner with Richard King of the fabled King Ranch, Texas' largest and richest ranch, then and now. The mayor beat up Kenedy who left and came back to town with murder on his mind. The mayor was out of town. Kenedy shot rounds into his cottage, killing a touring vaudeville singer named Dora Hand. Kenedy was seen riding out of town right after the shots.

Bat and one of his gambler's posses, including Wyatt Earp, figured out what route Kenedy would take back to Texas. They spotted him. Kenedy had purchased an expensive race horse to help him take it on the lam. Bat shot the prize horse and the prize Texan with his Sharp's Big Fifty. Seabiscuit couldn't outrun a Big Fifty. Kenedy confessed but later got off. He died in a year and a half, maybe from the huge wound to his arm. The Texas money and lawyers that got Kenedy off caused great anger in Dodge.

Two railroads, the Santa Fe and the Denver, were competing for the right-of-way to the big boomtown, Leadville, Colorado. They had lawsuits flying, but each railroad hired a group of armed men. The Santa Fe hired Bat Masterson to recruit an army of thirty-three gunmen, including Doc Holliday and Ben Thompson. The Kansas sheriff led his little army into Colorado, but nothing much happened. However, it led the folks of Dodge to again question their sheriff's close association with a couple of the most famous gunfighters of all, Ben and Doc.

In 1879, Bat was defeated in his bid for re-election as sheriff. He was madder than a broke pimp. Of all these Old West Gamblers I write about, I like Bat the most, easily. He was the most ethical and humane. Bat started his career as a caustic, angry, humorous, provocative, and thin-skinned writer. Bat would write letters to the editor in different cities, attacking his political enemies, and Dodge itself. At one point, Bat put out a one issue newspaper called *Vox Populi*. Bat attacked all the candidates running for office on the opposing slate with outrageous stories, gossip, and lies. He said one man had starved his own father to death. All of Bat's candidates won. Bat had tasted the self-affirming power of being a writer.

In 1880, Bat was called on for a rescue. Ben Thompson asked Bat to travel 250 miles north to Ogallala, Nebraska to attempt to rescue his brother Billy, who had shot the thumb and three fingers off a prominent citizen. Billy had been shot with a shotgun in the ass, and was stove up. Ben was already in trouble in Ogallala, and could not go himself.

When Bat arrived by train, the sheriff was very suspicious that Bat would attempt to help Billy escape. Bat offered bribes to what he called, "the thumbless one." That didn't work. On a Sunday night, the fiddling sheriff was playing for a town dance and left one lone deputy to guard Billy in his hotel room. Bat got the bar tender to drug the deputy's drink, and he passed out. Bat carried Billy to the train out of town. Billy could not sit a horse.

America's most famous showman, Buffalo Bill Cody, lived in North Platte, Nebraska, fifty miles away. Bat had met Buffalo Bill in Dodge. Cody was to become a good friend later to Ben Thompson. Cody agreed to protect them from any posse. He had a group of some twenty, wealthy European dignitaries coming the next day for a tour of a ranch. He gave Bat a fine new wagon he had ordered specially built for his wife and a fine horse.

The whole group took off the next day with expensive, gourmet foods, and a great deal of liquor. There were frequent stops to drink, and Cody passed out. That night, at a big ranch, there was an elaborate dinner. Cody put on a show of horsemanship and shooting. Bat and Billy Thompson rode into Dodge in a driving rain. Bat never liked Billy at all. He was just returning a favor to Ben, who had saved his life in Mobeetie.

After Dodge, Bat lived in Kansas City awhile, toured the boomtowns of Colorado, and developed his gambling skills and reputation as a high roller, especially at poker. As a young man, he tried the best of his day.

The New York Sun printed a story that would follow Bat Masterson for life. It said he killed 26 men by the time he was 27 years old. Bat would always ward off questions about that with jokes, but he never really denied it. Doc Holliday did the same with his inflated record for killing people. A fierce reputation was good for a gambler at that time. It kept the bullies away, and the cheats off. These gunfighters were the rock stars of their day, written up in newspapers, magazines, and the lurid dime novels. That reputation, and Bat's previous position as a gambling hall manager, and expert faro dealer, meant he had jobs waiting in any boomtown, if he wanted them.

Wyatt Earp left Dodge for Tombstone, Arizona, a silver-strike boomtown. He convinced his brothers and Doc Holliday to move there also. The biggest, fanciest gambling joint was the Oriental Saloon. They gave Wyatt one-fourth of the gambling concession to keep out the rowdy element. Doc asked Bat, Luke Short, and Doc Holliday to come there and go to work as dealers, and they all did. Their collective celebrity kept the joint packed with high rollers.

Bat had a close friend, Charles Storms, who was a legend as a gambler and gunfighter. Storms got in a squabble with Luke Short over a faro game at the Oriental. Bat separated them, and urged a drunken Storms to get some sleep. As Bat was talking to Luke, Storms returned, grabbed Luke's arm and went for his long-barreled six-gun. Luke was faster with the gun from his back pocket and he shot Storms dead. Luke Short had his tailor-made suits specially designed with a soft-leather lined back pocket, and longer vests to conceal his barking iron. He lubricated the pocket with talcum powder. Luke had reasoned long ago that a gambler needed a short-barreled pistol since disputes would be at close range. It comes out of a holster or pocket faster. Bat testified for Luke and Luke got off. Luke returned to Dodge soon after this to manage, and later own, the Long Branch Saloon.

While in Tombstone, Bat got a cryptic, unsigned telegram saying two named men meant to kill his brother, Jim Masterson, a city policeman back in Dodge. It was Bat to the rescue by the very next train, as usual. When Bat got to Dodge, he got off the train early only to see the two men he was looking for. He spoke a few words, and they all started shooting. All three took cover, and some friends entered the fray as backup for each side. Bullets were going into bars and buildings. One of the men Bat was seeking was severely wounded, but the shot did not come from Bat. When the smoke cleared, Bat was jailed, fined $8, and told to get out of Dodge and stay out of Dodge. Run Bat Masterson out of town for good? Fat chance.

Bat went on to Trinidad, Colorado and opened a faro game. He became city marshal. After the gun fight near the O.K. Corral and the nationally newsworthy Vendetta Ride, Wyatt and Warren Earp, and Doc Holliday went to Trinidad. They were now wanted murderers back in Arizona. Wyatt set up the faro in nearby Gunnison, Colorado, and Doc drifted on to Denver, where he was arrested, and faced extradition to Arizona. Wyatt Earp pleaded with Bat to do a rescue.

Bat wrote of Doc, "his whole heart and soul were wrapped up in Wyatt Earp." Bat didn't like Billy Thompson, and he really didn't like Doc, but he left immediately to captain a brilliant, nation-wide press campaign. Bat got an audience with the governor who refused to extradite Doc. Bat had saved Doc's life. Doc spent the rest of his life in the safety of Colorado.

Back in Dodge City, Luke Short owned the Long Branch Saloon. His competition, the mayor, had Luke's employees arrested. Then a lynch mob-like group escorted Luke and the gamblers they did not like to the train station, and forced them to leave town. Luke wired Bat. Bat wired Wyatt. What became known as the Dodge City War began. Word spread that Luke Short, Bat Masterson, Doc Holliday, and Wyatt Earp were leading a group of desperate men to Dodge. The town folk were near panic. They appealed to the governor of Kansas for the militia to be sent. Luke and Bat went to see the governor to explain Luke's position. This was the second state governor Bat had appealed to successfully for a friend. Doc wasn't really coming because he was not about to leave Colorado. Wyatt arrived first with a few men. He spoke to the city council group with demands that Bat and Luke be allowed in town, Luke's property, including the Long Branch, be returned, and he be left alone. They all quickly agreed. Later, Luke sold out when reform threatened gambling. Bat went with him to Fort Worth, Texas where Luke bought the fanciest gambling joint, the White Elephant.

At a celebrity-filled poker game there, Wyatt, Bat, and Luke were playing. Also playing in the game was famed gunman, Long Haired Jim Courtright. He was a hit man and trying to extort money from all the gambling house owners in a protection racket. Luke would not pay. Bat was standing there when Jim called Luke out of the White Elephant. Jim was slow with the long gun, and Luke shot him to death. Fast draw shootouts were very rare in the Old West. Bat had seen Luke win two of them. Luke was put in jail, and a mob formed. Bat went to the jail and persuaded the sheriff to allow he and Luke to share a cell and each have two handguns. When the sheriff told the crowd the famous gunmen were armed, they went home. Luke got off, again, thanks to Bat's testimony.

At the July 4th celebrations in 1885, Bat Masterson was voted as Dodge's most popular man and given a gold watch chain and a gold-tipped cane. One newspaper said he was one of the most famous men in the Old West.

Later, Wyatt and Bat, worked in Denver for boss gamblers, Big Ed Chase and Square-Shooter Johnny Hughes. Having a healthy bankroll, Bat bought the Palace Theater, a vaudeville house. His old friend, Eddie Foy, did many performances there which helped Bat book other big acts. Bat married a performer named Emma Walters, and they stayed married for life. She had been married to a foot racer, and they put on an act where she ran against her husband. She also did a dance routine.

Bat began to write a column on boxing for a newspaper, and he went to every major prize fight after that for the rest of his life. In boxing, Bat served as time keeper, body guard, purse keeper, corner man, manager, promoter, and mostly as a gambler. In Denver, Bat owned a fight club. When Bat was for a fighter, he would have them heavily insult their opponent in the newspapers, as he did in letters, interviews, and columns. Newspapers reported he knew as much about boxing as anyone in the country.

Reform movements always sent the gamblers on to the next wide-open boomtown. Bat sold out in Denver, and badmouthed the whole town in print, just as he had when he left Dodge. Bat Masterson moved to the silver-strike boomtown of Crede, Colorado to manage its biggest gambling house, the Denver Exchange. Celebrity gamblers that came to Crede included Poker Alice, Calamity Jane, Soapy Smith, and Bob Ford, the man who shot Jesse James in the back for a reward. He was killed in Crede.

There was little trouble in Bat's gambling house in Crede. Bat was known for his charities, and as a soft touch. A civil war veteran, dying of consumption, came in to beg a meal. Bat took up a collection to send him by train back east where he came from. When a crazed, itinerant preacher came in, asking Bat if he could give a sermon. Bat beat on the bar with his pistol, and asked for silence. The games all stopped, and the preacher gave a sermon on the Prodigal Son. He ended by singing *Rock of Ages*, and the crowd joined him. Many had tears in their eyes. Bat suggested a collection, and the Preacher suddenly had $350. After he had left for his tent on the edge of town, some of the gamblers said they didn't give enough. They wanted to double it. Bat didn't know how much it was, and sent a man to find out. He found the preacher asleep and stole his pants. The Preacher came into the bar in his red, long handles saying he had been robbed. Bat gave him his pants which now contained $700. The happy preacher bought a round of drinks for the house.

Bat Masterson was a better, finer, smarter man than any of the other Old West gamblers that I write about. One night in Crede, with a packed joint, a drunk walked up to Bat and slugged him in the face. The whole place got suddenly still and totally silent. Bat paused and then roared with laughter, as did everyone in the whole casino. Wyatt would have pistol whipped him brutally. Doc might have killed him. Bat sent him on home.

Many years earlier, Bat had met two writers who were brothers, Alfred Lewis and William Lewis. They would have a tremendous influence on his life. Bat moved on to New York to write a thrice-weekly column for 18 years for William Lewis' *Morning Telegraph*. That is over 4,000.000 words. It was called "Masterson's Views on Timely Topics." Alfred was a magazine writer and novelist who wrote about a heroic, mythical Bat Masterson. He was one of America's best known and highest paid writers. Bat's column was about boxing, but also theater, restaurants, politicians, and anything he cared to comment on.

When Bat Masterson first arrived in New York in 1902, he was arrested for a crooked faro game. A Mormon elder from Utah, John N. Snow, the son of the president of the Mormon Church, had taken a big loss and accused Bat and others of cheating. He was lying and did not show up to testify. Bat sued him, saying his reputation as "a square gambler" was well known. Bat won money in an out-of-court settlement. Several New York newspapers supported Bat and said he had always been a "square gambler." This got nation-wide news, and the victory was sweet for the sporting fraternity.

When a rival newspaper said that Bat had made his reputation in the Old West by shooting Mexicans and Indians in the back, Bat sued them. The newspaper had as their attorney future Supreme Court Justice Benjamin Cardozo. Bat won when two Army generals, Baldwin and Miles, testified to his courage and reputation. Bat had been an Army scout for a few months, forty years earlier. He was awarded $3500 in damages.

Each time Bat would be back in the news, the old story of him killing 26 men would surface, but it did not seem to hurt him. When President Theodore Roosevelt was elected in 1904, Bat became a regular visitor to the White House. Roosevelt appointed Bat a Deputy Federal Marshal for the Southern District of New York. This was a part-time political job that did not interfere with his newspaper work, boxing promotion, or gambling.

A whore's breakfast was defined as "a cigarette and the *Morning Telegraph*." Several famous writers, including Gene Fowler, Heywood Broun, Louella Parsons, and Bat's protege, Damon Runyon, wrote there also. Runyon has said Bat would buy old six-guns from pawn shops, carve notches in them, and sell them to collectors as guns used in famous gunfights.

Bat died at his desk at the newspaper of a heart attack in 1921 when he was sixty-seven years old. His last column was ready to go. Here is a bit of the last thing Bat Masterson ever wrote: *There are those who argue that everything breaks even in this old dump of a world of ours. I suppose these ginks who argue that way hold that because the rich man gets ice in the summer and the poor man gets it in the winter things are breaking even for both. Maybe so, but I'll swear I can't see it that way.*

Benjamin "Ben" Thompson: The Old West's Deadliest Gunfighter Was An Englishman

It is doubtful if in his time there was another man living who equaled him with a pistol in a life-and-death struggle...He had in his career more deadly encounters with the pistol than any man living and won out in every single instance...Bat Masterson

Ben Thompson (1843-1884) was born in Knottingley, Yorkshire, England. His family moved to Austin, Texas when he was six. He was to gain national fame early in life as a gambler and gunfighter. At age 15, he shot another boy with a shotgun, and served sixty days jail time. He learned the printer's trade and started his life-long association with newspapers. When he was 16, he met Dick Clark, one of the Old West's highest stakes poker players and gamblers. Ben knew he wanted to be a gambler. At 17, in New Orleans, Ben came to the defense of a woman he'd never met being abused by a Frenchman, whom he killed in a knife fight. This became a pattern in Ben's life, going to the defense of others. While still a teenager, Ben joined the Texas Rangers to chase Comanche Indians. He served there with Buckskin Sam Hill, later to be a famous dime novelist that often used Ben as one of his heroes.

Ben enlisted in the Confederate Army in 1861, and served along the Mexican border where he and gambling partner Phil Coe dealt and banked Spanish monte, not to be confused with the sleight of hand game, three-card monte. They worked both sides of the border. Ben had a troublesome brother, Billy, who enlisted and joined their company. Ben was dealing monte to Mexican soldiers and had won a lot of money. One held out a card and a dispute arose. Billy, the lookout, had forgotten his gun. Ben killed two men when they drew on him, and they barely escaped with their lives, if not their money.

Back in Austin, Ben killed a man who had a shotgun pointed at him on Congress Avenue in a dispute over a mule. He was jailed, but escaped to Mexico, where he served as a mercenary for two years under Emperor Maximilian when the French controlled Mexico. He rose to the rank of major. When he returned to Austin, Ben shot his brother-in-law for abusing Ben's pregnant sister and did two years in the penitentiary.

Starting in 1870, Ben followed the gambling circuit of West Texas and the Kansas cattle-drive towns. His partner, Phil Coe, had a good bankroll. They opened the Bull's Head in Abilene, Kansas. They were known as square gamblers, and high-stakes poker players. For the rest of his life, Ben would be known for running the biggest, squarest, and best poker games for the Texas cattlemen. The city marshal in Abilene, was Wild Bill Hickok, now in the Poker Hall of Fame. Wild Bill was connected to a different gambling house, and they all were making lots of money. Wild Bill was nationally famous. His exploits were written up and magnified in *Harper's Weekly*.

Ben Thompson was also well known, and there was speculation about having the Old West's top two shootists in the same town. Once Wild Bill came into the Bull's Head with a shotgun. He said the citizens objected to the sign which showed a bull with over-sized private parts. Ben and Phil agreed to allow Wild Bill's workmen to paint over the offensive part of the sign.

The customers in the Kansas towns were rough Texas cowboys who came in the summers with the trail drives. The Bull's Head was the top gambling spot. Ben was personable, popular, and admired. Phil Coe, Ben's tall, good-looking partner had stolen the affections of a dance-hall girl from Wild Bill. When Coe and the lady were sitting at a table, Wild Bill rushed in and struck her in the face. Coe beat the hell out of him. Ben sent for his wife and children. In Kansas City, they were all injured in a buggy accident. While Ben was recuperating from his injuries, Phil Coe went into the street with a rowdy group of Texans at the end of the season. He fired his pistol. He said it was at a stray dog that had tried to bite people. Wild Bill Hickok came running up with both famous six shooters drawn. Words were exchanged, and Wild Bill shot Phil Coe twice in the stomach, killing him. A private security guard came running though the crowd, and Wild Bill turned and killed him accidentally. Wild Bill was fired and went on to Deadwood. A Texan killed him in a poker game when Wild Bill was holding two pair, Aces and Eights, which became the "Dead Man's Hand." Phil Coe was the last person Wild Bill killed on purpose. Wild Bill left town before Ben returned.

In 1873, Ben and his hapless brother, Billy, were running a gambling joint in Ellsworth, Kansas. There was a dispute over a poker game. Ben had staked a man who would not give him his half of the winnings. The fight spilled into the street, and Billy came with a cocked shotgun to back up Ben. Their friend, Sheriff Whitney, came to stand beside a drunken Billy. Billy's shotgun accidentally discharged and killed the sheriff. Ben yelled, "My God, Billy, you've just killed our best friend!"

Ben and a few Texans held off an angry crowd with rifles while Billy made his escape. Only a drunken Billy rode out of town very slowly, and returned to hide. He escaped later. Billy was captured in Texas and returned for a trial. He was acquitted. Billy killed two sheriffs and a soldier at different times, and Ben always paid for top legal talent. Ben moved on to Wichita and then Dodge City where he dealt faro in the famous Long Branch Saloon.

In 1875, Ben and Billy opened the Lady Gay, the fanciest gambling joint in Sweetwater, Texas, later called Mobeetie. It was in the Texas panhandle. When the town folks found out there was already a Sweetwater, they asked a Comanche for the Indian name for sweet water, and he told them *mobeetie*. It really means buffalo dung. It was a gambling boomtown because of the buffalo hunters, the cowboys on the trail, and the soldiers from nearby Fort Elliott. The Lady Gay had a band, dance floor, pool table, saloon, and gambling tables. Mobeetie was a legendary poker town with many of the Old West's most famous gamblers passing through: Poker Alice, Wyatt Earp, John Wesley Hardin, Bat Masterson, the Thompson brothers, and Pat Garrett, the man who killed Billy the Kid.

By 1875, and for the rest of his life, Ben Thompson was a well known figure near the Austin capital. He wore the finest, tailor-made Prince Albert coats, a stiff white shirt, a tie, and a huge diamond stickpin, called a "headlight." He wore a silk top hat and walked with a gold-tipped cane. Ben was known as an easy touch and shared his wealth. Later, he would be well known for his favorite hobby of getting drunk and shooting out street lights.

When a friend of Ben's was thrown out of the Capital Theater, owned by Irishman Mark Wilson, Ben returned with him. The friend had helped Billy escape from Kansas. When Wilson and his aides again jumped his friend, Ben came forward. Wilson, got a shotgun, and the bartender a rifle. Ben shot them both, killing the owner. It was judged self-defense.

There were large silver strikes in Colorado, and all the circuit gamblers went. Leadville was the largest gambling town of all. Ben Thompson had a good bankroll and was looking for investment opportunities. He was playing poker and "bucking the tiger", playing faro against the house. One night he got drunk and lost $3000 at faro. He shot out the lights and the crowd fled. Of course, he paid the fine and damages, as always. Later, he was successful with his gambling concessions in saloons in Leadville. He wrote a long piece for the *Austin Statesmen* about the high price of everything in Leadville.

When Buffalo Bill Cody's stage play and shows played Austin in 1979 for three weeks, he and Ben Thompson became fast friends and did public shooting exhibits there and in San Antonio with rifles and pistols. A newspaper picture showed the two riding in a buggy.

When Buffalo Bill's show returned to Austin, he gave Ben a gift of the largest buffalo head ever mounted, which had been killed by Russia's Grand Duke Alexis on a famous buffalo hunt that included Wild Bill and Col. William Armstrong Custer. Wild Bill also gave Ben a fancy target pistol with a long, artistically carved barrel. It had gold and pearl handles and was inscribed, "From Buffalo Bill to Ben Thompson." A private collector now owns it, but it is shown in museums.

Back in Austin, Ben opened his most famous and successful gambling joint, the Iron Front, at Sixth and Congress. He had the gambling business upstairs. It was a few blocks from the capital and had the legislators and ranch owners in the big poker game. Ben was incredibly popular and a darling of the Texas rich. Once when the powerful Texas Livestock Raiser's Association was having a luncheon meeting, Ben held twenty of them at gun point while he lectured them on insulting a friend of his, by throwing him out. He broke a few dishes, and paid the fine and damages.

Ben Thompson always ran a square game. When he found his faro dealer had a crooked dealing box, he shot the chips off the table, then shot up the dealing box in his own gambling establishment. He said, "I don't think that set of tools is entirely honest, and I want to help Mr. Lorraine, buy another." Of course, being Ben, he shot out his own fancy chandelier and all the lights. He then went next door and shot up the keno "goose" that holds the balls in a crooked joint owned by a rival. He left that place dark also, as was his custom. Later that same night, Ben went to another part of town, and shot out a few street lights. He was quoted in the newspaper as saying they could buy some honest gambling equipment. The *Statesman* had an editorial praising Ben. As usual, he paid the fine and damages.

With employees to run all the games of faro, keno, Spanish monte, and chuck-a-luck, Ben played high stakes poker each evening from eight to two or three a.m. The Iron Front had one of the best known poker games in all Texas. It was through this game, Ben met many of the rich and powerful who would come to his aid later. He had purchased his family a beautiful house right across the street from the University of Texas. Ben would always have dinner with his family. He had supported his mother since he was 17, and she lived with Ben, his wife, and two children.

Once an undertaker went broke in the poker game. He asked for credit on a fine marble tombstone. Ben agreed, and won the tombstone, which he had put in the basement. It was found there in 1910, when the building was torn down.

In 1880, at the urging of many, Ben Thompson ran for Austin's city marshal. The *Austin Statesman* endorsed him saying, "He is well and favorably known to everyone in the city, and is in every way worthy of the confidence and support of the people." He lost the first time, but was later elected to two terms. In his first campaign announcement, he wrote truthfully, "the difficulties of the independent life I have led were the result of an impulse to protect the weak from the strong." When the noted gunman, Johnny Ringo, was in Austin flashing a pistol, Ben walked up alone, and arrested him. While he was marshal, the crime rate was the lowest in years, with no murders. Congress Avenue was especially quiet, because Ben was there playing poker, and might go for a stroll.

San Antonio was Austin's rival, and only four hours by train. In 1880, Ben went there and lost $4000 at faro in the Vaudeville Theatre, owned by Irishman Jack Harris. They had served together in the Civil War. Ben grumbled and made some threats, but left. Unlike so many Old West gamblers, Ben was not a pimp. Harris was, and Ben badmouthed him for living from the soiled dove's sorrow. Later, Harris put out the word that Ben was barred from his gambling house. This made the newspapers. Ben was, after all, known for shooting up gambling joints, and killing an owner. Harris was a political boss and gambling boss with investments in several gambling houses. He was seen as one of San Antonio's most important, respected, and admired community leaders.

Later, Ben did return to San Antonio and the Vaudeville Theater. Harris knew he was coming and hid behind a Venetian blind screen near the door with a shotgun. He planned to kill Ben and had said so. Ben saw him from outside through a window and went in. After words were exchanged, Ben fired through the screen and killed Harris. Ben was reputed to have had 14 gunfights, 11 in Texas, without a loss. He had faced shotguns and rifles successfully with his pistol. He never took unfair advantage, shot anyone in the back, or committed murder, according to Bat Masterson.

The San Antonio newspapers hated Ben. The Austin papers loved him at first and endorsed him at first, but they eventually turned against him and called for his resignation as city marshal. There was a great deal of expensive legal maneuvering and Ben spent six months in the San Antonio jail. The Austin City Council, at first, refused to accept his resignation. Ben was finally acquitted of killing Harris. He arrived back in Austin to a hero's welcome. A group took the horse off his carriage, and pulled it up Congress Avenue to the capitol building in a parade. The streets were lined with people cheering. They had an African-American brass band, local and state elected officials, and huge crowds. Like my own father, Ben Thompson was very active with the Knights of Pythias, a fraternal organization that raises money for orphan children. The Knights and the children were there leading the parade. However, Ben was drinking heavily in the days after that and on several occasions, he went out at night to shoot out street lights. Austin was getting tired of this. He was arrested three times in March for discharging his pistol and once for invading the *Statesmen* offices and waving his pistol around.

One of the new owners of San Antonio's Vaudeville Theater sent Ben an invitation to come back there. Ben said, "If I were to go into that place it would be my graveyard." His premonition was precisely correct.

Ben ran into King Fisher, another noted Texas gunfighter. After being on trial for killing four men and cattle rustling, Fisher faced six hung juries in a row. They let him go and he became a deputy sheriff. Ben and King took the train to San Antonio. They were drinking heavily. Ben bought a new hat. First they took in a play and then, Ben wanted to go back to the Vaudeville Theater. There he exchanged a few words with the new owners and was directed upstairs to a theater box to wait for the main owner. The theater was crowded, and dancers were performing on the stage. Ben Thompson and King Fisher were ambushed by as many as five people firing rifles and pistols from nearby theater boxes. Ben was hit nine times, Fisher thirteen. Each of the new owners ran up and shot them in the head with a pistol. One of the assailants shot himself in the leg and later died.

A rapid San Antonio inquest ruled self-defense, and newspapers state wide let out a howl. Ben's death was a front-page story in the *New York Times,* and nearly every Texas newspaper.

Ben Thompson's funeral was one of the largest in Austin's history, with another parade, led by the Knights of Pythias in full uniforms, with orphans from the homes they funded. They put his top hat on the coffin. The funeral was held at the Pythian Lodge, like that of my own father. Ben had been married to the same woman for twenty years and had two children. He was buried in the Oakwood Cemetery.

III.
My Best Short Fiction

The Man Who Knew Jack Ruby

In 1963, I formed a strange friendship with this old gambler named Soft Shoe O' Shea, or just Shoes. He was a regular fixture around the lobby of the Adolphus Hotel, the fanciest hotel in all of Texas. The lobby was a beehive of activity and a real power center. There were several lush, leather couches that sat beneath these huge oil paintings of western scenes. There were often big oilmen there looking at maps, trading leases, or listening to another story from Shoes. The oil men wore the big hats and boots. Soft Shoe O' Shea was always nattily dressed in an older suit and tie, french cuffs and cuff links, a dress fedora or porkpie hat, and highly-shined, often two-tone shoes. Very often, he had a rose bud or white carnation in his lapel. He was a tall man, too thin for his suits, very agile and athletic. He was eighty and seemed to know everyone in downtown Dallas. I was only twenty-three, and that age difference became the reason for our friendship. Sometimes when he'd walk up, one of the oil men would sing out, "It is Soft Shoe O'Shea." He'd do a few dance steps.

Shoes had been an early partner in a dice game with Rowdy Martin. He got big rich as a wildcatter. Rowdy was chasing oil in the sky, but his two sons, Little Rowdy and Sonny, with more money than good sense, seemed to keep Shoes in money. They ran a big poker game weekends in a plush suite in the Adolphus Hotel. They'd chippy there too. I got to playing lucky there, even though it was over my bankroll. Shoes never played, but he would be up there telling stories while we waited to get our first hole cards of the day. Once the game kicked off, he mummed up. The Martin boys both had displeasing personalities, even for *nouveau riche* Texans. They often teased Shoes.

Once, Little Rowdy asked Shoes to "tell that story about Bonnie and Clyde." There were four of us waiting for enough to start the poker game. Shoes pulled his chair up closer to the poker table where we were sitting. He hitched up his trousers. His watery, blue eyes began to shine. He took off his black fedora, exposing a full head of snow-white hair. I'd never seen him so excited.

"Well, I was working the stick at a crap game on the north edge of Dallas around Christmas of 1933. One night the boss said we was gonna stay late and fade this high player. About one o'clock in the morning, Clyde Barrow and Bonnie Parker and two other guys show up. Clyde and the boss went way back, so Clyde knew we wouldn't snitch them off, and we hoped they wouldn't rob us. Clyde goes to shooting and drinking whiskey. We didn't have nothing to eat but Vienna sausage, crackers, cheese, and onions and he ate his own self two plates full.

"They was real famous and in the newspapers and all robbing them banks, when banks were unpopular. I asked Bonnie for something to remember her by. We didn't have a pencil for an autograph. She pulled this little pair of scissors out of her purse and gave me this, a lock of her hair." Shoes leaned up on one cheek and pulled out his ancient billfold. Inside a piece of hotel stationary, there was a lock of brownish, dry hair. He passed it around for everyone to see. "It was just a few months later, the Texas Rangers shot them down like dogs on the street. Don't seem legal, the Texas Rangers ambushing folks in Louisiana." Little Rowdy was rolling his eyes and mocking Shoes.

After that, Shoes and I sat in the lobby and talked nearly every time I played in the poker game. He had a key to the suite, and we go up there and make coffee some mornings. Sometimes he would be in the lobby in the middle of the night. I thought he lived at the Adolphus, but he lived in a residential hotel a.k.a. flop house where old men paid by the week and you heard coughing all night. Shoes could sign for room service up at the suite, and he often got a chicken-salad sandwich or egg-salad sandwich to go. He'd drink half a beer in a glass, and put the bottle back in the suite's refrigerator. One night late, I ran into Shoes in the lobby when I had $84 left in the world and dark, low feelings to match the occasion.

"Poker money ain't got no home." he said. "When I was young, every time I pumped a healthy bankroll, I never dreamed that I would get broke again, but I did lots of times. If you ain't got enough character to be broke, go to nine to fiving it. Get a job. Be a square John, 'cause a gambler has to know how to be broke in style. Yes sir, in style."

Jack Ruby was a regular in the Adolphus lobby, walking around fast, giving away passes to his strip club. Ruby and Shoes seemed to be absolutely best friends. When Ruby came in, Shoes would walk toward him, and they'd often laugh or do a little dance. Shoes gave conventioneers passes to Ruby's joint. I heard at the poker game, but Shoes never told me, that Shoes ran football bets for Ruby, who was a bookie.

One time, Jack Ruby got in a fist fight in the Adolphus' big fancy Burgundy Room and was arrested. Folks were talking about that big time, and Little Rowdy guessed we'd not see Ruby again in the hotel. The next day, there were Shoes and Ruby strutting around the lobby as if nothing had happened.

Another night, I ended up bigger behind than a cotton patch spider. Shoes wanted to talk and I didn't, at first. He told me that he once had a big joint on the Jacksboro Highway in Ft. Worth during World War Two. They had three dice tables and sometimes a roulette wheel. Then the Texas Rangers raided. "That was the best bankroll of my life, but every shiny dime went for crooked lawyers and crooked politicians. I barely stayed out of the pen." He said.

When Kennedy was assassinated, I was playing poker in Hot Springs, Arkansas. When I saw a familiar figure, Jack Ruby, blasting away at Oswald on TV, I headed for Dallas. It wasn't as if I had a boss, or a budget, or a schedule. I went straight to the Adolphus, figuring Shoes would tell me all about it. Only I never saw Shoes again. Not ever. Neither did anyone else, best I could tell. As the days passed, even the Martin brothers showed concern. I found the fifty-cent limit poker game in the back of a pool hall that Shoes had told me about. No one had seen him. I found the Dallas Arms, the flea bag where he had lived for some years. They had carefully boxed up his impressive wardrobe, but no one had seen him since the assassination.

Little Rowdy didn't take any convincing to file a Missing Person's Report. The police checked the morgue and hospitals and found nothing.

The bellhops at the Adolphus were these old, black men, in maroon uniforms. I had often seen Shoes talking to them. I asked one of them if they had heard any thing about Shoes.

He said, "The FBI and the Dallas detectives asked around about Jack Ruby and about Shoes, but we haven't seen him. I told the man that if he found old Shoes, to ask him to show him the lock of Bonnie Parker's hair."

Those Grifting O'Malleys

"Tough times make tough people," Benny Binion

Being an O'Malley, I was learning the grift by age fourteen, and I drove a car across Texas, all by myself in 1937. You go ask any old person in the Southwest if they've seen my uncle Sky O'Malley's act. They'll laugh and remember. They had this biplane in the depression. They'd go to county fairs, and rodeos, and such. Sam Hogan, another uncle, would do some trick flying. Then when he was off on break, Sky would come out acting real drunk, with a fifth of rot gut in his hand, and he'd pretend to steal the plane. Well, he'd fly all over, doing tricks, and he'd let go this here smoke trail and go flying toward the audience, and all until he *crashed* it right in front of a fair size crowd in Oklahoma City. He had some broke bones and what not, and this deputy sheriff didn't know it was an act, and handcuffed him.

Sky had done some flying bootlegging before I went on the road with him and Sam Hogan. They'd bring booze from El Paso and Mexico to Dallas, and that is how him and Benny Binion got to be real close friends, when they was very young bootleggers. When Bonnie Parker and Clyde Barrow got gunned down by the Texas Rangers over yonder in Louisiana in 1934, they were the most famous bank robbers in America. They'd killed some folks, including some laws. Benny was only thirty years old, but he was already big in outlaw circles. He had big dice games in Dallas, and just kept getting bigger until he had twenty-seven dice games in downtown Dallas during the war. He had a piece of some fancy casinos too. You know how most outlaws keep with their own kind for telling stories, and such, but Benny would show out, even early on.

So, Benny comes to Sky and says he wants to hire him to fly a plane over Clyde Barrow's funeral, and drop a floral wreath of fifty yellow roses. They went back and forth on it all one day, but Benny could talk a frog up out of a log. Clyde was real unpopular with the laws. Sky did it and it was in the Dallas newspaper, but it didn't mention Sky or Benny.

Sky and Sam Hogan were my uncles. Sam was married into the O'Malleys with my aunt Grace. I'd been practicing cheating with cards since I was eight, but I wasn't really ready to do anything. I went on the road with them when I was fourteen. They'd leave out of Duke, Oklahoma and work every little town all the way through West Texas down to El Paso as gamblers. They both could play most anything pretty darned good. This was 1937. Sky wore these old painter's clothes, and had said he was headed for a big job, but he'd tell folks he'd lost a fortune gambling in his life. Him and Sam would shill up at dominoes, or pool, or poker if they could find it. Every town had a domino hall. They were both good players, and they'd take the O'Malley edge. They could false shuffle dominoes or playing cards, but they weren't good for any cold decks or big moves. In dominoes, Sky could hold the double six under his palm when he shuffled and throw it by Sam or himself every time, and I couldn't even see it. He'd leave some cards on the bottom of the deck and false shuffle. I could see that, which kept me half scared the whole trip.

When we first left out of Duke, Oklahoma, they both got nearly broke in a poker game in Amarillo, Texas, and nearly got in a fight. Any time trouble came up, Sky would say he was a classical pianist and couldn't hurt his hands, but Sam liked fighting, and did the fighting for the family. Both of them were average-size guys, but wiry and strong. Sky'd give a grand speech, and there wouldn't be a fight, or I never saw one. Sky had a lock box with a bankroll over in El Paso, a fair spell away. Anyways, when they are acting, Sam does the winning, and Sky seems like an all-day sucker. If there was a movie house in any of those towns, we'd all three go to the movies, which wasn't smart for looking like we didn't know each other. Sky would say he looked like Errol Flynn, but he didn't.

When we got to El Paso, they were good winner, and each had given me a few bucks. Being the depression, sometimes they were gambling for change and a few lonely singles. Sky traded for this slick Ford Roadster, shiny black. He dressed up real fancy. O'Malleys have this genetic weakness for clothes they don't need. On the way back, he'd tell how he won thousands off this banker in El Paso. Sam would tell them he was cold trailing Sky because he knew he'd blow his boodle. Well, the greed of the mark is my family's stock in trade, and it was hard to belly up to the table for all the folks hustling Sky. He'd flash a lot of cash. And Sam would win it off him, or appear to. Sometimes, Sky would figure out the best producer in a town, and end up playing him one on one something. They'd gather up all the money open, and get ready to go. Sometimes, Sky would soak a fake diamond ring to somebody right before we left.

Even with a nice, plump bankroll, Sky is always doing short cons. He'd steal milk off back porches with five hundred cash on him. We'd go in a cafe and Sky would go to praying, and Sam is calling him Reverend and all, and he'd get a free meal or something. He'd keep a dead fly in his coat pocket and slip it in the soup, and raise hell with the owner. In this pretty nice cafe, considering the depression, right outside Wichita Falls, he'd did the fly con, and the owner got madder than a hatter. He started grabbing the change out of the cash box and slamming it on the counter. Sky was scooping it up, and putting it in his handkerchief. Sky got out of there with a big bunch of coins, but he could have got killed. That man was red as a fire engine.

So, they were my teachers, and wouldn't much leave me be. Sky's always yacking about my education. He'd always say he was gonna buy me a new suit of clothes, and a hat. Young guys like me wore a cap. In any town, I wanted to go find some folks my own age, mostly girls. We made a big circle around hitting several towns, and got to some little town just north of El Paso, in New Mexico, but right by Texas. There was about thirty of them bad women, bootleggers, burglars, big 'uns, gambling at dice, poker, and pitching quarters at the line. Well, I was good at that, and Sky and Sam got to betting on me, but it wasn't much, just the experience. It was mostly a dice game, and there was no edge, except fading the square dice. They even let me fade, and I was fourteen years old.

So, this deal came up where Sky is going to take this guy's plane and fly it to Dallas. Sky says it is a big money deal. I could tell you of several times he got flimflammed his own self. They were all drinking. Sky wants me to ride with him to make sure he stays awake. I'm not getting on any airplane with Sky O'Malley, drunk or sober, either one of us, even if I have to walk back to Oklahoma. So Sam goes, and they leave me to drive the car back. They were drinking, and they just flew off. I'd been driving lots on the highway, but I'd never driven alone. That fancy black roadster could get you robbed or killed in those bad lands and hard times. At first it wouldn't even start, and I went to walking, madder than I have ever been before or since. Then I went back and it started easy.

I drove right to the bridge to Juarez, Mexico and parked the car, and walked over there. In a half a block, I bought a whiskey and coke for a nickel. It didn't take much to get me drunk, being only my fourth of fifth time. I bought this big sombrero, and two fifths of fancy, but cheap champagne. That was a mistake, because I had to carry them everywhere, and if I wore the sombrero, folks would hurrah me. It was as big as a wagon wheel. I bought this gold watch that turned my wrist green. I barely remember finding the car, and going to sleep in it. The next day, this man in a filling station is showing me how to get to Carlsbad, New Mexico and on to Lubbock. I'd never read me a road map, and the man just gave it to me. When I started to put it in the glove box, there was over five hundred dollars cash in there, and not a bill over a ten. I went back and gave that filling station man a ten spot, probably two weeks pay for him in those tough times. It was coming a golly whopper of a rain storm, so I figured to spend one night in a fancy hotel. O'Malleys were always hanging around the lobby of a swell joint looking for some action or live ones. I stayed down town at the Plaza Hotel four days. Each morning and evening, I'd know I should call the farm in Duke, but somehow I never did. In order to avoid the law, and look like a fellow who was not driving a bent car, I bought a new suit of clothes, and my first fedora. Everyone knows the laws will leave a rich man or his son alone. I even got a tall-collar, stiff, white shirt, but I only wore it once. I'd eat at the hotel in a fancy dining room with a table cloth and all. They had a lamb and potato dish I still remember.

Well, they joke about that trip when they swap O'Malley family stories. I tried to marry a gal in Big Spring, and her daddy came at me with a deer hunting rifle. I lost $100 in a poker game at the domino hall there, and I tried to claim me being only fourteen, it wasn't fair. I looked all growed up, and I nearly got whupped over it. I stayed at a motor court in Lubbock about a week, and ate at a cafe every single night. I'd go downtown to the picture show every afternoon, and buy something, a shirt or shoes or something. And I took to wearing a suit, tie, and a hat. I bought another black fedora with red, green, and brown feathers. It had a white, silk lining. They say the people in Lubbock, Texas are the friendliest in the world, and I found no reason to question that.

Never said it, but I'm Pat O'Malley, not the famous wrestler. He was my cousin. The main thing about that trip was that I was alone for the very first time, and I had lots of time to think or daydream. I got to liking just driving down the road. Being the depression, there were lots of hitchhikers, bums by the rail yards, and general misery. So, I'd pick 'em up, sometimes three at a time. I'd buy a big loaf of bread, some onions, some bologna, and some soda water, and they'd wolf it down. Lucky, I didn't get heisted.

I'd been just stopping in towns and lollygagging around for about three weeks, when I finally decided to go on to the farm in Duke, and see what was up. I'd decided that for sure Sky wouldn't know about the money or how much anyways. I had two hundred left, and the whole back seat full of new clothes, shoes, real fancy clothes. I had two fedoras, the sombrero, and a porkpie hat. Thinking he might not even know he'd left money there, I had made up some good stories about me winning gambling at everything all along the way. Sky was at the farm. Must have been ten of the family came out into the yard. Sky knew to the dollar how much was in that glove box. I gave him a hundred, and held out a hundred, even though he was really yelling. I knew he wouldn't hit me or anything with a yard full of laughing O'Malleys around. They still quote what I said, "Well, just chalk up a few hundred to the price of your education."

Author's Note: Benny Binion really did hire a plane to drop a floral wreath at Clyde Barrow's funeral in 1934, when Benny was thirty. This was patterned after my gambling, grifting, great uncles during the depression. When I was fourteen, I went to Juarez alone and bought a big sombrero and two bottles of champagne immediately.

BLUFF EUROPE MAGAZINE

The Hero of COINTELPRO

Austin, Texas, 1968

It was a rather generic anti-war rally: the usual speakers, slogans, loud bands, and the smell of cheap Mexican dope in the air. The surveillance photograph that changed first-year FBI Agent Hank Trueblood's career and life showed Assistant Professor Richard Borden standing with the three most prominent leaders of the Students for A Democratic Society (the S.D.S.). They joked with him and let him speak first. Richard's longer-than-the-Beatles mop top of curly, black hair was known to hippies that showed up at rallies, vigils, protests, marches, rock bands, and some pretty cool parties. He was the guy at every lecture or meeting that would stand up with a very long question that was really a self-advertisement.

If you asked folks about Professor Borden, they'd reply, "the guy with the gorgeous wife?" Twas so true. Perky Peggy Borden had a *Playboy* bunny figure, and a new convert's absolute devotion to all things hippie. Her bouncy walk, auburn pony tail, and twinkling blue eyes made her appear a little more happy than seemed normal. Folks were new to getting stoned. Unexplained joy and suspicious laughter were everywhere. Peggy stood by the stage gazing adoringly at Richard as he shouted, "Why do we care about the government of far away Vietnam? Why should we waste lives and money on a war that does not impact our national interest?"

Borden was a much-published poet, thanks to Peggy, who mailed submissions to academic presses and tiny journals three days a week. She seemed to make incomprehensible, self-centered word play slide by many a committee. When FBI Special Agent Trueblood discovered that Peggy and Richard had attended a poetry conference in Moscow, he freaked. He

| 139 |

also discovered that Richard had an unused short-wave radio, a hobby in high school, and their bank account was always holding many thousands of dollars. Richard had inherited oil wealth. They had the mandatory Volkswagen van and had inherited the "perfect hippie house" just two blocks from Austin's drag, Guadalupe, the main street by the university. The house was 100 years old, red brick, with high ceilings, a wood-burning fire place, and antique oak furniture. The Bordens hosted frequent small parties. The open consumption of dope made Richard very nervous. He'd pretty much do anything his wife wanted him to do. Agent Trueblood had other duties harassing *The Rag*, the underground newspaper, and scores of self-appointed, movement leaders, but he'd go peek in the Borden's windows a few nights a week.

Peggy was best known in Austin for this incredibly sheer blouse that meant her breasts were basically exposed. She'd start to walk down the crowded, carnival-like Guadaupe Street, the Drag, and unbutton her shirt to expose the blouse underneath. If anyone was looking, she always wore her wedding ring. After talking with street vendors, giving some change to the "spare change, Mister?" guys, and grabbing some free newspapers, she'd end up in the restaurant/coffee house, Les Amis. Les Amis was so 1960s! If Peggy was at a large table with "movement leaders" and loud discussions, Hank Trueblood was often nearby. Peggy noticed him, but thought he was just another guy that wanted to look at her breasts. Hank Trueblood wrote a long memo just about the Bordens to FBI headquarters. He said Richard had taken many Russian books from the library, spoke Russian, had been to Russia, and was expert at short wave radio. He had a large bank account and seemed to disperse funds to varied movement groups. It said he was a key, but hidden, leader of the S.D.S. and the Young Socialists. It also listed a long list of underground newspapers, and left-wing magazines that the Bordens subscribed to. It said they were small-time dope dealers.

At the time, COINTELPRO was this FBI nation-wide program to disrupt anti-war groups, civil rights groups, and spy on writers, movement leaders, and politicians. Memos would come from J. Edgar Hoover's highest flunkies saying to look for certain things. Foreign connections, faculty connections, underground newspapers, and movement leaders were some of the largest imaginary targets. Phones were tapped, mail was opened, houses were broken into, and thousands of campus informants were recruited.

Trueblood's memo caught the eye of J. Edgar Hoover who wrote on the margin, "Good work. Keep me informed," in his girlish, scratchy hand. Trueblood was elated. His Austin bosses were more than skeptical. He asked them for permission to do a "black bag" job, of entering the Borden residence without a search warrant. They said, maybe later.

When a memo arrived that said to be on the lookout for religious cult groups that used sex in recruiting, Hank Trueblood had a flash. That's why Peggy was always in Les Amis so proudly showing her breasts. Peggy would go with a group to an apartment or a dorm room to smoke weed and listen to music, but she was careful not to go with any guys alone. Hank trailed along behind and assumed wrongly it was an orgy. Her breasts were the most recognizable icon on the Drag in 1968. When Richard was around, she covered up, like everybody else. More than once, he came home to find the stereo blasting and strangers getting high. They argued over it. Richard seemed to be one of the few who saw a connection to the many movement leaders and left-wing writers that had been arrested for pot. When a prominent movement leader was murdered in an Austin convenience store where he worked, Richard assumed correctly that it was a political assassination. It was 19 years later that one of those FBI informants was arrested and still had the gun.

Trueblood wrote a follow-up memo about sex parties at the Borden's house, and using sex to recruit more "communists." He wrote about Peggy's really far-out exhibitionism. He wrote that she did not wear panties, and often sat exposing herself to men on purpose. This was not true, but it reached the desk of the head voyeur, J. Edgar Hoover, who was known to keep sex files on many congressmen. This report went in with 178 photographs of Peggy Borden exposing her nipples through the sheer blouse. Some were shot on Guadalupe, and some in Les Amis, and some had Peggy with her head cut off, but every single one had both nipples. The sameness and sheer volume of the photographs raised some questions and snickers at the FBI.

Once at Les Amis, Peggy asked if she could join Hank at a table where he was sitting alone. She asked if he was interested in politics and he said, "no." She said he was free to join their conversations at the big table anytime. When another of her friends came, Hank left. Peggy had seen Hank walking by their house but thought nothing of it.

All over the country, the FBI were visiting employers to make left wingers, even simple Democratic Party members, look bad. A couple of older agents came to the Chairman of the English Department at the

University of Texas to share their suspicions about Richard Borden possibly being a foreign agent, even a financial conduit. The Chairman thanked them, and said they would deal with it quietly. He never told another living soul about it.

The assassinations of 1968, Martin Luther King and Robert Kennedy, shocked Richard into a morose period of depression. He quit going any place except to teach and work in his office. He asked Peggy to stop having the twice-weekly parties. Hank Trueblood noticed this and reported that he thought the Bordens were going "underground", as radicals were doing. Hank was certain that Richard Borden was someone very important and far different than he appeared. He thought all Borden's routine actions were part of a giant ruse.

Agent Trueblood began to fictionalize his reports even more. He reported seeing Richard speaking Russian to the same man on three occasions on campus. Although Richard did not speak Russian and had never checked any Russian language books out of the library, Hank was convinced. He saw himself as a true patriot, his lies serving his beloved country.

In 1969, on a trip to see her parents in Abilene, Texas, Peggy ran into her old high school sweetheart at a car wash. She'd been Homecoming Queen. He'd been captain of the football team. Even though Austin offered sexual temptation every few minutes and every few feet, neither of the Bordens had ever broken their wedding vows until Peggy crawled into the back seat of a red Pontiac Firebird on a dirt road just north of the Abilene Country Club and ended up a dentist's wife. Richard told her she would only stay gone a short time. He was wrong. After Perky Peggy had been gone three months, divorce papers arrived. Richard began to withdraw more and more into his depression. He canceled all his subscriptions, and phone service. He hired a maid who would also do grocery shopping. He returned to his hobby of short wave radio, often talking at 3 or 4 a.m., when insomnia ruled him.

Hank Trueblood wrote his longest, omnibus, summary memo about Richard Borden going underground, having meetings in small towns, and rarely driving the V.W. van. When he did leave in the van, he was often gone a few hours. However, the stack of reports about Richard Borden were becoming a big joke around the bureau. There was no one left that thought Hank Trueblood was anything but an obsessive who was way off base. After being ordered to drop all investigation of Borden, Hank broke into his house. He found a stack of poetry books, and critiques that focused on

Russian, English, and American poets of World War I. Borden got his start on A.E. Housman and Rupert Brooke. He also found three months worth of uncashed oil company royalty checks, explaining Borden's wealth.

The FBI transferred Hank Truelock to Dallas and white collar crimes. He still managed to get to Austin on weekends to sit down the street from Richard Borden's darkened house. If he did invade the flower bed to peek in the window, as he did often, he'd see that Richard was watching some cop show on TV, alone and catatonic, in his one enormous chair.

One night while Hank sat in his car on his lonely vigil outside Borden's house, a drunk driver plowed into the side of his car. The Austin police report went to the local Special Agent in Charge of the FBI. Seeing the address and Hank's name set up first a request for a psychological evaluation, and then before the first session, Hank was fired. It went on his record that he involuntarily resigned. He started a higher paying, promising career in private security. Hank never drank until after he left the FBI. If he has a few beers, he can really bend your ear about America's premier, underground, Russian spy. He can tell you all about the nefarious ways the agoraphobic recluse, Richard Borden, hides his true calling and mission.

Hank Trueblood never had any impact whatsoever on Richard Borden's life. Richard Borden ruined Hank Trueblood's FBI career and left him nutty as a fruit cake.

Author's Note: This short story won an Honorable Mention in the 2012 *Texas Observer* short story contest. There were several hundred entries.

The O'Malley Family Tonic

SARATOGA, NEW YORK, 1925. A FICTIONAL MEMOIR.

*The hardest thing in the world is to find an honest
partner in a skin game.....Arnold Rothstein.*

S ean O'Malley pulled his new $3150 Pierce Arrow Coach up in front of
the American Hotel. He limped slowly into the busy lobby, leaning on
his cane, and stopping to rest every few paces. His left arm, and leg weren't
aligned right, as if he had been a stroke victim. His neck was twisted to
the left, and his face seemed pinched in agonizing, and heroic pain. Sean
could only make it as far as a couch near the front desk. On the other end
of that couch sat Clarice Biddle, the single most prolific gossip on the east
coast. Sean summoned the desk clerk, with a slow, tortured motion.

"I'm Sean O'Malley. I have a suite reserved and paid for. Will you
check to see if a parcel has arrived for me? It is my family medicine. It is
urgent." His voice was strained, and he seemed not able to raise his head.

"I'll go check. So, you are Sean O'Malley, the man who will play any
card game. I've heard the gamblers talking about *you.*" The desk clerk was
loud and enthusiastic. Saratoga Springs, New York in August was the
gambling capital of America in the 1920s, with the horses, the spa waters,
large and ornate casinos, and America's wealthiest citizens in a gilded age,
when money and wine were treated like water.

"I need to rest here. Go see first about the family tonic. Has it arrived?
I can't play any one until I get my health back." Sean O'Malley had bribed
this desk clerk, though his cousin Patrick who was *persona non grata*
in New York, due to his successful stock scams. They were part of five

generations of the Traveling O'Malleys: gamblers, con men, musicians, medicine show owners, carnival barkers, and snake-oil salesmen. For generations, O'Malleys were around hotels, conventions, county fairs, golf courses, country clubs, and race tracks, selling little bottles of O'Malley's Family Tonic: Secret Irish Herbs.

After explaining to Mrs. Biddle that the tonic was not for sale, Sean spoke knowingly of holly, fennel, oak, hemp, and secret herbs that bonded the rest. His dear grandmother, Grace, grew the herbs in Duke, Oklahoma, but they had been grown in his family in Ireland and America for eight hundred years. Telling the hard of hearing Mrs. Biddle something was much like radio advertising. She would repeat it all through the day. "Now, I know and can *prove* the family tonic helps to heal, by changing the blood. But in Ireland, there were secret herbs that led to good fortune and luck. I can't prove that, but I *believe* it, and that is why I am a gambler. I am living proof the luck it brings works."

That afternoon, Sean limped up to a croquet game on the lawn. Nearby, some men were pitching washers, and were quite animated and verbal in their obvious gambling pleasure. One of the men asked Sean if he would like to join in, and he declined due to his health. Now Abner Cosden asked directly, "So, you are Sean O'Malley, the man who will play any card game?"

Now Sean told them he was a traveling gambler that would bet on almost anything, if his health came back.

Harold "Mike" Vanderbilt, from one of America's richest families, asked, "Do you play bridge? We were looking for a fourth."

"I'd play for mild stakes. At the Biltmore in Atlanta, I ran into three of them playing in together. My partner would bid high, get doubled, and go down as much as possible. The card room manager said I did not have to pay. I like one on one games, any form of poker, rummy. I'd throw those washers, if I was well. These other fellows look like they are on the square, but I'm not so sure about you."

The desk clerk came running across the lawn with the earth-shaking news. The tonic had arrived! He took Sean's arm and helped him back to the hotel. A pitiful sight. He stopped twice to rest on his cane.

The next morning, Sean O'Malley, athletic, and amazingly cheerful bounded down the stairs and into the lobby, the very picture of robust health at thirty-three. His thick, curly, auburn hair had been pressed flat the day before. He jumped into the air and clicked his heels. He sat with Mrs. Biddle, and repeated often his thanks for her kindness, before the tonic worked its expected, and proven rejuvenating magic. This was a Friday. Sean confided to her that he was a betting agent for New York's biggest gambler, Arnold Rothstein. He would be betting only the fourth and fifth races the next day, and then leaving town. He sold her two, quarter-pint bottles of the tonic at $100 a bottle, but told her he only had a wee, tiny supply.

That afternoon, Sean purposively ran into Vanderbilt, Cosden, and their group at the race track club house. "I've got me health back, and I can beat any of you guys at anything," Sean said, almost up in Vanderbilt's face. Vanderbilt was six years older, forty pounds heavier, and three inches taller than Sean, who was cocky, at best. Again, Harold Vanderbilt started a discussion of bridge, and then gin rummy. The brash newcomer was invited to their box. Cosden asked if he was really Rothstein's betting agent, and in the same breath, what horse might A.R. favor.

Sean O'Malley didn't seem to even notice the first two races, telling bawdy jokes, and boasting about his big poker wins, and then losses, in the Dallas Petroleum Club. He sang parts of "Danny Boy" in a fine Irish tenor, and danced a jig. He spoke to Harold Vanderbilt as if they were equals, and he was a bit insulting to a man that was used to everyone catering to his every whim, and agreeing with his every opinion. In the first hour they met, Sean told him he was wrong often, and he liked it. Sean read Harold Vanderbilt's sky-blue eyes intently. He knew the man had a great sense of and enjoyment of humor. They hit is off instantly.

Now after swearing them to secrecy, which Traveling O'Malleys did several times in any given day any place wealthy folks gathered, Sean said honor forbade him telling them Rothstein's selection of a horse, but he'd share the mechanics. "I'll meet this big fat man in a white coat right out there, about five minutes before the bell. I'll hand him a signed bet chit, and he'll sign a chit for me." The traditional bell at Saratoga rang seventeen minutes before post time.

Before the fourth race, Sean O'Malley ran back to the box, frantic, visibly upset. "He didn't show up. Something went wrong. I don't have much money on me." And after clever conversation full of O'Malley stock phrases: *promise, guarantee, cross my heart, opportunity, chance of a lifetime, swear on the Bible, trust me, and decide now.* Abner Cosden and Richard Barton rushed off to the bookmakers and wagered $10,000 each on Gaelic Mist to place. The filly was rated second in the betting odds at three to one. They had agreed to pay Sean, "a wee finder's fee, the customary steerer's fee in any gambling joint, saw-dust or rug, twenty per cent." An O'Malley steerer would hang around outside a dice game, and follow a live one in with his finger in the air, the old high sign.

Harold Vanderbilt had remained silent, with his arms crossed, grinning. An O'Malley can smell skepticism, their worst enemy. "You can sell them some snake oil when they get back," he said. "I liked the way you did that. You have that Irish gift of gab." Vanderbilt didn't wager on the race.

"You should have bet something. You might be walking around real lucky and not know of it," Sean said.

Sean said he was going to make a bet and walked down into the crowd. He could hear the announcer with no good news about Gaelic Mist. He was contemplating an O'Malley standard: Take a gypsy's leave. He walked toward the exit, and then the announcer said the scarlet and black silks were moving up fast on the outside. As Gaelic Mist was headed for the winner's circle, Sean was back in the Vanderbilt box. "Did you cheer? Oh, did you *cheer?* We will not forget this day. Did you see her come from behind?" After back slaps all around and some conversation, he noticed Vanderbilt whispering to the others, and they paid him over six thousand in cash for a few minutes work, with no risk of his own funds. Typical O'Malley proposition.

On the fifth race, Sean went through the same elaborate routine, repeating each O'Malley stock phrase like an ancient litany. He finally confided that Dublin Morning was Rothstein's choice on a place bet. Again, Barton and Cosden went to bet, this time even more eagerly. Vanderbilt did not, but enjoyed the whole mini-drama immensely, calling Sean correctly, "a world-class tout, but a tout none the less."

Sean told him that he really believed that the secret herbs in the tonic brought good health, and that he could prove it. "And there are herbs some Irish long ago knew brought good fortune. *Good luck.* Now, I can prove the tonic restores health, but I also believe it brings good luck. A gambler has to believe in luck to enjoy his life. You can book me on this filly." He wanted to get Harold Vanderbilt gambling with him personally.

Sean O'Malley ended up betting Harold Vanderbilt three thousand dollars on Dublin Morning to place, the way he always bet horses to run second or first, at track odds. Again, it was an Irish-named filly that showed all the other horses their backside. Cosden and Barton were eager to pay Sean his "finder's fee." And now Sean O'Malley and Harold Vanderbilt bet $1000 on each of the next three races, and Harold wrote down the bets. Then Sean left, saying he had run out of the tonic, trusting his new friend to tell him the outcome of their wager back at the hotel. Harold won all three. Sean's trap was set and baited. Not all trappers wear fur caps.

Right before sundown, a messenger woke Sean from his nap with a knock on the door of his suite at the American. Mr. Vanderbilt wanted to play some cards, and collect some money he was owed on the horses.

Sean took all the money he had in the world, thirty-two thousand dollars. Sean didn't know they made hotel suites the size of Vanderbilt's. They played cards with blue and red Bicycles, and decks with Rembrandts and Titians. There was a card table, with padded, leather chairs. They played high draw poker at first, using no chips, just money. Vanderbilt sent this silent, pained, hulk of a man servant/bodyguard for plenty of ten, twenty, and one-hundred dollar bills. He stayed out in the hall. Sean knew an O'Malley principle: With a rich man, don't let him get off winner. Keep him behind. He cares about the win or the loss, not the money. They played stud. When Vanderbilt suggested deuces wild, Sean said, "I'll play a *children's game*, but I'd rather try gin rummy. You aren't any good at any thing we have tried yet. So far, it doesn't look like you could beat Rin Tin Tin."

Sean took off the coat of his tan, silk suit, and put it on the back of his chair. Harold walked the length of the room, and hung his coat in a closet, turning his back on Sean, who could have peaked at his hand.

When Sean would shuffle, he would do so very, very slowly, with lots of slow cuts to make it apparent his hands were easy to see. He was not cheating, in case they had heard of his cousins. Sean never cheated, but he sure knew how.

Soon, Sean was calling his new friend Mike at his suggestion, and telling colorful stories of his family, admitting they did the shell game, and sold worthless gold mine stock, but he swore the tonic was not part of any con. He would get passionate about only the tonic. He told of an uncle who went nearly crazy finally believing he actually could make it rain, driving and driving, and always hitting rain sooner or later. He told of the time he had hopped freight trains from Dallas to Kansas City in a race for a $300 bet, and lost. He said he'd never cheat, citing the time his own father was thrown from a moving train nine miles from Albuquerque for suspected cheating at high draw. MIke was laughing so hard he stopped the game when Sean told of being a failure in his three week career as an Irish tenor in vaudeville.

When Mike dealt, he'd put Sean's hand on the bottom, flash cards, and shuffle poorly, against a man with this skilled, practiced, most amazing ability to memorize the card locations from another man's shuffling. When he was two games of gin rummy ahead, Sean knew he could beat Mike like a broke drum, anytime he wanted. They both sipped Irish whiskey over ice slowly. Mike played his hand. Sean played both, knowing what cards Mike needed, and playing defense masterfully.

They agreed Arnold Rothstein was the model for F. Scott Fitzgerald's *The Great Gatsby*. Mike kept score of all the bets in a neat, tiny lawyer's script with his Eversharp pen. The same hand ran several railroads. Once when he blitzed Sean, with Sean's help, Mike called out, "Irish need not apply!"

The next time Sean won a hand he called Mike, "Yacht boy". Now Mike was angry for real, and Sean picked up on it. It was in the newspapers telling of all the major yacht races Vanderbilt had won.

When they talked of all the things they could bet on, they agreed to throw washers, shoot pool, and putt on a golf course, but not play the course. Sean traveled with horse shoes, washers, a pool cue, a bowling ball, and a golf putter. He was too busy around the club house to go for the full course. He had mastered prop bets, usually surrounding making a putt twice or three times. Mike would talk about bridge and bidding systems for bridge which bored Sean. They ordered Porter House steaks with all the trimmings, wine, Irish whiskey, beer, oysters, chocolate ice cream, and pheasant as an after thought.

They took a break while waiting for room service. Mike turned up the radio just as Al Jolson started singing, "I'm Sitting On Top of the World." Sean was on his feet, dancing the Jolson steps, and pantomiming the first verse. Then he started singing in his fine, schooled, Irish tenor, as loud as the radio. Mike was slapping his hand on the table, and then mid-song, he joined the singing, timidly at first and then louder with a rich, surprising baritone. After the song, Sean offered to bet $500 he knew all the words to "Danny Boy." Mike said, "There's a Mick in Herald Square will sing it all day long for a dime a time. No bet. No tonic. No Irish need apply."

After dinner, they threw quarters at the wall for $500 a throw. The one with the closest quarter won. Sean kicked off his two-toned Florshiems. Mike, clearly drunk, removed his own hand-made shoes, and threw his tie on the floor. This took on some great meaning for the drunken aristocrat. Sean could win at will. They threw cards into the hat, and Sean offered two to one odds, after the third round. Mike insisted that they use a homburg he had in the closet, and not Sean's fedora, which was obviously "a trick hat." When they were not doing anything else, O'Malleys practiced throwing things. Sean pretended not to be keeping exact track of all the bets, with Mike carefully writing every thing down. He knew he was up over $20,000 to a man that loved it. An O'Malley principle: If they are laughing and losing, they stole that money.

When Cosden and Abbot came by the suite in tuxedos, they were headed for the Brook, Rothstein's fancy casino and a midnight meal. Sean yelled, "Let them in, they might not win." Mike told them to come back later for bridge or poker. Sean thought he had died and gone to O'Malley gambling heaven.

Mike would mention knowing Jack Dempsey, the Astors, President Coolidge, Eddie Cantor, and Fanny Brice or having his own private railroad car in town, and the number of railroads the Vanderbilts controlled in a matter of fact, non-bragging way. Sean acted like he was talking about the weather.

"One time my family had more ships than yours. Grace O'Malley, the Pirate Queen's own family had a fleet that traded all over the world, around the late 1500s. She was bright, red-headed, and is well known in Irish history. She had lands, fleets of ships, castles, and lost them to the English. She sailed to England itself, and talked to Queen Elizabeth, the first one. They freed her brother and sons who they held captive, but they never returned her estate, as promised. The English were grabbing off Ireland little bits at a time. There is always a Grace in our family. My grandmother grows, and mixes the herbs."

"Why don't you sell that stuff mail order? Everyone is into health. Half the Whitneys eat Fleischmman's Yeast each day. It tastes horrible. They advertise Grape Nuts as a cure all in the *Saturday Evening Post*." Mike said.

The first time Mike invited Sean to visit, and stay at his legendary estate, Idle Hours, on Long Island, Sean said no, he'd just heard of a huge open poker game at the Palmer House in Chicago. Later, he showed more interest, realizing Mike was obsessed with bridge.

When Mike said, "The unions and the coal strikes hurt the working man. They hurt our railroads. They never help anyone..." Sean interrupted.

"Now you've discovered a subject on which we will always disagree, and for the sake of our new, dear friendship, we should not discuss unions, because I am firmly for the West Virginia coal miners, and the unions, and wonder why one man needs the whole top floor of a hotel." His voice was rising. The alcohol fueled a real anger.

"There are three suites up here," Mike said. It was after four a.m. and the alcohol had loosened tongues. They stopped to throw quarters at the wall again to wake up, and stretch their legs. Sean offered a proposition bet, saying he could throw forty playing cards in the hat, out of a fifty-two card deck. Drunk as he was, he was finally gambling, since he was not sure he could do it. He measured out sixteen paces from a large, leather chair and placed the homburg there. They agreed on three thousand as the wager. While Sean was in the bathroom, Mike moved the hat out another nine paces. Sean missed the first two throws, then realized what had happened. He let up a squeal. Mike was triumphant, gloating, laughing. An O'Malley principle: We are entertainers. Let the marks have a big time.

Finally, with the hat back in place, Sean won the bet with the O'Malley signature one card to spare. The two men played until six a.m., and Sean won $52,000. The next morning, Sean sold seventeen bottles of the tonic in the lobby, thanks to Mrs. Biddle, and the desk clerk. He stayed three more days, and never won another horse race bet with his bet them to place system.

A month later, Sean O'Malley arrived for a two-day visit at Idle Hours, the Vanderbilt estate on Long Island. He stayed nine days: playing bridge, gin, poker, pool, throwing things, and fishing, swimming, and yachting. Harold Vanderbilt invented contract bridge, developing many of his ideas playing with Sean O'Malley. They played in bridge tournaments as partners for several years. Sean had a lifetime pass on several Vanderbilt railroads. One day he ran into Vanderbilt on a Manhattan sidewalk. Vanderbilt took him to his tailor for a fitting, and ordered fourteen suits for Sean, in a array of fabrics, and conservative designs. Both won national bridge tournaments, but never together as partners. They were known for yelling at each other, but also for betting on every thing they could think of. MIke would call with bets on Ivy league football, major league baseball, horses, boxing matches, elections. Sean always knew Mike's preference in advance, and he coppered the odds.

In 1934, a sign was posted above a massive guest bedroom at Idle Hours that read SEAN O'MALLEY'S ROOM. The two were inseparable. Sean ran large, honest poker games at Idle Hour during the worst of the depression for some of the richest Americans, many when Harold and his wife were at another estate. Sean O'Malley married Mary Kerns, a table servant he met at Idle Hour, and the Vanderbilts put them on the invitation list for all manner of parties they rarely attended.

Sean O'Malley promised Mike that he would not sell the O'Malley Family Medicine: Secret Irish Herbs at bridge tournaments or to the Vanderbilt's society friends or on any of the Vanderbilt railroads, and most especially not to the guests and staff at Idle Hour, but Sean could not stop. When *Time* did a cover story on bridge tournaments in 1936, it quoted Harold "Mike" Vanderbilt as saying, "my closest friend and advisor, Sean O'Malley is the best all-around card player in America." From his side of the table, it sure looked that way. Both men lived until 1970, and remained the very best of gambling friends.

Bluff Europe Magazine

Was Joe Hill Guilty?

1913-1915

Ryan O'Malley had promised his singing partner, Lonnie Hogan, that he would keep mum about his past as a Wobbly soap boxer. Ryan sang the songs of the labor movement's best known songwriter, Joe Hill, in union halls across Oklahoma, Colorado, and Texas for pennies and beans. Ryan and Lonnie had met in the Amarillo jail and immediately recognized that Lonnie's perfect-pitch baritone and Ryan's perfect-pitch, Irish tenor blended together magically. Lonnie had secured them a permanent engagement three days a week singing at the La Fonda Hotel in Santa Fe, New Mexico. Ryan didn't as much as whisper about the Industrial Workers of the World or one big union to Lonnie after they worked that first glorious week. What a way to make a living! Both were most expert on guitar, and they continued to surprise each other on stage.

The two thirty-year olds were totally different. Ryan was 5'8" tall and diminutive. Lonnie was 6'2" and powerfully built from his hard-working days as a Texas cowboy. Lonnie was thoughtful, deliberate, and quiet. Ryan talked all the time and his humor often offended the wrong people. When a drunken Colorado mine manager yelled out several times while they were singing, Ryan told him during the break that he was a "pure fool." The man challenged Ryan to fight outside. Lonnie walked up very calmly and slowly. He spoke in a soft voice containing no excitement, "Now look here. This is my singing partner. I need him. He is a little bitty fellow and you are my size. I just hate fighting. Over in Texas, I had a couple of bare-knuckle prize fights, but I hate it. Got my eyes blacked and my lip cut up. Now, please, don't make me just have to fight." The man retreated silently.

Ryan resented it, and never spoke of that resentment, but Lonnie was the boss of the act. That was not verbally agreed on or spoken about. They still did many of the cowboy songs from Lonnie's Texas ranch days. Lonnie knew Ryan could really sell a song. His acting out and jumping around had led Lonnie to loosen up and join him. And it was contagious. They got that La Fonda crowd in a party mood. The bar manager, Mr. Curry, had given them two raises as the attendance steadily grew. Ryan would mention the tip jar a little too often. Some of the regulars sang along which Ryan liked from his old soap box days. Lonnie didn't like them singing along or clapping their hands or talking, but he was a realist. He did persuade Ryan not to encourage or start the clapping or sing-a-longs.

Ryan had written an article about quirky Santa Fe places. He sent it to *Harper's Weekly*, a big national magazine. He didn't really expect a reply but a letter came from E. Elton Eddy, a senior editor, who wrote, "This doesn't fit our current needs. Your writing is humorous and lively, a totally fresh approach. Please submit to me personally any dispatches from New Mexico you have."

When Mother Jones, the 83 year old labor leader that had been at strikes across America for nearly half a century, was making an appearance in Trinidad, Colorado, Ryan took a train there hoping to interview Mother Jones. He kept Mr. Eddy's treasured letter in his breast pocket over his heart. He told folks he was a writer for *Harper's Weekly*. Ryan was carrying his guitar when he tried to get in the back stage area in Trinidad where Mother Jones was about to make a speech. Some self-appointed union official asked Ryan if he could lead the crowd on a Joe Hill song and soon he was singing, *Long Haired Preacher,* often called *Pie in the Sky.* Many of the coal miners had the Wobblies' *Little Red Song Book* in their overalls or shirt pocket. The crowd sang along, and many looked on a neighbor's song book, like a hymnal in church. Mother Jones was hustled off the other side of the stage after her fiery speech calling for a strike against the Rockerfeller coal mines. That strike was to cost over 200 lives, and the miners essentially lost. After the speech, Ryan refused to do a newspaper interview or give his name. With this all going on in nearby Colorado, Ryan kept quiet back in Santa Fe. Wobblies were under attack all across America. Ryan hid his red Wobbly union card in an old gray sock in a box of clothes at Mrs. Cooper's boarding house where he and Lonnie each had a room.

When Ryan O'Malley's hero, labor icon, and songwriter, Joe Hill was arrested for murder in Salt Lake City, Utah in January of 1914, Ryan's life was transformed. He often made visits to the union hall just to read the latest copy of the national union movement newspaper, *Solidarity*. For months, it shouted that Joe Hill was innocent and being railroaded because he was such a high profile Wobbly symbol. Ryan shared with a few of the union members his idea to go to Utah to Joe Hill's trial or even to interview him in the jail. Ryan O'Malley had described himself as a writer for *Harper's Weekly* so often, he believed it.

As the interest in the Joe Hill case grew, it became a huge international story. The news stand at La Fonda carried *The Denver Telegraph*. When they ran a long, detailed story of Joe Hill's hearing and the few facts of the case, Ryan and Lonnie had their first contentious discussion of what was of deep emotional significance for Ryan.

Lonnie said, "Look here. A store gets robbed and two folks killed. One of the robbers gets shot. A little over an hour later, Joe Hill shows up at a socialist Doctor to get patched up. He has a pistol. Later, when they are giving him a ride home, he throws that pistol away. All he can say is it is a disagreement about a woman, and he won't name her or who was supposed to have shot him. That's it. That's all the real facts. The eye witnesses doesn't mean anything. A ten year old boy was in the back of the store. Doesn't make any difference about what he saw. They had on masks. And this woman on the street just saw a tall man in a hat. He isn't getting a fair trial, but he is guilty."

"He's an artist, a romantic. I believe him about the woman. They are jailing Wobblies all over the place. You are right telling me not to talk about that. I threw that union card away," Ryan lied.

"If a man shot you, the last thing you'd do is throw your pistol away. He might come back and shoot you some more." Lonnie said.

Ryan asked Mr. Curry is he could have one weekend off to go to an O'Malley family reunion in Denver. The Garcia Family Singers, who worked Tuesday through Thursday, had agreed to fill in. He was going to the end of Joe Hill's trial, but Joe Hill fired his attorneys, and put on no real defense. The trial was over before Ryan could finalize his travel plans. Joe Hill was sentenced to be executed. When given a choice between hanging and a firing squad, Joe Hill said, "I'll take shooting. I have been shot a few times in the past and I and I guess I can stand it again." Joe gained several stays of execution over the next few months. The President of the United States and the King of Sweden sent telegrams on his behalf.

Forty-thousand telegrams were sent to Utah's governor seeking a stay of execution.

As gamblers, Ryan and Lonnie were bored with the afternoon five-dollar limit draw poker game upstairs at La Fonda. When they first came to Santa Fe, the game ran all night sometimes, and the limit was often dropped at night when there was a lot of money on the table. However, the poker had dried up. They only played four or so afternoons a week, and stayed with the limit. Lonnie would often be partners with Ryan until he thought alcohol was becoming a factor. Then he would signal Ryan to end the partnership for the night. That was one reason Lonnie knew Ryan would probably be needing a loan if he was planning a trip out of state.

As the Joe Hill story became bigger and bigger internationally, Ryan O'Malley's desire to be a part of it became obsessive. The suspense of whether and when Joe Hill's life would be taken had him in a most agitated state.

Ryan lived at the end of a long hall on the second floor of Mrs. Cooper's because he feared robbery. Lonnie lived on the first floor near the front door because he feared fire. When Ryan came to Lonnie's room all charming and praising their mutual good fortune, Lonnie knew for certain he wanted something. Ryan mentioned the La Fonda Christmas party where Lonnie was a bit drunk, which he rarely was. Ryan would get drunk because it was dark outside. The altitude in Santa Fe enhanced the alcohol's impact. Lonnie had said they were like brothers, and Ryan brought that up. He wanted Lonnie to go with him to Utah. Maybe they'd find some poker or dice games along the way. A long train ride would do them good.

Ryan wore a new gray derby hat and a new gray suit on the train to Utah. He had his reporter's note book and sharpened pencils prominently displayed as props. Lonnie kept wondering why he had come along. He thought the derby hat looked ridiculous. He laughed but wouldn't tell Ryan why. They played gin rummy and Lonnie won, as usual. When they went for dinner in the club car, Ryan expressed joy and amazement that Lonnie bought them both the most expensive t-bone steak on the menu. Ryan had a couple of drinks and Lonnie pretended he did not mind.

At the Hotel Utah, Ryan registered as a writer for *Harper's Weekly*. A man in line behind him said the bar was full of reporters talking about "the few facts of the case which have not changed since the first day." Ryan threw his card board suitcase on his bed and ran for the bar to hob nob with his fellow reporters. Lonnie wandered the streets asking where the gambling was to be found. He was directed to a no-limit draw poker game in the back of a pool hall. There was much higher gambling on pool out front. The poker players told of pool games for $10,000.

Ryan was up casing the Salt Lake City jail the next morning at dawn. The reporters had told him Joe Hill had been allowed a number of visitors but he was scheduled to be transferred to the state pen any day to await the firing squad. By chance, he saw a young guard walking toward the prison. He told him of his journalistic credentials and asked if he knew the procedure to visit Joe Hill. The fellow said to come to that side door some time mid-morning to noon, and he would ask the sheriff. When Ryan explained it would be really easy or they would just say no, Lonnie agreed to go. Ryan handed him a reporter's note book, and five sharp pencils.

When Ryan and Lonnie knocked at the side door, they were allowed in. As usual, Ryan had a con ready, "We are the visitors scheduled to see Joe Hill. We are reporters for *Harper's Weekly*." Ryan was waving his sacred letter from E. Elton Eddy like a flag in the wind. In the twenty-two months Joe Hill had been in jail, most of the guards had developed a deep affection for him. His humor was the talk of the dreary dungeon. The grapevine said he was about to be transferred out, and the guards were agreeable to being nice to Joe, since their time for it was most short.

The guard walked them down a long corridor with Joe's cell at the end. The two cells nearest his on either side were empty. Joe Hill rose from his cot with some effort given his gaunt and emaciated frame. As he neared the bars, Ryan said, "We are so honored to meet you Joe. We are writers, hoping to get a story in *Harper's Weekly* if you want that. Just your words, what you'd want to say." Ryan held his hand up resting on the bars to disclose his palmed red card of the union. "Look Joe, see my Wobbly card. I am a singer. Was a soap boxer singing your songs. This here is Lonnie Hogan, and I'm Ryan O'Malley. We are singers now. We met in the Amarillo jail. They put me in jail for being a Wobbly."

"Me too." Joe Hill said.

"Joe, I led this big crowd singing your song, *Long Haired Preacher*, when Mother Jones gave a fire and brimstone speech in Trinidad, Colorado."

"She's been in a jail worse than this in Colorado. The governor is keeping an 84 year old woman in an unheated basement." Joe Hill's Swedish accent was most noticeable. Lonnie wondered why that had not been a factor in his trial.

Ryan handed Joe Hill a copy of the pocket-sized *Little Red Song Book*, the Wobbly hymnal, through the bars. There was silence as Joe looked through it, stopping to read. Both gamblers studied his blue eyes, which came natural to them.

Joe had the book open to *Long Haired Preacher*. He handed it back to Ryan and said, "Sing it for me."

Ryan held the book where Lonnie could read the words. Lonnie came in on the second verse when he got the melody. So did Joe Hill, and Ryan was crying without any shame.

Long-haired preachers come out every night
Try to tell you what's wrong and what's right
But when asked about something to eat
They will answer in voices so sweet

'You will eat, by and by,
In that glorious land above the sky
Work and pray, live on hay -
You'll get pie in the sky when you die' - that's a lie!

They sang rather softly. Joe Hill, like any musician that had heard them, noticed the perfect union of these two voices.

After the song, Ryan asked Joe Hill what he might say for the article they hoped to write. As Joe spoke, Lonnie wrote down his words. Joe Hill would watch his hands and pause to let him catch up. "I'm just the Tin Jesus in all this. It is not about me now, it is about the one big union and that is good. They had this big march in Chicago singing my songs. What is it all about? Me? My songs are about union brothers and sisters sticking together." Joe paused to let Lonnie catch up. "If my unfair trial and unfair death help the one big union to stick together." Now Joe paused again, as if searching for words. "So be it." he finally said. "I am an artist and you tell them I died like an artist. I died in love."

Ryan was weeping softly. Lonnie didn't know whether to speak or not. Finally, Joe Hill said, "Here's a song I wrote in here. Folks are singing it at these marches and meetings. Can you imagine?" Joe sang, in his raspy voice, older than its years.

It's a long way down to the soupline,
It's a long way to go.

It's a long way down to the soupline,
And the soup is thin I know.
Good bye, good old pork chops,
Farewell, beefsteak rare;
It's a long way down to the soupline,
But my soup is there.

The young guard approached them, but waited several feet away as Joe finished the song. Then he said, "I'm so sorry, but they told me your time is up. There are some officials here."

As they walked out, the guard told them they were Joe Hill's last visitors. He was to be transferred to the state prison that afternoon since all appeals were exhausted.

Lonnie gave Ryan the notebook and Ryan read over it when they were alone. "Did you look in that man's eyes? Those were the eyes of innocence, compassion, love for the working people. His eyes and his songs say he could never commit a foul murder."

"What I saw was the scar on his neck. A prominent scar. The eye witness talked about that scar." Lonnie said.

"You mean after seeing the man and hearing the man, you still think he might be guilty? Oh, Lonnie." Ryan was exasperated.

"I do think he is guilty, but it doesn't matter between us. He didn't get a fair. Joe was legally innocent but the facts are just too simple. Have you ever heard of Occam's Razor? The simplest explanation is most often the correct answer."

On the train back from Salt Lake City, they agreed not to talk about Joe Hill ever again. Ryan sent an article about their meeting to *Harper's Weekly* three times, and got no reply. After Joe Hill was executed, Ryan sent his article to the *Denver Telegraph*. They paid him $100 for his story entitled, "Singing With Joe Hill in Jail."

When Lonnie saw the article, he was furious. He had agreed that Ryan could use his name. Ryan promised not to mention ever being a Wobbly. He kept his word. The article said, "When *we* looked in Joe Hill's piercing-blue eyes, *we* saw innocence, intelligence, compassion, and his love for the working people. Just what *we* hear in his songs, innocence." The article ended by saying falsely that they all three sang *Rebel Girl* together.

Ryan brought Lonnie a copy of the original article as he submitted it, which said, "I looked in Joe Hill's piercing-blue eyes...I saw innocence."

The editor had added the "we" and the singing of *Rebel Girl*. Ryan gave Lonnie the $100 he got for the article. Lonnie Hogan and Ryan O'Malley remained partners for years. Lonnie was never sure he believed Ryan's story about the article on their historic meeting with Joe Hill.

Lubbock's Own: Larry "the Laugher" Larson

"Rough as hell, sweet as heaven, senior class of '57."

Nearly everyone graduating from Lubbock High School in 1957 planned on careers in show business, given Buddy Holly's success. Larry Larson's mother, Maude Larson, had started him out on steel guitar and juggling, and settled for the ukulele. By fifth grade, she had him costumed in this tattered straw hat, fake freckles, a tooth blacked out, a huge, polka-dot bow tie, and oversized overalls. The country corn pone, hayseed, stock-character comedian. And the kids laughed at Larry's laugh. He had memorized these old vaudeville jokes. He sang something like George Burns. It somehow attracted a rich cotton buyer's daughter. Her father had a red Cadillac convertible, a big mansion on Nineteenth Street, lots of fancy foods, and a Doberman that just hated Larry.

Larry was tall, gangly, awkward, with a big nose and Adam's apple, and orange-looking hair. It looked dyed, but was not. Lubbock High football players dyed their hair gold or black for the Spring game. Folks thought Larry was one of them. He wasn't good looking, but he could attract the girls. Maude made him tell folks he was a "song and dance man."

Large Mouth Maude Larson once beat a Hockley County man half to death with a bowling pin at the Cotton Club because she thought he stole her comb. Later, she found it in her purse, as all women do. She didn't feel a bit bad about it. The world-class bitch.

After High School, Larry and his Uncle Ferd expanded the act and took it on the road with a little tent show. Ferd's mother was dyslexic, so her spelling error followed Ferd for life. They went around West Texas to Floydada, Lamesa, Pampa, Justiceburg, and Ralls before they ran out of money. Larry lied to his dear mother about not getting paid, but you would have lied to the aggressive bitch too, if you had known Maude.

Somehow Maude got Larry and Ferd, that's what they called the act, Larry and Ferd, booked into the lounge of the Golden Nugget in downtown Las Vegas. Larry and the cotton buyer's daughter said their 1960 goodbye in the backseat of his Hudson on a full-moon night, parked on a dirt road right in the flight path by the airport. A big jet came over at exactly the right moment, for him anyway, if not for her.

Larry and Ferd were working this little bitty stage at the Golden Nugget in the afternoons to a little bitty crowd. Basically, Larry wore the same costume from the fifth grade. They had developed some physical comedy: fake fights, falls and all, but the stage was too small. When Larry juggled three golf balls, one kept rolling all around the casino floor. As he did in a panic, Larry turned up the volume on his famous laugh. It was this deep, "Ho. Ho. Ho.", followed by this high, "Hee. Hee. Hee.", and he'd repeat for a proper interval. It was infectious. You could not help but laugh at or with Larry's laugh. You could hear it all over the casino.

Little Buddy Blair, Las Vegas' best known comedian and front act, was in the gift shop with Sal Bella, who had juice at the Sands. They were drawn to Larry's laugh. A moths and flames prop going in. Buddy wanted Larry to come talk with him about being a "laugher." This was a plant in the audience of Buddy's show, a shill, someone who would start the laughter and had a funny laugh. Larry had always been especially proud of his laugh. He caught on to the idea immediately.

A couple of days later, Larry and Ferd were fired at the Golden Nugget. The boss said, "People don't come out here to feel like hicks." He refused to pay them, saying Maude had lied about their Los Angeles and New York tours. You would have hated Maude. I absolutely promise that you would have hated Maude!

Ferd hi-tailed it for the flat lands. Larry called Little Buddy Blair, explaining he had dry pockets on Fremont Street, America's worst place to be broke. Sal Bella made a phone call and the man paid Buddy for the whole two weeks, not thirty minutes later. Old Vegas. Juice. Much later, Larry asked Buddy about Sal Bella's visible power in Las Vegas. Little Buddy said, "He is one of those boys from Illinois." And he winked.

So Larry became Buddy Blair's laugher at varied clubs around Las Vegas. Larry was born for it. Best laugher in the history of the town! A legend! Maude was furious. Good! In no time, Buddy wrote a few lines for Larry. Buddy might have Larry interrupt, or be the mock heckler that lost every time to Buddy, just like Larry's bad-guy, wrestling uncle, Rowdy Pat O'Dowdy, would always lose in the end. Larry took to being a laugher like a duck takes to Scrabble.

Then Buddy provided Las Vegas native Jana Crawford, a six-foot, gorgeous chorus girl with natural, gigantic boobies, to sit with Larry. They'd do some bit of comic business: a fake fight, a walk out. Buddy, and the two brothers he had started out with, wrote new material every week. The couple looked funny, because Jana was so good looking and Larry was so not.

Little Buddy Blair got booked at the Sands to front the Rat Pack: Frank Sinatra, Dean Martin, Sammy Davis Jr., Peter Lawford, and Joey Bishop. Sal Bella never appeared on any papers as an employee of the Sands, but he had maximum juice. He wandered around, quietly telling folks what to do. He even went into the count room. That's juice! Sal, who had zero in common with Lubbock Larry, adopted him, Old Vegas style. He became his official "sponsor." Now Larry and Jana were eating comp lobster and steak and learning about the finer comp wines. Life was good. Larry was the only guy around who can't tell that Jana is falling for him, until she just flat laid him down.

Sal spent his off hours teaching Larry how to deal blackjack and work the craps table. He wanted to teach Larry to be a gambler where he could make something out of himself. Sal Bella had worked in every imaginable type of gambling joint starting out in Chicago.

Then the word came down, "Eighty-six the laugher." Somebody up high, with more juice than Sal, wanted Larry fired, and he was. He spent the rest of his life thinking it was Frank Sinatra, or maybe Maude someway. She'd do it. Gaff the prop.

Sal Bella placed Larry dealing blackjack right outside the showroom door. Some nights, Frank Sinatra and Dean Martin would take over dealing at a blackjack table. They'd just give the casino's money away, by not collecting bets or over-paying bets. One night Frank and Dean took over Larry "the Laugher" Larson's table, and kept putting tips and chips in his pockets. Sal was looking on, and Larry could not tell how Sal felt about it. Sal demanded and got his taste of the $12,000 score Larry tipped over, thirty per cent.

When Larry heard that casino manager, Carl Cohen, had knocked Frank Sinatra's two-front teeth out, he turned up that signature laugh, so that you could hear it up and down the whole Strip. Some Sands' employees applauded. Frank Sinatra was not kind to the little people.

A group from the Saudi royal family came to shoot dice upstairs in a private room at the Sands. Sal made somebody put Larry on the stick, even though it was above Larry's skill level. The Saudis loved Larry's laugh, and shoved so many tips and chips Larry's way, that Jana insisted they get married. Maude refused to come to the wedding, even though Sal offered to pay for her airline ticket. She sent some roses that were dyed black. Like the box office, Maude had no heart.

Larry started telling Sal Bella all about the cotton buyer's daughter and trading cotton futures. They put together a little bankroll and threw in partners trading cotton. Sal was very uncomfortable fading a proposition where he could not cheat, but they played lucky. It had nothing to do with Larry's barnyard patter about the weather, noxious chemicals, boll weevils, and drought in Mississippi. They made serious, lucky money for six years before Sal Bella vanished....*left no word of farewell. Will there be not a trace left behind?* Little Buddy, Jana, and Larry held a sad, little ceremony for Sal, but they never asked questions around town. Old Vegas.

Larry and Jana had a whole lot of money saved, until they decided to form a country-music singing duet. They tried it in Nashville awhile. They went broke making demos, and then records to sell in truck stops across the south. That made Maude really happy, the double-mean bitch. They limped back to Lubbock broke, and Maude took them in. Maude wouldn't speak to them. She left hurtful, vicious notes for them on a Big Chief tablet every morning. She made them go to the grocery store to get her a Moon Pie and an R.C. Cola, every *single* night. Maude kept a bowling pin on the mantle, right under an autographed picture of Jesus Christ. His eyes would move, and follow you around the room.

VIRTUALUBBOCK.COM, TRUCKIN' AND SEVERAL WEIRD WEB SITES.

A Gambling License for the Horseshoe

They call me Jersey O'Malley. Might as well tell it, I'm one of the Traveling O'Malley's, five generations or so of Irishmen out grifting in the Southwest. Making our living with our wits. But this is an important part of any O'Malley story. We are *not* in the muscle end of it.

I'd been working the dice north of Dallas, running with Sal Maceo, when he was just a kid. They had the gambling in Galveston, and we was talking about me a job. Dallas was too hot. FBIs. Lots of arrests. Reformers. Things had changed. I'd never work for Benny Binion in Dallas or Las Vegas. I'd drink back then. Lots. They beat folks up something fierce. Benny hired lots of Irish folks 'cause he was Irish.

A great dice man I knew around downtown Dallas was Lewis "Chili" McWillie who ran Binion's big no limit game at the Southland Hotel during the war. I could have got a job there. The Maceos owned the hotel. Then Chili was the manager of the Top of the Hill in Arlington, big swank joint Benny controlled, for several years. He went on to the Tropicana in Havana for the biggest of mob guys in the forties. I could have probably got a job for him. He ended up at Binion's Horseshoe some time later.

Anyways, Sal vouches me in some way, and I got a job at the Desert Inn in Las Vegas in 1951, the year after it opened. I'm figuring the bosses to all be Italians, but most were Jews, from the mid west. The biggest one strutting around was Moe Dalitz.

Being young, I bragged some and showed them some moves switching the dice, and told them they could put me in as a bust-out man. That's when Big Sid Wyman got to liking me. Nobody knew who was boss, or owner, or any of that. I learnt first rattle out of the box to ask no questions. It was a real whisper joint. They come on a little hard ribbing me on being

Irish, and having a temper and all. That's how they got to talking about Benny Binion, and his Irish temper. They were underestimating Benny. Let me tell you.

Well, I'd heard tell all about Benny, but I worked in a little crap spread north of Dallas that he didn't control. He controlled all the gambling, dice and policy wheels, especially around downtown. He had all the laws in his pocket. I told them some Benny stories. They already knowed about him killing some folks and trying to kill Cat Noble. I didn't tell them I knew Cat. Me and my uncle talked to Benny one time standing on a Dallas street corner. That was Sky O'Malley, the famous trick pilot folks called the Flying Bootlegger. Him and Benny had done some work. Benny was big even when he was real young. They flew booze in from El Paso they got over in Mexico.

Big Sid would take me right into the fancy dining room and we'd sit and talk. He liked stories about the O'Malleys and the grift. He was a top dice man, but he was the glad hander, carney talker for them mob guys. One day, and the only day, I sit there with Gus Greenbaum, Davie Berman, and Sid Wyman. After Davie leaves, Gus, not a suave man, most uncouth, tells me Davie has been in the pen awhile, and had killed seven men. I was real uncomfortable, and so was Sid, but Gus was telling me this where I'd spread it to scare the pit help, I figure. Sid had a lot of class. He wasn't like that. We heard Gus had killed some folks too. He got killed later in Phoenix. His wife too. Their heads was almost cut off! Everyone *knew* Marshall Caifano did it.

Now, Sid is having these here junkets fly in with high rollers, and Sid is talking it up with the press, and some movie stars come in there. Lou Costello. Lucille Ball. When Sid is in the pit, us dealers were happy. He called everyone by name. 'Course we had name tags. Sid was one of these larger than life guys.

If they wanted these high rollers out of California to stick around, they'd just tell them the airplane had troubles, and another was coming. That happens one night when the dice ran to the suckers like water down hill. It was a sight to see. Sid, Davie, top guys was looking at them dice.

They give me some six-ace flats and put me on the stick. I put them in, and they dusted out that crew. I wonder what would have happened if I had *spilled?* Sid got me in this here hall where we was alone, and give me a $500 bill. In a way that $500 was an insult considering the scores they tipped over. They was always acting more generous than being generous with the help. Sid would loan walking-around money to the help. I figured him for

| 166 |

a shylock, but he didn't charge vig. We'd beat a table real bad sometimes, and they'd put this "Irish luck" deal down as a joke, but Gus Greenbaum said everything in this irritating way. I sure knew how to act like I liked everyone around there.

While I was back in Texas, Benny Binion came out to the Dunes one night and raised a ruckus. I never heard of Benny drinking, and I don't know what come up, but this Security Guard named Tiny threw Benny out. Tiny weighed a good 300 pounds. Sid Wyman came up there pretty fast. He got $300 out of the cage and sent Tiny straight to the airport. They told him to take the next plane to anywhere, and call back. Sure enough, Benny came back, but Sid was waiting for him. Benny came alone, but he was packing heat. Sid said sit down and have a drink with me, and Benny did. Sid told him what he had done and said Tiny will never be back to this town or work in gambling anywhere. Benny went on home.

Anyways, a man my age gets sidetracked. Back to August of 1951.

One fellow coming around the Desert Inn was the lieutenant governor of Nevada, Cliff Jones, but I didn't know it until later. I knew something was up. Sid and Davy were treating him like a high roller. He goes to the cage and gets $5000 on the arm. He shoots on my table a couple of hundred a pop, leaves the chips and goes off with Sid. Later, he'd cash in for cash.

So, one night it was slow. Cliff Jones had been meeting with Sid. Sid came out and asked me if I would please drive the man downtown and wait around for him. He gave me the keys to his black Cadillac.

On the way downtown, Jones says he heard I'd worked the gambling in Dallas and knew Benny Binion. Well, I say I don't him, but knew he was the Boss Gambler, but that is about all. He goes to telling me all this stuff. He said Benny was "active in politics" in Texas. None of this seems to be gonna help me, so I plead ignorance, saying "Really. I hadn't heard that."

When we get downtown and park, he makes me come with him to this gambling license hearing for Benny Binion. Or it wasn't for him exactly, but a front, and everybody from there to the bus station in Henderson knows it. I snap. Maybe he is here to queer the deal. This hearing is going on. Dr. Monte Bernstein is doing all the talking to get a gambling licence off this city commission. Benny is sitting over to the side and eyeing everybody, like some damn king. Everybody knows that Benny has put big bankroll downtown with the Las Vegas Club, the Westerner and then the El Dorado which he is making fancy and going to be calling the Horseshoe. Benny is listed as the restaurant manager, but folks call joints "Binion's." Benny has brought in all these here Texas guys, some gun men, and the city boys is saying there are no local jobs come out of it. This hearing is not going good for Benny and his front man when they take a little break.

Well, Benny is all dressed up in a brand new gray suit. He is with two guys that must be body guards. He crosses the whole room and comes right up to me, "You are one of those O'Malleys, ain't you? Any other 'uns in town?" he asked.

Well, I say no, and tell him that I met him with my uncle, Sky, and I might want a job from him and wondered if I could come down and see him. He smiled as big as all get out and said, "Sure," and then he gave me the scariest, coldest, meanest look I've ever seen, before or since. I spent the rest of that August just thinking about that one look.

The big high point of the whole hearing is when Dr. Bernstein takes off his coat and gets real emotional, like he is about to cry. He's sweating like a whore in Sunday school. Finally he says, and he is puffing, "There is no one connected with the Eldorado Corporation that has a criminal record. No one." Then it got quiet. I thought someone might challenge that. Benny was giving that look to the whole damn crowd. To look at Benny, you might of thought he wasn't arrested for killing, gambling, and bootlegging and lots of times. Hell, he was under some warrants or indictments back in Texas. And some federal stuff.

Now, Cliff Jones, the lieutenant governor, is on his feet defending giving Dr. Bernstein the license and saying the Dr. had a piece of the Golden Nugget, and this and that. He acted like he didn't know Benny had the biggest bankroll downtown. I'm surprised, and began to get it. Benny *and* Sid had the fix in. Now the mayor chimes in and he is on Benny's side. They still deferred the gambling license two weeks to save face, but they gave Benny the liquor license. It said in the newspaper he was the restaurant manager.

On the drive to his house, Cliff Jones said this was all good for jobs and development and that Sid Wyman was "right on this one." He spoke of doing things for his "dear friend, Sid Wyman" because he knows what is best for Las Vegas, all of Las Vegas or something kind of like that. He's wanting me to tell Sid he said it.

Just two weeks later, Davy Berman comes running into the pit at the Desert Inn, and he is fuming. "Where is Sid?" You can hear him all through the casino. Sid weighed 260 pounds. He strolled up, calm as Wyatt Earp. Nobody rattled Sid. I figure it is about the count or the soft count room.

Three mob guys always go in the count room together. If there is only two of them, they wait. Gus, a real ass hole, is the late one usually.

Davy Berman is waving this copy of *Time* and yelling, "What did I tell you? That Irishman lied to me. To me!" There was a story about Herbert "Cat" Noble being killed outside Dallas when his mailbox was detonated from across the road. It left a four-foot crater. It said Benny had it done. Benny and the Cat had been trying to kill each other for a fair spell, years. These casino bosses went into the office, but these here mob guys seem to think this is very important. Black Cadillacs rolled up. By the end of the week, the story was in *Life*, with a bunch of pictures of that blowed up car. It showed a couple of playing cards, an ace of diamonds, and a joker, by the hole. It was in *Newsweek* too. Moe Dalitz came in. I knew he had a *big* piece of the joint, because he went in the count room. Later, I got to guessing they was thinking about killing Benny. You could tell Moe Dalitz was a bigger boss than Gus, Sid, or Davie.

I didn't know the whole story, and maybe I got it kind of wrong as to when, but sometime or other Davie Berman who they was calling "the toughest Jew in Las Vegas" goes to see Benny to tell him to end all that Texas killing. Whatever actually happened, Benny comes out of it smelling like a rose. He became good friends with all those Mob guys.

Bluff Europe Magazine

I Screwed Your Sister in High School: A Lubbock Fable

B illy Sue Bailey, well-known local Tea Party leader, and prominent member of one of Lubbock's founding families was standing at the checkout counter in the upscale grocery store, Market Street.

Dewey Huffknot was standing right behind her. "I screwed your sister in high school," he said loudly, "In the back yard of y'all's historic home."

The teenager at the cash register was a frozen statute, holding a can of Del Monte Sweet Corn in mid-air. Dewey's naturally buggy eyes and perpetual half-grin gave him a surprised, innocent expression. His perfect flat top, and short-sleeved shirt with a plain, black, clip-on, bow tie shouted out, "Square!"

"What did you say to me?" Billy Sue turned sharply, with a rattle of bracelets and ear rings.

"I've seen you around many years. I've always wanted to say that to you. We dated a while. Where is Wild Jenny? I heard she is in Santa Fe. I hear you on talk radio all the time. Me and Jenny didn't go together long but she wanted to screw in the backyard one summer night. I'll never forget."

Billy Sue Bailey still occupied the family home, one of the historic knock-offs of Tara, the plantation in *Gone With the Wind*, that face Texas Tech on 19th Street. Dewey always, always thought of Wild Jenny when he drove by there.

Billy Sue almost ran for the parking lot, abandoning her groceries and the startled clerk. She stood by her Lexus in the 100 degree heat calling her lawyer on her cell phone. Then she called her gossipy friend, Vic Jones, a great way to get the word out all over Lubbock! Billy Sue was known far and wide for the walkouts and demonstrations at the annual county and state Republican Conventions. Neo-Nazi *Lubbock Avalanche-Journal* blogger, Don May, a.k.a. Dr. Doom, was her ideal ideologue. She labeled most everyone socialists on a few talk radio call ins each week. She liked to point out correctly that she was farther to the right than everyone else, everyone. Of the talk show hosts, Chad loved her. Wade tolerated her. Jim and Dave went to a hard break or a Zogby Poll. At 38, she was a striking, even beautiful, brunette with the figure of a college girl.

Billy Sue hadn't spoken to her New Age, hippie, socialist sister in seventeen years, even though Jenny came to Lubbock often. In Santa Fe, Jenny was a crystal healer and channeled a five-hundred-year-old Navajo woman named Velvet Hands who was a massage therapist. Billy Sue didn't doubt for a minute Dewey's backyard humping memory.

Dewey's life was crashing down before his eyes. For sixteen years, he had been the Life Skills teacher at the Tornado Christian Military Academy, funded almost entirely by the late Asa Sheridan, Dewey's best friend, mentor, and Bacardi Rum and Diet Coca-Cola partner every single Sunday afternoon. Dewey told folks, and it was very true, that Barack Obama killed Asa Sheridan, and therefore the Academy, which needed killing.

In the early days, Asa wanted the students to wear uniforms to celebrate the combat experience he had in World War Two, which was a lie since he entered the Army two years after the war ended. Asa was thrown out for bed wetting, sleep walking, and an outrageous, false charge of public masturbation stemming from a technicolor world-class wet dream he had in the barracks. The Academy parents resisted uniforms and most tuition increases.

Dewey had a wife, Ariel, the first four years he taught at the Academy. With him gone every Sunday, she began an affair with the young man who drove an ice cream truck through the neighborhood playing, "Pop Goes the Weasel" over and over. When Ariel changed Dewey's pet name from Cuddles to Caliban, he should have known the jig was up. Ariel and the ice cream man moved to Longview, Texas and opened a wildly successful Chuckie Cheese franchise. Any time Dewey would see an ice cream truck or hear any of their songs, he'd cry.

The Academy students were a joke all over town because they all marched for one class period a day outside if the temperature were above

25 degrees and the wind was below 90 miles per hour. Kids tagged them the "Tornado Marchers." The Academy, for seventh to ninth graders, was down to 164 students even though they hosted the annual Easter egg hunt for "home skooled" students hoping to meet some other right-wing white folks avoiding the socialist, government-run schools and minorities. The did have five old non-operative M-1 rifles and some students developed drill team skills twirling them around. Dewey took them over to Asa's house for delivered pizza, and they got drunk and watched them left face and right face around the yard. Dewey didn't really like rum and coke and would never have ordered it in a bar. However, he had lied to Asa on that first afternoon and it became their personal tradition.

In the early days, Asa and Dewey watched football with the rum and cokes, but since Obama's election, Asa, 81, when Obama finally killed him, left the television turned to Fox News 24 hours a day, even when he slept. When Bill O'Reilly was on, Asa would stand very close to the set, militarily erect, almost as if at attention, but more like a trance. Asa had ordered O'Reilly's book for all the Academy parents, whether they could read or not. When Obama was elected, Asa was the model of health, and had five million dollars he had inherited from his father's lumber yard chain. He promised each Sunday that the Academy would be taken care of by the mysterious and generous will he spoke of often as a sick, old man's con. About three quarters way down the rum bottle, he'd let it slip that Dewey would get "a nephew's share" in his will.

Actually, telemarketers in Las Vegas who had "proof" that Obama was a foreign-born Muslim and Manchurian Candidate Muslim plant beat Asa out of most of his fortune, and he gave the rest to Sarah Palin. He had a series of strokes starting with Obama's election and became most profane at cursing the TV. Dewey thought it was Alzheimer's. Asa was the maddest man he had ever seen. He was popping Lipitor and Atenol like popcorn. Fox News was helping him secure some eye-popping blood pressure numbers.

When Dewey got home that afternoon, Todd, a lawyer and his younger brother, called with a "deal." He had to stay away from Billy Sue, not mention their family and get counseling or she would file stalking charges for holding her up to public ridicule. Billie Sue had also told Ronda Eloyd, the principal of the Academy, who couldn't make payroll anyway. Dewey protested that he really did screw Billy Sue's sister and that he was just telling the truth.

As a sideline, Dewey spoke in small high school assemblies on Life Skills which was basically an anti-sex lecture. He'd started out with twenty small town high schools a year, but most didn't invite him to return. Dewey, with the same flat top he'd had in high school, would sit in the middle of the stage at a table with his yellowed, veteran index cards and warn the teenage girls that boys will tell any lie, do anything to touch *certain spots*. He'd talk about hands outside clothes, hands that would unfasten bras, hands and the dangers of drive-ins and parking. He'd tell of a boy driving a girl out in the country and saying, "If you are not here after what I am here after, you will be here after I am gone."

He'd say that every boy, every single boy, will go into that locker room and tell that you went all the way whether you did or not if you let him touch *certain spots*. If he feels of your breast, he tells. Boys hated him as a gender traitor. When Dewey repeated his signature phrase, *certain spots*, he'd drag the words out and pause as he made eye contact with the prettiest girls. More than one high school counselor noticed that Dewey liked to hug the girls and that he held the hugs with the chubby ones way too long. Dewey was steadily hitting up on the young chicks in those small towns, often in the oil fields south of Midland.

Ronda asked for and received Dewey's resignation and a small retirement party was held at the Academy for the faculty. Ronda had heard talk that Dewey was a lecher with the girls in small towns. She had lost her own husband, an evangelist, when they were teaching at a Christian summer camp in New Mexico. Her husband had been caught giving two teenage girls LSD and malt liquor. They were thrown out that night. Their marriage did not survive the long, painful bus trip back to Texas.

For Dewey Huffknot's retirement party, they had a white cake from a bakery, some Fritos and bean dip, and this fire-engine red punch they served at every occasion. Ronda said some of the expected things, then Dewey began to speak.

"This place was founded by Asa Sheridan who promised me long-range funding one thousand times. Hey, we're all turning a page, huh? It's honesty time. When I'd go give those anti-sex lectures in the little towns, it would make me horny. I nailed me twelve of those young Texas beauties but none were underage, nothing illegal. I'd wait. One girl worked at the Dairy Queen in Crane. I started courting her when she was only fifteen. Single roses and Hallmark cards. I would drive 100 miles out of my way to see her."

It was the summing up of his years of teaching, and he chose his favorite memories. The room began to empty rapidly. Ronda's fists had balled up and she couldn't open them, just like on that dreaded last bus ride with her ex-husband.

Dewey's brother agreed that he would attend a therapy group. This was someday-Doctor Nina Hemply's on-going group, last labeled anger management. Everybody there had made some deal to go there to keep from criminal charges being filed against them. Nina started out going over the rules for the new members, although Dewey was the only new member. Confidentially. Free expression. Cooperation. Share your feelings. No seeing other members outside the group.

Calvin, an outrageous gay dude with so many piercing's he couldn't pass though airport security, had stabbed his roommate in a dispute over a floral arrangement. He chimed in, "Why is that Big Nurse? What if I want to see Mr. Wilson or Jose for a beer or something?"

Nina went into this carney pitch about being a Rogerian explorer helping them map their untapped inner feelings.

Mr. Wilson's son had attempted to have him declared incompetent in order to control the worthless oil rights on the old family farm. He had traded away the cotton farm and kept the mineral interest in order to invest in exploration and 3-D seismic surveys that indicated there was no oil. Mr. Wilson said it was the greatest hot weather for a record cotton crop after record rains. The price of cotton had nearly doubled in a year, the highest in twenty years. His family wouldn't harvest a single boll. Not one boll because of his idiot son. Mr. Wilson had fired both barrels of a shotgun over his son's head in his front yard when he came out to get his *Lubbock Avalanche Journal* one morning.

Nina was a large, tall woman, not fat, more like a big, muscled man. She ran the group with an iron fist and a soft heart. She was very, very good at what she did although few of the clients knew that. She warned Mr. Wilson that "graduation" from the group was based on her report to the district attorney's office. It depended on progress in "owning and authenticating and using your anger."

Ernest Watkins and his wife were locked in a bitter child-custody battle. Neither he nor his wife wanted their black-clad, heavily tattooed, nail-polish sniffing, expert shoplifter, twin girls. He was the maddest man there.

There was also a wife abuser, a man who was abused by his wife, a hard-shell Baptist church youth minister, a parolee, an ambulance driver, and a Catholic priest, all men.

When Nina asked Dewey to reveal the source of his anger and how his anger brought him to the group, he said he didn't hear about anger until after he got there. Then he told the story of Billie Sue at the supermarket, and his confession at his retirement party. The other guys roared with laughter. Nina saw this as as cohesion building and a critical stage in the group developmental process. She was curious about the sex part. She left for the bathroom.

While she was gone, Mr. Wilson invited them all over to his house that very evening to grill steaks outside, drink beer, shoot pool, and break Nina's rules. All but Jose Alvarado accepted. He was on parole and a member of a lesser-known, out of favor, prison gang.

"I can't be hanging out with all you outlaws," he said. "I'd end up back in jail."

That first night, Dewey brought his old index cards with the famous quotations, and jokes from old issues of *Reader's Digest*. Calvin immediately asked him about his twelve sexual conquests in the little towns. Mr. Wilson echoed that question. They liked to talk about sex and the group bonded, just as the absent Nina intended. There was Dewey, just as he was supposed to be, just as he felt called to be, up before a group talking about sex, only now, he could tell the truth, finally.

They continued to meet each week at Wilson's house, and even took up a collection for a gift for Nina. Wilson went to the Tornado Gallery and selected an oil painting by Austin artist, Leola Perez. It showed Ponty Bone and his accordion. Nina cried. Life-long friendships were developing. Mr. Wilson funded a used CD and book store for he and Dewey to own together. It became a hangout for the group members who often came for coffee and talk in the mornings. Dewey Huffknot had another rich mentor and another job, for awhile.

TRUCKIN'

Jack Burk is in Heaven!

J ack Burk, a man *loved* by so very many, has passed away. When a hippie arrives in heaven, there is a hell of a party. Jack woke up puzzled, walking down this dirt road. He thought he was dreaming. The dirt road looked just like the road to "The Farm", the home and legendary party house shared by Jack and his brother, Mike, for many years.

When he heard Jack was coming, God warned Saint Peter to watch out for some jokes and heavy insults around the Pearly Gates. God said, "Those Burks were the most devoted brothers I ever created!"

Jack could see a dog running toward him. It was Cracker. There were more dogs: Red Dog, Black Dog, Yeller, and Sapphire. A pickup truck was kicking up some dust. Jack thought that if this is a dream, is certainly is elaborate. Ricky "L.B." Martin drove up, and said, "Hop in, Jack. There's some folks up at the Farm you are wanting to see." The sun was just going down on the beautiful flatlands. He watched a pump jack pulling up that oil. The ditches and the CRP land were lush and green. They don't have droughts in heaven.

As they got near the old house, Jack asked, "What's going on, L.B.? This *is* the Farm, isn't it?"

"That's right, Jack. This is your very own special heaven."

The first thing Jack noticed were the laughing, happy, smiling people. There were beautiful women in the hot tub. One was Helen Hodges. Harold Akin was standing next to her, holding his guitar. Harold pointed to a suckling pig roasting in the pit. Jesse Taylor and Joe Don Davidson were just kicking off a tune on their guitars. Les Jones was playing the key boards. Jack began to understand the whole journey of life. Everyone was laughing and crying and telling Jack about the Farm all at once. It was twilight and a big camp fire was going.

"Jack wants to know about his couch," Les laughed, "It is the same and your old piano and banjo are waiting for you." The dogs were going crazy with wagging tails.

Jack thought it was great that the coke machine that dispenses beer was there. L.B. took him walking out back to see the pens with rabbits and chickens. "We have been up here in heaven watching, Jack. We know what a hard year you had. You faced it with admirable courage and humor. More people would call you their best friend than almost anyone. We've all been hurting for Mike. You guys define brothers. Best pair of brothers, ever. Those folks that took care of you, including Mike, Mark Hirst, Cindy Walden, Miz Ayn Bowron, Michele Denham, and Brent and Sherry Harper, are angels. I am proud of these upstanding and fine examples of the very best of West Texas. We'll party all night and walk that dirt road in the morning, just like old times."

"Well, " Jack said, "There is something I have to ask."

"I already know what it is, Jack. Yes, they have Marlboros and Canadian whiskey in heaven."

The Sandstorm Scholarships

Way out here they have a name for wind and rain and fire
The rain is Tess , the fire's Joe, and they call the wind Mariah.

Henry Foster awoke to euphoria for him: the howls, sighs, whimpers, and groans of a full-scale, West Texas sandstorm. Gusts to seventy miles-per- hour changed the tones and sounds that danced up and down the musical scale. He opened the drapes to welcome the orange-gold glow of the sand in the air. The trees in his back yard were swaying like Stevie Wonder. Henry was known for the millions in oil revenue the Foster Ranch generated, but also for what mean, gossipy folks called his "sandstorm fetish."

This was the day Henry would march through the sand to the English Department at Texas Tech University to answer questions about the $100,000 dollars a year in scholarships he promised to donate for the "best writing about sandstorms: fiction or nonfiction." This was the fifth year. Three times Henry had given four awards of $40,000, $30,000, $20,000, and $10,000 for short stories, folklore, literature reviews, and what he had called, "personal life experience philosophies." One anorexic, sorority reject made wind chimes a character in a short story and wrote about spousal abuse. She got $30,000 for her first short story, which made absolutely no sense. Last year, Henry had to travel for Sufi dancing lessons in Taos, and gave 13 awards of $10,000 each. Everyone that entered won. He didn't really read all the entries.

The old-Department-Chairman-out-of-power and his bitter gang of four had filed urgent "emails of concern" with the Second Interim Assistant to the Interim Vice Deputy to the Provost about how the vague guidelines for the so-called Sandstorm Scholarships broke many university rules. They realized there were three hundred and twelve administrators between this clown and the Provost, all afraid of donors, even the legendary Henry Foster. The grad students called him "the Sand Man."

Having a rare, hard sandstorm on the day he was to appear at the English Department seemed like a giant omen to Henry, but most things did. Given to magical thinking, he had spent nine years as an undergraduate in the English Department, during a time of spiritual retreats in many states. He studied channeling, self-awareness, aroma therapy, and crystal healing in Santa Fe, fasting, Jungian hypnosis, walking backwards, and bowel cleansing in Sedona. He lived in a silent, macrobiotic, sexless, all-meditation ashram in South Austin, until boredom overcame him. And Henry believed strongly that all this made him a better man, recluse, weirdo, and talk of the town.

Henry had four suits tailor made in Dallas that were sand-colored silk, and fit like O.J.'s glove. He always wore one in a sandstorm, with a matching cashmere neck scarf, and some really ugly, bright-orange swimming goggles, and matching soft, foam ear plugs. Henry was very good looking. An eye witness would mistake him for George Clooney's younger brother. Henry had been engaged three times to women who could not bring themselves to believe that God was about to say something really profound, even for God, to Henry at any given moment.

English Department grad students drank Friday afternoons at Cricket's Grill across from campus. A few times, Henry had wandered in, paid all tabs, ordered more munchies than anyone wanted, and answered questions in a monosyllable that hung there in the air. Shyness was mistaken for aloofness. One drunken Doctoral candidate's wife cornered Henry for her Oprah-size tale of woe, with her father out of work and facing foreclosure on his house. Later, she put an Alka Seltzer in Henry's white wine.

When Henry was eleven, his father wanted him to spend time with Jiggs Monroe, the 90-year-old former foreman of the Foster Ranch. Jiggs insisted on sitting outside the ranch house on folding chairs in a raging sandstorm. Henry's two older cousins fled to the house. Jiggs said, "You can judge a man by a sandstorm. We'd watch a young cowboy, and see how he acted. We'd see if he complained. You don't complain. You are tough."

Henry believed that and believed in that and had told about a thousand sensitivity group members, life-style coaches, other overweight counselors, and self-appointed Gurus about that in seven states and Cancun, Mexico.

When it was his turn to talk, he trotted out Jiggs-on-sandstorms every single time, like patting for a dance.

Corky Hargrove III was a third because his granddaddy, a bootlegger, was called Corky and named his son Corky, also a bootlegger. They lived in Dickens County, near Spur, Texas, and delivered beer and spirits across three sparsely populated counties and about 3000 square miles. The laws all knew about the Hargroves, and knew they were righteous, ethical bootleggers with regular clients that needed them. They barely scraped by. Three generations of Corkys had made the unprofitable 130 mile round trip to take Widow Jennings her quart of cheap Vodka once a month, and now more often, for twenty-seven years.

Corky III's momma ran off with the government man taking the U.S. Census in 1990, when he was four. Corky II has a rabid hatred for the government and vents on talk radio several mornings a week. He is an ill-read conspiracy theorist that sees the loss of his cheating-heart, Thelma Jean, as connected to many things, including the current economic problems. He eats St. John's Wort like it is popcorn.

When Corky III went to college, he changed his name to James and sailed through the business school, but could not land a job in the aftermath of Cheney/Bush. He was waiting tables at Cricket's when Darlene Jeffers put the Alka Seltzer in Henry Foster's drink. James heard all the student gossip about Henry, and the money they were chasing. James a.k.a. Corky went to the English Department to read what he could of the old Sandstorm Scholarship entries. Most were very negative about sandstorms, often plagiarizing the driven-crazy-by-sandstorms theme.

James Hargrove enrolled as an English major in Grad school and started writing. He wrote truthfully about the men in Spur gathering at Dink's Texaco and Domino Parlor when the weather was too bad to work outdoors to swap stories, often about the wild West Texas weather. He wrote of the wisdom of the oldest cowboys from the Pitchfork Ranch, and their tales of the worst sandstorms of the depression. He included J. Frank Dobie's story about folks finding a hat in a sand dune. They started digging, only to find a man under the hat. The man said, "Keep digging boys, there is a good horse under me." James wrote of St. Elmo's fire, the bluish, static electricity that could be seen on the horns of cattle during a sand storm.

James told of the long drives with his father, who had a bad right knee from his early rodeo misadventures. He'd drive with his left leg. They liked to run loads of whiskey on full-moon nights with their lights out.

They were called a Comanche moon, because the Comanches would raid when the moon was full, in this same West Texas wonderland. Just like the Comanches, the Hargroves knew all the back roads. Their 1988 Ford Pickup was always in top shape, with good tires. James wrote about the eccentric, regular customers that lived alone in isolated areas, often on what was left of their old family place. James told about meeting the Pitchfork Ranch cowboys at the fence line with a tornado headed their way.

However, James wrote all of this without mentioning bootlegging. He knew it didn't make any sense, three generations of them driving all over this big, near-empty chunk of Texas. He began to search sandstorms on the Internet. He was consumed. He wrote several drafts, confident that Henry Foster liked sandstorms. Most natives didn't really mind or too much notice the sandstorms, compared to the Yankee imports on the English Department faculty, whose whining had given Henry the idea for the scholarships in the first place.

James lost sleep and didn't eat properly. His mind was in a frenzied, manic fog. He couldn't get sandstorms out of what was left of his mind. He wrote poems, songs, essays, and a short story set in Spur, Texas in 1933. Finally, James wrote his final lead, "My daddy and granddaddy are bootleggers, and damn proud of it. I am a bootlegger too." He said he loved sandstorms because the men would gather at Dink's Texaco and Domino Parlor for the philosophy and oral history that guided small town life. He wrote about how glad the thirsty customers were to see them come driving through a sandstorm when the visibility was so low you couldn't see the hood ornament on the pickup, which they lovingly called, Spot.

The very night the English Department T.A. delivered all the entries to Henry Foster, he saw a 1953 movie entitled, The Naked Spur, with James Stewart, Janet Leigh, and Robert Ryan. James Hargrove's entry was on the top. When Henry saw the words, Spur, Texas, he took it as an omen. He decided to give the whole $100,000 to Corky III. He most especially liked the fact they were bootleggers.

The old-department-chairman-out-of-power and his bitter gang of four wrote angry letters to varied administrators and co-signed a letter of protest to The Daily Toreador. A rude reporter called Henry to ask his reasons for giving the whole award to a self-confessed bootlegger. Henry announced he was doubling the award to James Hargrove.

The attention Corky III got made him uncomfortable, until the nubile coeds starting acting really friendly. He bought his daddy a 2006 Ford pickup, and the bootlegging route stayed exactly the same. Henry Foster showed up to ride with the bootleggers in the worst sandstorm. He loved it, although he didn't know what Corky II was talking about with A.I.G., Fannie Mae, Thelma Jean, and Freddie Mac. They made friends for life.

Everybody's happy except the old-department-chairman-out-of-power and his bitter gang of four.

VIRTUALUBBOCK.COM, TRUCKIN',

All Those Things That Don't Change, Come What May

We were young and drunk and twenty and knew
that we could never die...Thomas Wolfe

Jake inherited the Magic House when his drinking uncle tried to empty a rabbit out of a long irrigation pipe. The pipe hit a high-line wire. The 1940s furniture clashed with Jake's beatnik, coffee-house conversational monologues sanctioned only by the weekend wannabe artists, singers, writers, and actors from the college that came to his regular parties, called Jake Parties.

Stilt Momma took me to one of Jake's scratchy–jazz-records-spilled-red-wine-bullfight-poster-smoky rent parties. Pseudo intellectual was the pose du jour. Over one hundred optimistic souls, mildly costumed, loved each other there every weekend of 1964 and 1965. Faded blue work-shirt was already the uniform of the day for this flock of alleged nonconformists. Magic House and the parties were Jake's life and livelihood.

Jake would meander regally to small groups of impressionable college kids, pontificating and pretending to speak knowingly. His weapon of choice was the caustic, shocking insult, a brief cryptic challenge. It was Jake's gig. He was the only legend in town that year. I thought he was a con, and sometimes cruel to his drunken guests/suckers.

It was cheaper to go to the strip for your own booze and hide it somewhere in the spacious Magic House than to be badgered by Jake to chip in for his profitable trips to the strip or later to buy beer outright from him. My first night there, two gorgeous, blond, ironed-hair bookends were glued to Jake reading aloud from Kerouac's *On the Road*.

For them, being hustled by, buying wine from, and ultimately being Jake's temporary girlfriend would be the adventure story to take back to Dallas.

"I have a right to tall women," he gloated. Jake was five-eight, not good looking, with this bramble patch of thick, black curly hair which he conditioned and fussed over to get the exact, unkempt look. His flashing, chocolate eyes stayed hidden by his signature shades day and night until he needed to remove them dramatically for effect. His wispy and uncooperative goatee betrayed him.

The Magic House was Jake's rice bowl. Revenue trickled in from love offerings, a volunteer cover charge, bootlegging, and the sale of you-cook-your-own hamburgers and pork chop sandwiches. At two bucks, I'd buy one right now. The place always smelled of the variegated stale of red wine, tobacco, and pork chops. Usually, Jake had compelling reasons not to actually cook or clean or hold a job over three weeks or a fiancée over a semester.

Some of Jake's stories originated with trips to Selma, Denver, Mexico City, North Beach, and Venice. He did the Beatnik grand tour before he was self-incarcerated in the never ending party of Magic House. For some, graduation was delayed. For others, the dream of graduating was partied away. I feared I'd miss some folk singers or some heartbroken freshman girl rejected by rush or some radical politico with news of the outside world. Magic House was my flame. I was the moth, returning, returning.

Karen began to pretend to love me during the third verse of a group sing-a-long of "Four Strong Winds" and I really believed her. Under the year 'round Christmas tree lights and the spell of the song, "twelve voices glued us together," Karen later said. I cooked her a pork chop sandwich. The black leotards, oversized men's dress shirt, dishwater ponytail, and copy of Kahil Gibran made Karen seem ordinary that year. She was a skilled romantic with little notes, poems, morning toothpaste kisses, worn pink wool pajamas, and small shoplifted gifts. We'd have romantic dinners at fancy restaurants, dressed to the nines, and walk the check. She'd pout and cry and leave and I'd go after her and keep going. Her elitist belief in Ayn Rand's objectivist philosophy somehow justified her life of petty crime.

Her notes, presents, day and night phone calls, and obsessive, controlling jealousy convinced me of the ocean floor depths of our love.

Stalking wasn't known then. Karen climbed a winter-brittle elm tree to the second floor window of my alley pad to leave a lime on my pillow. Jake's unvarnished warnings all slid past me. She secretly tape recorded my drunken benedictions.

Three months into it, Karen quit me in a Furr's supermarket produce section. We were shopping for French bread, noodles, garlic, and tomatoes. "I don't like you or Jake or your so-called friends," she said.

A business major with a long slide rule on his belt observed all this and drove me back to Magic House. He baked the garlic bread, drank half a gallon of red wine, and left a new, tan corduroy coat with leather elbow patches. Jake claimed it, as he often did with lost articles.

When the mean blood-alcohol level of the Magic House was precisely right, Jake led a group sing-a-long to the Beatles' first album and everyone knew every word. He was shaking his own mop top and dancing on the couch. I had thought Karen and I were engaged. No one saw me cry.

Sororities warned penitents about Jake and Magic House and his well-intentioned but ephemeral engagements to a parade of young women, dissimilar in appearance and background but remarkably alike in their intense need to prove their intellectual worth and unbridled devotion to the dawning of the counterculture. Jake's future bride of the semester always had a car to loan, but Magic House was hard on monogamy.

My last semester, I was so broke that I had to move into Magic House. My clothes always smelled of cigs and pork chops. After a few weeks, Jake wanted me to go with him in Karen's car to steal food from deep freezers in richie neighborhoods. Sometimes, he stole beer or whiskey which was amply stored in a dry town. I wouldn't go but knew Jake and Karen were an item. I baked one of the stolen, frozen cherry pies the next morning and moved out before Jake woke up.

A couple of years later, on my way home from Vietnam, I ran into a guy from the Tech debate team in the Los Angeles Airport. He said the Magic House, and the parties, and Jake were still the same. On the airplane, a reed-thin, textbook salesman, who smelled of Old Spice, provided his opinion of the manhunt for James Earl Ray. "He'd been to New Orleans just like Jack Ruby and Oswald. Probably been to Cuba too." he said.

The flat, flat land of home and the checkerboard fields glided by outside the airplane window. While filling out the papers for a rental car at the Lubbock Airport, I began to have jagged, second thoughts about a reunion with Jake. The kitchen door of Magic House was open when I arrived. The walls had the same tired, printed slogans I had seen in magazines, "Hell no, we won't go." The college-bar smell welcomed me. From the next room, I could hear Jake reading aloud from Kerouac's *On the Road*. A youngish female voice said, "Wow." I retreated, silently.

Truckin'

The Big Empty

"They say you went off to Dallas for good," Irene said.

"I'm back. Working for Dowd. He took me under his wing," Cotton said. "I haven't seen you in a coon's age."

"You remember Irene, don't you Cotton? From the school house," Buck said.

"Sure, how old are your kids now?" Cotton said.

"The boy is twelve, the girl's nine. All I hear is Pokémon. Wanta be a good Mom. We got her the video game. We catch her watchin' *Beavis and Butthead* all the time. You and Michele have any kids?" Irene asked.

"Nope," Cotton said.

"Where is she these days?" Irene asked.

"Now, Irene, Cotton don't want to be bothered by that. Our boy wants his own web site," Buck said.

"No kid needs a web site," Buck said. "The government wants everbody on computers. You've heard of the long ear of the law."

"They say Horace already put you in jail again since you come back," Irene said.

"That was Mutt's doings. We run out of gas on the back side of the lake. He walked up to the highway and a trucker carried him home. Horace come up or I would have froze to death. If the wind would of been blowing, we would be there still. Felt like a record cold. Blue norther overdue," Cotton said.

"They can't stop you without reasonable doubt," Buck said. "How did you get out of jail?"

"Dowd wanted me on a combine and I called him," Cotton said.

"Ever time I see Dowd, he gets shorter. Used to be taller than me. They say he puts a drop of honey on everything he eats, and he gets Chinese herbs from a chiropractor. Dowd has farms all over Crosby County," Buck said.

"They say he is on his third divorce and they are fussin' over farms and houses and all that," Irene said.

"I've got a map," Cotton said.

"Did Maureen die?" Irene asked.

"Naw, she's livin' in a little house in town," Cotton said.

"What did she get out of all that?" Irene asked.

"They say she didn't get much more than what the little boy shot at," Cotton said.

"What happened to your arm?" Irene asked.

"He set his own self on fire lighting a bar-b-que grill," Buck laughed.

"You better get that looked at. It is beginning to fester," Irene said. "Looks awful."

"You must have been arrested with the first hard freeze. Did you get any snow?" Buck asked.

"None that stuck to the ground. I was combining guar for Dowd before my arm got hurt," Cotton said.

"They say Maureen didn't even get no lawyer," Irene said.

"Farming guar is like raising gravel. Little hard balls. You combine it. They use it to make cosmetics and candy," Cotton said.

"They say Dowd got the insurance on all his hailed-out cotton and will make more off of guar than cotton anyways," Irene said.

"That's right. I got a map printed of all his farms. His lawyer don't seem to know that when and how he got each farm counts," Cotton said.

"They say Beauregard's name is on those farms he stole off families on four sides of Crosby County," Irene said.

"I'm glad we are out of farming. You glad, Cotton, to be out?" Buck asked.

"You won't be so glad when the United Nations takes all your guns," Cotton said.

"Oh, Cotton. They say you come on some weird political beliefs when you was off in Dallas," Irene said.

"Just wait. Hide and watch. There are a lot of people that can see what is happening. There was four cars followed me plumb across the big empty all the way to downtown Jones," Cotton said. "How come there aren't any people our age left in Crosby County?" Cotton asked.

"They say that guar will grow in ever which kind of weather. They use it for electrical insulation," Buck said.

"They say Dowd comes out to the farms in any kind of weather," Irene said.

"Yeah, he is there to count ever boll of cotton. Dowd is tight. It would take the jaws of life to open his billfold. He is a great old man but he ain't really got no right to the farms that other people's great granddaddy broke out. It is the damndest thing since Roy stuffed Trigger," Cotton said.

"Him and Beauregard know when a boll weevil belches in Crosby County. You better mind your beeswax," Irene said. "You know Michele and I rode the school bus together for years. We'd pray and sing gospel."

"There is gonna be a brand new government. Hide and watch," Cotton said.

"Hope you ain't one of them racists," Irene said.

"Naw, David was the first fellow I looked up when I got home. He don't smoke or drink and he married this woman from his church," Cotton said.

"They say he drank in Las Vegas. That's where they went on the honeymoon. He is one of the only people our age that has hung on in Crosby County. He is at the gin office of a morning telling stories," Irene said.

"Crosby County will be one of the last places the United Nations will try to take over. A different government between now and then would more than likely return our farms. Your farm and mine," Cotton said.

"My double lucky prodigal-looking brother has a good farm where it rains all the time and he is buying another," Irene said.

"They say he is a bootlegger and a gambler and everthing else now," Cotton said.

"Well, you know what they say about what they say," Irene said. "We could use our farm back."

"Don't file these liens yet but keep them and study on them. I take St. John's Wort now. Things have to change fast. Ain't no accident we had the hottest winter anyone remembers," Cotton said.

"Pecan trees got a bright gold like them tourist trees in New Mexico," Buck said. "It was great weather."

"You better not let anyone catch you with these South Plains Fair legal papers," Irene said.

"I knew I could trust both y'all not to tattle on what we was talking about," Cotton said.

"Absolutely," Irene said. "They said you would never hire on as a hand for Dowd what with what happened with Michele and all."

"Irene I swear. You are noisy as a hog eating charcoal," Buck said. "You play the lottery, Cotton? Me and Irene always plays the date she first come into the bar."

"They say Dowd keeps a big old chicken house and gives red pepper to all those hens," Irene said. "If you ain't got no prior engagement, we would like to invite you to our house to watch the big game."

"Yeah, we would love to have you. Irene is a great cook just like her mama." Buck said.

"I already promised Dowd I'd watch the big game with him. He wouldn't have nobody to watch it with if it wasn't for me," Cotton said.

"Is Michele coming?" Irene asked.

"Nope," Cotton said.

THE TEXAS OBSERVER

Hard Luck Harry and the Owl

Harry believed in luck more than any gambler you have ever met. If the Dallas Cowboys lost in the final seconds of a football game, Harry thought it was because he'd spilled the salt shaker at the truck stop. Harry had lost steadily at no-limit Texas Hold 'em for twenty-three years. His favorite hands were ace-jack and ace-ten. That's kind of unlucky by its own self. By playing very tight and quitting when he was ahead, Harry managed to win one out of four times, year after year. If you asked Harry about that, he'd tell you he played too many hands and called too much on fifth street but he really believed he was snake-bit, permanently unlucky. It started in junior high flipping coins odd-man with guys that cheated him.

Harry was walking up to Williard's poker game when he spied a Great Horned Owl staring him down from a fence post. A shiver went down Harry's spine like a rabbit had run across his grave. It looked to Harry like the raptor might attack at any minute. He stood there frozen trying to decide what it meant. Since these owls are nocturnal, Harry had never seen one before. The owl let out its distinctive mid-winter mating call, "Who? Who? Who?" the owl asked. Then it flew off with a great clapping of the wings.

Harry knew the owl was a bad omen to the Plains Indians who roamed the West Texas flatlands before the buffalo hunters, barbed wire, Texas Rangers, U.S. Calvary, windmills, and massive ranches ran off the Indians. That's why we don't have Indian casinos like the Okies. Sighting an owl was a sign of death to some Indians. Harry was spooked big-time. He wasn't his usual friendly self when he got his chips and a chair. On the third hand, while he was still thinking hard about the significance of the owl, he caught two black aces. The ace of spades is the death card. He almost threw the hand away. Harry smooth called the ten dollar blind. He only had $150 in chips.

Even Harry knew that Dylan always raises on the button and always makes a follow-up bet. Dylan was one of these college-aged players with a torn, battered hat and sunglasses. Dylan ran over the game like water over the lowlands. Harry called Dylan's predictable $30 raise. When the flop came 8,7,2 rainbow, Harry checked and called Dylan's $60 bet after a long study. Dylan could read and smell Harry's fear but he only had $50 left. When Dylan paired queens, he bet the last $50. All Harry could think of was that owl. He only called to confirm his primary interior vision of his bad luck. He looked surprised to win the pot. Fireman couldn't keep from laughing.

Then Harry caught a little rush, calling fearfully with some monster hands. If the owl was right, Harry thought, I am a doomed man in this poker game. Then Harry caught the ace-eight of spades in the big blind. No one raised and it came ace, eight, deuce. Harry held the ace of spades and the dead man's hand. His heart pounded. He called Dylan's small wager crying. When another ace came on fourth street, everyone checked it down. Harry cashed in $1,240, his best winning since two years ago Christmas at Sandia Casino when he held more hands than any manicurist in town.

As Harry walked toward his car, the Great Horned Owl was sitting on the same fence post. Harry avoided eye contact and ran for his car. His feet shuffling on the gravel startled the owl and it took off flying just over Harry's head as he opened his car door. He jumped in and locked the doors. By the time Harry reached his place of employment at the Purple Coyote Liquor Store, the story had grown. "It came right at my head." Harry said. "I ducked behind the car just in time. Sighting an owl is a really bad omen."

For a wrong-way gambler, Harry lived a very orderly life. He rented a small furnished apartment, He got all his clothes at garage sales and all his food at Walmart. He didn't have a phone or cable TV and he didn't want them. Clyde would always let him work overtime on big football weekends. Harry religiously studied his dog-eared back issues of *Bluff Magazine*, but he still had a weakness for a weak ace. The guys around the liquor store made little $10 bets with no juice on sporting events. Harry budgeted $6 per week for the Texas lottery. He knew it was in support of the school children of Texas.

After his winning at the poker, Harry went back to betting football at eleven to ten pick 'em. The first week he had six $100 winners on the college games and three $200 winners on the pro games. He won every bet. If this wasn't lucky, what was? But Harry couldn't shake the thought of the owl. He dreamed about the owl clawing his face. He drove by Williard's poker game every day looking for the owl. It was a no-show. Then Harry went down to the library in a howling dust storm to read up on owls. He found out that some Indians believed owls have powers of prophecy. They represent helpfulness and wisdom. So the owl meant good luck, Harry thought. He sure was on a hot streak. The Greeks thought it was a sign of victory in battle if an owl flew over their troops. They revered owls and put them on their coins.

The Romans viewed owls as sinister, a very bad sign. They thought the sighting of an owl meant a defeat in battle. The Roman Army suffered one of its greatest defeats at the sight of the Garden of Eden between the Euphrates and Tigris rivers in what is present day Iraq. They saw an owl before the battle. Some American Indians saw owls as a sign of death. So did people in the middle ages. But many other cultures saw owls as signs of wisdom or good fortune. The English are divided on owls as they are on most issues. In early English folklore, the call or screech of an owl was a sure sign somebody's number was up. In Northern England, an owl is a sign of good luck. Harry was confused by all this. Was the owl a sign of bad luck or good luck?

Somebody said that if you don't get a bet down, you might be walking around real lucky and not even know it. That was about as close to a core value as Harry got. He bet on sixteen football and basketball games and won thirteen bets. He won four times in a row at the poker game, rarely getting his money in the pot with the best hand. He went to the Mall and bought a whole new outfit, with a shiny blue Italian cut sports coat and gray wool pants. He got a shine and a manicure and had his thinning hair styled.

As Harry approached Williard's game, he didn't really see the owl fading away in the twilight but he thought he did. That night he played super tight and caught way more than his share of big easily played wired pairs. Harry convinced himself this was the certain signal that his life-long streak of bad luck had ended. This was his time. He would never see another poor day. Harry kept winning at every thing he did for a couple of months. He bought a 1993 red Cadillac Eldorado, moved into a new apartment, and got a small, multi-colored tattoo of an owl on his left forearm.

The paste boards returned to normal and obsessive loyalty to ace-jack and ace-ten began to grind away at Harry's bankroll. If anybody got lucky, it was Harry's bookmaker. He couldn't pick 'em. Harry decided to have the tattoo removed by this quack with a laser. It left this weird bluish scar, but you can sure tell it is an owl. Nobody calls him Hard Luck Harry to his face.

BLUFF MAGAZINE

IV.
Memoirs and Secrets

Learning to be a Professional Gambler: The Hard Road

If you know poker, and you know people, then you got the whole dang world lined up in your sights.. Brett Maverick.

I was too lazy to work and too nervous to steal, so I became a gambler. As a teenager, I met the best and most knowledgeable gambler I ever met, Curly Cavitt. He taught me more than any other person about all-around gambling, because he knew more than any man I ever met, before or since. I wanted to learn to be a gambler where I could make something out of myself. Curly Cavitt was the model for Moody O'Malley, a major character in my novel, *Texas Poker Wisdom*.

Lubbock, Texas was a real poker and gambling center. No need to travel, but we did, often. Johnny Moss moved to Lubbock in 1938 for the poker for a while, before my time. In the 1950s, and early 1960s, many big gamblers moved to Lubbock, and the poker was fantastic. Dallas and Ft. Worth had gambling turf wars with many killed, grand jury indictments, law crackdowns, and vicious hijackers. That sent a few gamblers to West Texas.

Big gamblers would live in a town, and play square there, but on the road, they only got the suckers one night at an Elk's, Moose, Eagle's, Country Club stag, or gambling night, so anything goes. The old saying was, "Get the money before it walks." Curly Cavitt traveled around gambling for sixty years, more miles than any gambler. At the gambling nights held by fraternal organizations, every form of imaginative dice came in and out, moved by the top magicians. Card cheating was expected.

All those guys older than me that came out of the great depression knew how to cheat, but not anything at all like Curly and Titanic. Without a bankroll, losing is not an option.

The big open, always no-limit Texas Hold 'em game at "The Shop" in Lubbock, Texas lasted thirty-five years. There were a steady supply of "road gamblers" coming and going. Nearly all lost. We called them "cross-roaders" or "scufflers", which implied cheaters. After winning the World Series of Poker at different times: Amarillo Slim, Sailor Roberts, and Bill Smith came to the Shop, and lost. Same with Bobby Hoff, who was at a few main-event final tables. Far better were the really slick, all-out con men in hot Cadillacs and nice, hot clothes. The con men just could never handle the square poker, but they tried, and tried, and tried. They could always pump money, and how was none of our business. I knew some of them with incredible cons, but most were almost child-like at the poker.

The road gambler and con men slicks stole on the road, but not at the Shop. The biggest poker games were honest, because everyone knew the moves, and of course, some killers were ever present. We knew nearly all the home and road poker players, and we welcomed any well-dressed stranger. The Shop was West Texas outlaw central for all manner of traveling thieves. I loved it. I wish it was open. It was my favorite place on earth, Binion's in Las Vegas second, and Texas Tech third, a weak third.

The road was way cheaper than it is today, even counting inflation. I stayed at the fanciest, legendary hotels. They had an off-room, cheap-price, or commercial-rate room. The Adolphus and Baker in Dallas. The Texan in Fort Worth. I stayed in the same suite at the Cortez in El Paso that President Kennedy had stayed in a couple of days before his assassination. They charged me $9.

I'd travel to bridge tournaments and play with clients a few sessions, and get paid. We'd bet all the old ladies $5 a piece, a gift. I was a Life Master, the highest rank at that time, in my early twenties. We'd bet higher, but only good players took the action. But we still seemed to limp home broke. I left a lot of towns broke: Ft. Worth, Dallas often, Acapulco, Mexico City, Longview, El Paso, Joplin, Oklahoma City, Las Vegas, Austin, Del Rio, Los Angeles, Nashville, San Francisco, and more. Being broke on the road brings out one's inner creativity. As Benny Binion said, "I'll tell you the truth, but I won't tell you everything."

Nobody wanted to miss the big July 4th Regional Bridge tourney that alternated between Dallas and Ft. Worth. One year I was flat broke, and hitchhiked there. My golf hustler, bridge expert, complete con artist mother passed me three times with her rich, lady friends. I had spent a fortune in poker money taking her to bridge tourneys. Often we'd fly someplace and take the long, long overnight bus home. I could sleep anywhere: buses, trains, planes, jail, back seats. I slept in a gambling joint until I was twenty-six, often while the chips rattled.

But on this trip, I was relegated to the Ft. Worth YMCA. I railed, kibitzed the bridge great, Oswald Jacoby, hit the buffet, played a few sessions, got drunk often, and had a big time. Bridge tourneys were very big, like poker tourneys now. Mother promised a few bucks walking around money, but no. On the last night, I get way to drunk to remember that my pockets were drought dry. I start marching back to the YMCA about 4 a.m. Being July the 4th, there were large flags everywhere. I stole one on a big, heavy pole. Now, I'm really marching. Some Ft. Worth rowdies stopped and hassled me, but I had the flag pole, the zeal of patriotism, and firewater courage. A cop car came my way, but I ducked into an alley. And I never abandoned Old Glory.

The next morning, I woke up broke on the third floor of the Fort Worth YMCA and owed them for several days. I put the flag in my old suitcase and threw it to the street, far below. It sounded like a bomb when it hit. The suitcase broke open, and the flag unfurled on the side walk. I ran on down. Thumbed a great ride who bought me breakfast. Kept that big flag for years, as a bed cover. My old suitcase had a huge double T for Texas Tech on the side. That made it easy to get around Texas very fast hitch hiking. Someone would pass you and come back because of some Texas Tech connection. I'd dress nice to hitchhike, wearing a tie and sports coat.

Another time I go on the road with one of America's very best bridge players, Butch Adams. We drive 500 miles to Tyler, where the bridge tourney is canceled. We drive to Dallas, and there is a Calcutta. You bid on the pairs, and a pot forms with big cash prizes. The most famous bridge player of all time, Oswald Jacoby, bought us cheap. You buy half and split the winnings. There is a huge amount of richie, Dallas popularity bidding and the pot got large. We blew it on the first few hands. Amazing, Butch had won everything, with everybody in tournament after tournament. We had won often. That same year, Johnny Moss staked me at auction bridge in Odessa, Texas. So, I had the best-known men in bridge and poker as stake horses, then and now, stake me, and I lost for both of them. I was not a stake horse. I was a stick horse.

So, now Butch and I head north to Oklahoma City in time for the tail-end of a big bridge tournament. In the large open pairs, we knew only three pairs to bet with, so we got down for all the money we had left. There were hundreds of people. We placed fifth, and lost all three bets, to 1st, 2nd, and 4th. Broke again! We drove 1500 miles or more to get broke, when we could have gotten broke much cheaper in Lubbock, Texas.

Once a major sucker catches two aces, and my partner did too. They moved it to the center in the middle of winter. My man begged for a split. Sucker said no. He hit a flush, and flew to Dallas. We flew after him, and found a triple-draw low ball game with thieves. Dallas and poker thieves went together for decades. The next morning, I am walking down Commerce Street, when a slick grabs me by the arm. He says he is a "colorologist" with a college degree, and he had a perfect sports coat to match my "ruddy" skin. So, I follow him into this fancy men's store, and he breaks me for my half of the traveling boodle. Coat, pants, shirts, belts. However, when I was broke, I was one of the best dressed gamblers in all of Texas.

When I went in the Army at age twenty-two, I had to tell them about my string of gambling arrests, and they listed me as a professional gambler. They told me if I played in the barracks poker game, I'd go to the stockade. It was a six-month active duty, six years reserves program. I didn't want to play in those nits and lice games anyway.

When I got out, right before Christmas of 1962, I had only my Army dress uniform to wear. I bought some fancy Signal Corps adornments, and a garish, orange sash for my shoulder, which I was not supposed to wear, bloused my boots like the paratroopers, and headed to Ft. Worth for another regional bridge tourney. This time I was staying at the Texas Hotel, like the quality folk.

With a pint of bootleg booze behind me, I went to the legendary Cellar, a beatnik, coffee house joint run by Pat Kirkwood, the son of one of Ft. Worth's biggest gamblers, Pappy Kirkwood. He had owned the fabled Four Deuces, the 2222, a full-tilt casino on the Jacksboro Highway when the gambling ran wide open, with the help of the law.

The Cellar sold fake booze. Syrupy rum and coke without alcohol. I raised a loud fuss, and they threw a United States Army soldier in uniform out. From Kipling, "they let a drunk civilian in, but had no room for me." I have been thrown out of a lot nicer joints than that.

Joe Ely, a singer I later managed, worked at the Cellar, as did ZZ Top. They'd rotate playing all night. Ely said that the owner of the Houston Cellar pointed a pistol at him rather than pay up.

One time coming out of Mexico with my pals, we had the cash stashed for the 300 plus miles home. Smuggling rum brilliantly, we had the backseat floorboard covered in bottles of rum. It was brutally cold, and we had our coats over the rum. The guys in the back had their knees up real high, and we got caught. It was only a $40 smuggling fine and the rum or my car, an easy choice. Case forty, oh Lordy, broke again!

Two of my best friends and first two partners and I opened a little gambling joint. We had pot cut Texas Hold 'em poker, and we dealt fast, very fast. Previously, college-age folks played dealer's choice, but Hold 'em makes the rake stronger than Grandma's breath. We had blackjack (21), and we dealt fast, very fast. We bootlegged beer and sold mixed drinks, whiskey and coke. When we got drunk, the hangers on got drunk. Once we made a light score, and decided to go to Juarez, Mexico, as we were prone to do. Being only 320 miles, we took no suitcases, clothes, or dock kits. We did take the little joint bankroll. When three people share a road bankroll, you tend to spend.

In Juarez, we went one block past the international bridge to a favorite bar, San Felipe's. We drank a long time, and hired this band to play and sing songs at 50 cents a pop. Every fourth song, we requested *La Cucaracha*, the Mexican Revolution corrido, and we sang loudly in fake Spanish, but on key. Finally, we went broke to *La Cucaracha*. We didn't eat in the fancy restaurant where each guy gets twenty-seven waiters, and five courses. We saw no dancing girls. We just sang *La Cucaracha*. We went in only one bar. Broke again.

Later, we slept in the car awhile, and headed home. We saw two giant strippers standing by the road. Their car is broken down. If we will take them to Hobbs, New Mexico, they will get us into an Elk's Stag with food, booze, and a show. Only we have to take the carnie-talking promoter, and they go in the car in front of us. Bummer. In Hobbs, we last four minutes inside the Elk's Lodge, and are thrown out. Broke again!

During my youngest years as a gambler, my folks moved around, especially Daddy, looking for oil. The Philippines. Colorado. Michigan. Indiana. The boom towns of Texas. Once Daddy was in Ozona, Texas near the border. I got Buddy the Beat really drunk, and headed there to take Daddy my 1954 Ford. He gave me $20, and we hitchhiked on to Villa Acuna, Mexico with that our total bankroll. Some whores beat us up in the Number Eight bar, and threw us in the mud. We got separated, and I caught a flop house in Del Rio to wash my clothes, and sleep. The next day I found Buddy in Acuna. He had organized a minor search for me. Touching. We headed home broke. He was terrible to hitchhike with, even though he had more miles than anybody. I have hitchhiked away from the Mexican border a couple of times, and nobody trusted you, even back then.

When I was twenty-one, a buddy and I got a job shilling at the poker at the Golden Nugget in Las Vegas for the great Bill Boyd. Seeing broke around the corner, I wrote to my con-artist mother, recalling the time they actually gave me four silver dollars when I was nine to go the South Plains Fair. I pleaded for a loan. There were many con artists and gamblers in her family, and many upright, successful professionals.

Finally, a letter came to General Delivery, Las Vegas. There was no money. There was only one sentence from mother. It said, "The only thing worse than being a gambler is thinking you are one when you are not."

English lyrics:
The cockroach, the cockroach,
can't walk anymore
because it doesn't have,
because it's lacking
marijuana to smoke.

PLAYER IRELAND MAGAZINE

Poker in a Texas Whore House

Texas Hold 'em became the major poker game in West Texas sometime in the mid- fifties. It created a lot of action and a good many poker professionals. There were poker games available day and night in Lubbock. Many of the road gamblers that are pictured in Doyle's *Super System* of the first two World Series of Poker were the gentlemen I started playing against when I was twenty years old. This included Jack "Treetop" Straus, Amarillo Slim, Johnny Moss, James "Tennessee Longgoodie" Roy, Bill Smith, Pat Renfro, Sailor Roberts, Skeet Childress, Joe Lloyd or Floyd, and Doc Ramsey. Back then, professional gamblers spent a good deal of money on clothes. As a matter of pride, they dressed better than almost any other group whether they had any money or not.

A woman named Dolly ran a game six days a week for many decades, until it was robbed. On Tuesdays, Dolly closed her game and the game moved over to Morgan's brothel, the best known brothel in all West Texas. When the houseman played, you would say, "The tea is live." Morgan was of average height, about fifty, with a thick head of jet black hair. He was a big man, around three hundred pounds. He always wore an expensive Stetson, a nice, white shirt, and bib overalls with a door knob-size diamond stick pin on the front pocket. If you were still out at dawn, as I often was, you might see Morgan with a Cadillac full of "his nieces" returning from the best hotels.

On Tuesdays, the trick room was closed and the poker was on. The trick room actually had a little red light lamp on the floor in the corner. Morgan was called a "nookie bookie" or a "knot salesman" and the young ladies were called working girls, soiled doves, or Morgan's nieces. Morgan was always at some poker game. His heart-of-gold wife, Bell, ran the place.

She also used a whip cup, a cheating device, to dust out many drunk suckers shooting high dice. Morgan was a slow, but steady loser at poker and a real calling station who only raised on two Kings. I have never seen anyone else play that way. Morgan's and Dolly's were open poker games with everyone invited: cross-roaders, scufflers, scamps, bookies, loan sharks, dice men, con men. Usually, there were several out-of-towners at the poker table.

My first game at Morgan's, the cards ran over me and I was out of there with a large winning for someone my age. Usually I'd run down to Coach Brown's Varsity Shop and spend way too much on wool coats and slacks after any nice winning. I'd travel and high roll and usually be broke by the middle of the summer. Fall in Lubbock means lots of money: The cotton harvest, the college students are back, and everyone is betting on football.

Right after I discovered Morgan's game, there was a fight on a non-poker night and Bell shot a fellow on purpose once and Morgan twice in error. The game was only closed about three weeks for Morgan's recovery. We were all really pulling for him.

Bill Smith, the world champ of 1985, was one of the top poker players in his early twenties. He was one of my early mentors. Bill warned me to stay away from Morgan's if there were any drunk folks. Unlike Dolly, Morgan sold beer. The place was well known to laws and outlaws. Morgan was friends with the detectives who parked at his place for long periods of time in the mornings. Rumor had it he let them know which characters were passing through town. Morgan carried five thousand dollars or more in the top pocket of the bib overalls which made him a juicy target for robbers, cheats, and better poker players like me.

Morgan's friendship and discussions with the police were incredibly suspect and unpopular with almost everyone. Poker players are different from other outlaws but they are forced by the laws to be outlaws in Texas.

One night I did stay too late and was drinking and gambling and the cards were striking me. I had failed to notice that Morgan was getting drunk. Sometimes it was hard to tell about several of the players. E.W. "Ol' 186" Chapman would slip pills into his coffee and just get weirder and weirder and bet more aggressively than anyone. Calvert would stash five or so olive jar bottles full of vodka somewhere on his person. He was a skinny fellow in an oversized baggy suit who got a little drunker as the night wore on. Gene Bass had a flask and slipped whiskey into his coffee.

He got so mad one night that he took the card that busted him and put it into a sandwich and ate it.

I slow played two kings against Morgan's king-three and the flop came K,3,3 giving up both full houses. It was around two in the morning and we got all in for around a thousand dollar pot. At show down, Morgan stood up and yelled, "You cold-decked me, you son-of-a-bitch. Bell, get my lead pipe." She was standing behind me and the big pot was just sitting there in the center of the table. I knew not to say anything, move, or make eye contact. I'm guessing Bell will ignore him. There was a little pawn shop pistol in my car but there is no way my partner, Jerry, is going to be making any John Wayne movements. Neal the Carney and Sharptop, Homer D., Friend of the Working Girl had only recently busted out. They were still sitting at the table. Neal asked, "Kid, will you loan me forty dollars?" I nodded yes and he got two twenties out of the pot. Neal said, "Sit down, Slim Jim. And shut up." Morgan sat back down. I finally raked in the pot. I also loaned Sharptop forty bucks. Neal dealt a hand. Sharptop was a real ballyhoo man, everyone's favorite grifter. As usually happens, no matter what, the poker game goes on. After I folded a few hands, Morgan appeared to cool down. I said I was leaving. Morgan apologized and said, "I wasn't mad at you. I was mad at myself."

My parents had moved off. On Thanksgiving, Morgan and Bell invited me to a wonderful feast of all the things you associate with the family holiday. There was fantastic food, wine, lively and humorous conversation, and five working girls. Back then there was some kind of system the "talent" traveled "the wheel" which included Ft. Worth, Dallas, Midland, Ruidoso, and Lubbock. They said they were from Ft. Worth or, at least, considered it a second home. One young woman spoke of how lonely she was without her children who lived with her mother. She said, "I'm gonna buy them a big color T.V. for Christmas, if I don't get arrested before then."

Another lady said that her fantasy was to rent a bus and "fill it with beer and whiskey and a wash tub full of pills. We'd get all the characters and just ride around Texas." They paid tribute to Morgan, because he only took forty per cent when his competitors routinely took fifty per cent.

One week, we were raided by the Lubbock Police and arrested at two different poker spots. At Morgan's, they raided these bootleggers next door first and gave us plenty of time to put up the cards and cash. They asked if anyone had a job and no one did, so the charge was vagrancy by association. The fine was $15 for playing poker and $20 for sweating a game to trap the liars who said they were not playing. Morgan's was very well known. Cab drivers had a rate card for the hotels, the airport, "The Flats", and Morgan's. The police were very nice and friendly. They never drew guns or used handcuffs or any of that. They would make us empty our pockets into a property envelope, take our belts, fingerprint us, and photo us and either put us in a cell for less than a minute or just collect the fines. Usually a bail bondsman miraculously appeared. Some court case back then had ruled that cash or currency is not evidence and the police could not confiscate it.

The next night they arrested us again at a bigger game. They would ask each of us if we had ever been arrested before. I would follow the older guys lead and say no even though the police found it hilarious. The police had all these old photos of everyone they had arrested before. There were thirteen of us. Three of the guys had been arrested together way back in the twenties. The photos showed these roaring twenties era gangster suits. Back then the players at the large game came from all over. They also dressed up with sports coats, slacks and hats, with no ties.

We laughed because they had Sherman down with an a.k.a. as Stinky. They had me down as John Hughes a.k.a. Johnny. The police would put KG for known gambler by your name.

Later, the Supreme Court threw out the vagrancy laws and a goodly portion of gambler's arrest records. When I entered the Army, I told them of my gambling arrests while seeking a Top Secret Clearance. They just laughed them off and I got the clearance.

A few years later they built Ruel C. Martin Elementary, a grade school, right across the street from Morgan's. He kept on operating the best known whore house in these parts but closed the poker. Having a whore house across from a grade school was all right, but not a poker game. Morgan's was located in the 3300 block of East Broadway on Lubbock's eastern edge. It was the edge of town then and it still is.

BLUFF EUROPE MAGAZINE

Elvis Presley, Buddy Holly, Joe Ely, and the Cotton Club

Elvis Presley was leaning against his pink, 1954 Cadillac in front of Lubbock's historic Cotton Club. The small crowd was mesmerized by his great looks, cockiness, and charisma. He put on quite a show, doing nearly all the talking. Elvis bragged about his sexual conquests, using language you didn't hear around women. He said he'd been a truck driver six months earlier. Now he could have a new woman in each town. He told a story about being caught having sex in his back seat. An angry husband grabbed his wife by the ankles and pulled her out from under Elvis. I doubted that.

Earlier, at the Fair Park Coliseum, Elvis had signed girl's breasts, arms, foreheads, bras, and panties. No one had ever seen anything like it. We had met Elvis' first manager, Bob Neal, bass player Bill Black, and guitarist Scotty Moore. They wanted us to bring some beer out to the Cotton Club. So we did. My meeting with Bob Neal in 1955 was to have great meaning in my future. I was 15.

The old scandal rag, *Confidential,* had a story about Elvis at the Cotton Club and the Fair Park Coliseum. It had a picture of the Cotton Club and told of Elvis' unique approach to autographing female body parts. It said he had taken two girls to Mackenzie Park for a tryst in his Cadillac.

Elvis did several shows in Lubbock during his first year on the road, in 1955. When he first came here, he made $75. His appearance in 1956 paid $4000. When he arrived in Lubbock, Bob Neal was his manager. By the end of the year, Colonel Tom Parker had taken over. Elvis played the Fair Park Coliseum for its opening on Jan. 6th, with a package show. When he played the Fair Park again, Feb. 13th, it was memorable. Colonel Tom Parker and Bob Neal were there. Buddy Holly and Bob Montgomery were on the bill. Waylon Jennings was there. Elvis was 19. Buddy was 18.

Elvis' early shows in Lubbock were:

Jan 6th 1955, Fair Park Coliseum. Feb 13th. Fair Park, Cotton Club. April 29. Cotton Club June 3. Johnson Connelly Pontiac, Fair Park October 11. Fair Park. October 15. Cotton Club. April 10, 1956. Fair Park. Elvis probably played the Cotton Club on all of his Lubbock dates.

Buddy Holly was the boffo popular teenager of all time around Lubbock. The town loved him and gave me a ton of support! He had his own radio show on Pappy Dave Stone's KDAV, first with Jack Neal, later with Bob Montgomery, in his early teens. KDAV was the first all-country station in America. Buddy fronted Bill Haley, Marty Robbins, and groups that traveled through. Stone was an early mentor. Buddy first met Waylon Jennings at KDAV. Disk jockeys there included Waylon, Roger Miller, Bill Mack, later America's most famous country DJ, and country comedian Don Bowman. Bowman and Miller became the best known writers of funny country songs.

All these singer-songwriters recorded there, did live remotes with jingles and wrote songs. Elvis went to KDAV to sing live and record the Clover's *Fool, Fool Fool* and Big Joe Turner's *Shake Rattle and Roll* on acetates. This radio station in now KRFE, 580 a.m., located at 66th and MLK, owned by Wade Wilkes. They welcome visitors. It has to be the only place that Elvis, Buddy, Waylon, and Bill Mack all recorded. Johnny Cash sang live there. Waylon and Buddy became great friends through radio. Ben Hall, another KDAV disc jockey and songwriter, filmed in color at the Fair Park Coliseum. One video shows Johnny Cash, Carl Perkins, Elvis, Buddy and his friends.

Wade's dad, Big Ed Wilkes, owner of KDAV, managed country comedian, Jerry Clower on MCA Records. He sent Joe Ely's demo tape to MCA. Bob Livingston also sent one of the tapes I gave him to MCA. This led to a contract. Pappy Dave Stone, the first owner of KDAV, helped Buddy get his record contract with Decca/MCA.

Another disc jockey at KDAV was Arlie Duff. He wrote the country classic, *Y'all Come*. It has been recorded by nineteen well-known artists, including Bing Crosby. When Waylon Jennings and Don Bowman were hired by the Corbin brothers, Slim, Sky and Larry, of KLLL, Buddy started to hang around there. They all did jingles, sang live, wrote songs and recorded. Niki Sullivan, one of the original Crickets, was also a singing

DJ at KLLL. Sky Corbin has an excellent long article about this radio era and the intense competition between KLLL and KDAV. All the DJs had mottos. Sky Corbin's was "lover, fighter, wild horse rider, and a purty fair windmill man."

Don Bowman's motto was "come a foggin' cowboy." He'd make fun of the sponsors and get fired. We played poker together. He'd take breaks in the poker game to sing funny songs. I played poker with Buddy Holly before and after he got famous. He was incredibly polite and never had a big head. The nation only knew Buddy Holly for less than two years. He was the most famous guy around Lubbock from the age of fourteen.

Niki Sullivan, an original Cricket, and I had a singing duo as children. We cut little acetates in 1948. We also appeared several times on Bob Nash's kid talent show on KFYO. This was at the Tech Theatre. Buddy Holly and Charlene Hancock, Tommy's wife, also appeared on this show. Larry Holley, Buddy's brother, financed his early career, buying him a guitar and whatever else he needed. Buddy recorded twenty acetates at KDAV from 1953 until 1957. He also did a lot of recording at KLLL. Larry Holley said Niki was the most talented Cricket other than Buddy. All of Buddy's band mates and all of Joe Ely's band mates in his original band were musicians as children.

Buddy and Elvis met at the Cotton Club. Buddy taught Elvis the lyrics to the Drifters' *Money Honey*. After that, Buddy met Elvis on each of his Lubbock visits. I think Elvis went to the Cotton Club on every Lubbock appearance. When Elvis played a show at the Johnson Connelly Pontiac showroom, Buddy fronted him. Mac Davis was there. I was too.

The last time Elvis played the Fair Park Coliseum, on April 10, 1956, he was as famous as it gets. Buddy Holly, Sonny Curtis, Jerry Allison and Don Guess were a front act. They did two shows and played for over 10,000 people. Those wonderful I.G. Holmes photos, taken at several locations, usually show Buddy and his pals with Elvis. Lubbock had a population of 80,000 at the time. Elvis was still signing everything put in front of him. Not many people could have signing women as a hobby.

Many of the acetates recorded at KLLL and KDAV by Buddy and others were later released, many as bootlegs. When Buddy Holly recorded four songs at KDAV, the demo got him his first record contract. It wasn't just Lubbock radio that was so supportive of Buddy Holly. The City of Lubbock hired him to play at teenage dances. He appeared at Lubbock High School assemblies and many other places in town.

Everyone in Lubbock cheered Buddy Holly on with his career. The newspaper reports were always positive. At one teenage gig, maybe at the Glassarama, there was only a small crowd. Some of us were doing the "dirty bop." The *Lubbock Avalanche-Journal* had photos the next day showing people with their eyes covered with a black strip. Sonny Curtis mentions that in his song, *The Real Buddy Holly Story*. When Buddy Holly and the Crickets were on the Ed Sullivan show, the newspaper featured it. The whole town watched.

Buddy was fighting with his manager Norman Petty over money before he died. They were totally estranged. Larry Holley told me that Norman said to Buddy, "I'll see you dead before you get a penny." A few weeks later, Buddy was dead. When Buddy Holly died in a plane crash, it was headline news in the *Lubbock Avalanche-Journal*. Over 1000 people attended the funeral on February 7, 1959. Buddy was only twenty-two years old. His widow, Maria Elena Holly, was too upset to attend. The pall bearers were all songwriters and musicians that had played with Buddy: Niki Sullivan, Jerry Allison, Joe B. Mauldin, Sonny Curtis, Bob Montgomery and Phil Everly. Elvis was in the Army. He had Colonel Tom send a large wreath of yellow roses.

In 1976, I was managing the Joe Ely Band from Lubbock. They had recorded an as-yet-to-be-released album for MCA Records. I was in Nashville to meet with the MCA execs. They wanted Joe to get a booking contract and mentioned some unheard of two-man shops. Bob Neal, Elvis' first manager, had great success in talent managing and booking. He sold his agency to the William Morris Agency, the biggest booking agency in the world, and stayed on as president of the Nashville branch.

I called the William Morris Agency and explained to the secretary that I did indeed know Bob Neal, as we had met at the Cotton Club in Lubbock, Texas when he was Elvis' manager. He came right on the phone. I told him the Joe Ely Band played mostly the Cotton Club. He said that after loading up to leave there one night, a cowboy called Elvis over to his car and knocked him down. Elvis was in a rage. He made them drive all over Lubbock checking every open place as they looked for the guy. Bob Neal invited me to come right over.

Bob Neal played that, now classic, demo tape from Caldwell Studios and offered a booking contract. We agreed on a big music city strategy: Los Angeles, New York, Nashville, London, and Austin. Bob drove me back to MCA and they could not believe our good fortune. The man had been instrumental in the careers of Elvis, Carl Perkins, Johnny Cash,

Roy Orbison, Johnny Rodriguez, and many others. The William Morris Agency sent the Joe Ely Band coast to coast and to Europe, first to front Merle Haggard, then on a second trip to front the Clash. The original Joe Ely Band were Lloyd Maines, steel guitar, Jesse Taylor, electric guitar, Steve Keeton, drums and Gregg Wright, bass. Ponty Bone, on accordion, joined a little later. The band did the shows and the recording. The recorded tunes were originals from Joe Ely, Butch Hancock, and Jimmie Dale Gilmore. These three are the Flatlanders, a group founded in Lubbock in 1971. This marks their 40th year of touring and making glorious, legendary CDs, available on Amazon.

However, some of the William Morris bookings led to zig zag travel over long distances to so-called listening clubs. When I complained to Bob Neal, he'd recall the 300 dates Elvis played back in 1955. Four guys in Elvis' pink Cadillac. When Buddy made some money, he bought a pink Cadillac. Joe Ely bought a pristine, 1957 pink Cadillac that was much nicer than either of their pink Cadillacs.

When I'd hear from Bob Neal, it was very good news, especially the fantastic, uniformly-rave, album and performance reviews from newspapers and magazines every where. *Time Magazine* devoted a full page to Joe Ely. The earliest big rock critic to praise Joe Ely was Joe Nick Patoski, author of the definitive and critically-acclaimed *Willie Nelson: An Epic Life*. After one year, MCA was in turmoil. Big stars were leaving or filing lawsuits. We were told they might not re-new the option to make a second record. MCA regularly fired everyone we liked. Bob Neal thought the band should go to Los Angeles for a one-nighter.

He booked the Joe Ely Band into the best known club on the West Coast, the Palomino, owned by his dear pal, Tommy Thomas. We alerted other record companies. They drove back and forth to L.A. in a Dodge Van to play only one night. Robert Hilburn, the top rock critic for the *Los Angeles Times* came with his date, Linda Ronstadt.

The Joe Ely Band loved to play music. They started on time, took short breaks, and played until someone made them stop. Robert Hilburn wrote that Ely could be "the most important male singer to emerge in country music since the mid-60s crop of Waylon Jennings, Merle Haggard and Willie Nelson." The long review with pictures took up the whole fine arts section of the biggest newspaper in the country. Hilburn praised each of the band members individually. He was blown away when they just kept playing when the lights came on at closing time. After that, several major record companies were interested.

The last time I saw Bob Neal was at the Old Waldorf in San Francisco on February 22, 1979. Little Pete, a black dwarf who was always around Stubb's Bar-B-Q, was traveling with the band. To open the show, Little Pete came out and announced, "Lubbock, Texas produces the Joe Ely Band!" Then he jumped off the elevated stage and Bo Billingsley, our beloved, giant roady, caught him. Bob Neal, the old showman that had seen it all, just loved that.

THIS ARTICLE APPEARED FIRST ON VIRTUALUBBOCK.COM AND TRUCKIN', AND THEN ON OVER 200 WEB SITES IN COUNTRIES ALL AROUND THE WORLD.

I've Been Lucky, Very Lucky: Memory Highlights

In gambling, no one is supposedly luckier than anyone else over the long run. In life, so many things depend on luck: historical events, the times, and for other people, hard work. I never worked at anything over about three hours per day once I quit gambling full time. That is with the exception of research and writing which I do not consider work. I worked hard as a poker player, but when there was no poker, I found a strange happiness in the idleness and freedom of time. Time gets all that more mysterious when you have a lot of it free to do as you wish. I've had more free time than any man listed as working. I was always totally honest about money, but I stole my time back from my employer.

I live in the place of my birth, Lubbock, Texas. I've never wanted to leave here, and turned down several opportunities elsewhere. Folks knew I was creative about being lazy even as a kid. I got this job at the grocery store on double stamp day carrying out groceries. Another lad and I decided to hide under these large cardboard boxes in the back to avoid work. I was fired. I had a lawn service with two other guys. One would mow. One would edge, and I'd get them the job. One summer, we stole watermelons from this store that left them outside and sold them door to door to get the money for the swimming pool.

When I was 14, a group of guys went bowling and played poker after that. I was the big winner and hooked. In high school, we'd play poker all night Saturday nights after our dates. I always won. From the very earliest, poker always brought in extra money. I have never had a losing year. In high school, I'd deal blackjack at the various annual signing parties, and win all their money. At 18, I won $300 in a poker game and was off and running. The lucky part here was that *Maverick* was on TV, a series about a poker player. This was a big advertisement for the poker games I ran. My parents went broke and poker put me through college.

When I got out of college in 1965, I got a job as a traveling salesman for McGraw-Hill Book Company. I sold textbooks to colleges, high schools, government programs, and private schools. It was at the time of Lyndon Johnson's War on Poverty with a great deal of government money going into adult education. Our sales soared. My territory was all of New Mexico and about half of Texas, a land I adore. It was an easy gig. I bought a new Mustang and loved it. I got married then, way above my head, to a beautiful, smart woman. That lasted ten years. McGraw-Hill was the industry leader. I got to travel all over: New York, New Orleans, Miami and many states. I was proud to be part of them, and they were the very best dressers, wearing all wool suits, or sports coats, and slacks. Being a gambler, all I had to buy were ties. I already dressed better than most of them.

Again, I got lucky, I entered graduate school in 1969 in time for the Sixties upheaval of protests, hippies and all that. I wrote for the *Catalyst*, an underground newspaper. Several of us sued the university on a first amendment case in federal court when the newspaper was banned from sale on campus. I was the second to testify at the trial. The banning was because of a satire article I wrote mocking the new football coach, Jim Carlen. He was this fat, pot-bellied guy who said he would have "no fat players or coaches." We had a picture of his fat gut, with the title, *Morality Fats*. We won the lawsuit.

When I finished my Ph.D. in 1974, I wanted to stay in Lubbock. First my wife got me a job selling radio advertising for country station KEND, run by Lew Dee and Paul Beane. A few months later, she got me a job with KCBD-TV, the NBC affiliate as an Account Executive. This was so easy. There were three local TV stations, no cable, and we got commissions on national sales. In 1975, my wife told me she had seen the Joe Ely Band at Main Street Saloon, and I needed to go. The first night, I told Joe I wanted to be his manager, which I became. I was the manager for the Joe Ely Band's first three classic albums on MCA Records. Again, luck was there.

This was the Willie, Waylon, Jerry Jeff time with Austin being huge. I gave Ely's demo tapes to Big Ed Wilkes, a radio DJ and local celebrity, and Bob Livingston, bass player for Jerry Jeff Walker. As luck would have it, both tapes arrived at the same A & R meeting at MCA Records in L.A. With Butch Hancock's help, we arranged a live audition in Austin at the Split Rail, as they were looking for Austin bands. Many of the crowd in the small club were former Lubbock residents. Doug Sahm came and gave a little speech welcoming Joe. Alvin Crow and Butch Hancock set in. Elyse Gilmore Yates, Jimmie Dale Gilmore's and Jo Carol Pierce's daughter, sang Butch Hancock's classic song "If You Were A Bluebird." She was twelve. The MCA guys loved the Joe Ely Band and negotiations began. After all the numbers for the recording contract were agreed on, some guy from MCA called me to tell me that the A & R man and attorney, Bob Davis, had been fired and the deal was off. Wow!

I called the MCA Records Company President, Mike Maitland, to express my righteous West Texas outrage. We had been doing what they said, which meant no bookings because we were to leave for the studio any day. We had verbal agreements with our lawyer as witness. I told him we would sue him here in Lubbock, where we were most popular. I knew he was up to his ass in lawsuits already! However, I offered a fair compromise. If he would come to Lubbock to see the Joe Ely Band at Fat Dawg's, I'd make no claim if he did not want to sign them. I'll never forget what he said, "I can't come to Fat Dawg's. I have to go to Japan with Elton John. *O.K. then.*"

"O.K. what?" I asked.

"O.K. we'll do the deal." he said. And we had a record contract

After one year, MCA was in huge upheaval with lawsuits and stars leaving. We heard Joe might be dropped, even though he had the best reviews of anyone on the label, and sales were fine. Through Bob Neal, our booking agent and Elvis' first manager, a booking was arranged at the famed Palomino Club in North Hollywood. Robert Hilburn, the major rock critic of the *Los Angeles Times*, gave them a rave, amazing, long review and saved the contract again. Luck is always there.

In politics, I became very close friends with Helen DeVitt Jones. With her sister, they were the richest people in town. They owned the Mallet Ranch, 54,000 contiguous acres in four Texas counties: Hockley, Terry, Yoakum, and Cochran. There were 1100 oil wells. and It is still pumping.

Helen was a magnificent person all around, one of the very best people I have ever met. She was a graduate of Berkeley and a real liberal. She donated money to fabulous causes. She allowed me to drive her Cadillacs or use her swimming pool any time I wanted. She had a unique and precise common sense wisdom developed from age and experience. We would have long visits where she told me her history and the history of the Mallet Ranch. Once, Sasha and I went out there when Sasha had first started grade school. Helen got out childhood pictures of her beautiful daughter. She wept. With her age, wisdom, legendary generosity, and fortune, she was above ordinary self-interest or self-centered motivations. I loved her as a very, very dear friend. I'd go with Helen to the hospital to visit her sister, Christine DeVitt, who lived there five years. The two richest women in town might yell and argue and actually show anger, but they loved each other deeply. Both lived until 97 or 98.

After ten years in television, I was fired after a merger. You get a pension after ten years. I left there and went to Texas Tech as a visiting professor the next day. Helen Jones was one of Texas Tech's biggest donors already, but she pitched my department over a hundred thousand, which was chicken feed, considering her donations. She gave away $27 million that I know of. I was a visiting Professor for two years, then I proposed a deal. I'd drop to the next lower rank, lecturer, but I'd keep the professor's salary. That was agreed. That was heaven. I didn't have to go to meetings with the world's most boring humans. Though never tenured, I lasted twenty years. I had only two jobs and was never out of work a day the last thirty years of my work life. And there was plenty of time for literature, and poker, and staring at the sky.

When I was fired off the TV job, I had a minor arrest record, but the Tech Management Department did no real background checks. I listed as references several of the richest women in West Texas: Helen DeVitt Jones, Jane Livermore, Mary Belle Macy, Elizabeth Masterson, and the most powerful political guy in Lubbock, banker Charley Pope.

Teaching at Texas Tech University for twenty years was absolutely wonderful for me! As a child, I'd played all over the campus. I had three degrees from there and love it. Like my father and mother before me, my ashes will be spread on the beautiful Texas Tech University campus when I die. Being lucky, the university just built a chapel about thirty yards from the Hughes family burial site. Free perpetual care, and now a chapel. Thanks.

Teaching at Texas Tech was the luckiest career thing of my life. Right off, they assigned me to teach two classes a day, three days a week, with 430 undergraduate students in each one-hour class. I called the class, Leadership and Management. Earlier, I had wanted to be an actor, and had done several stage comedies in local theater. There was a big stage, and I roamed it all speaking without a microphone. That allowed for bigger gestures, more histrionics, and more *acting*. I did "some" comedy, usually sure-fire monologues a few minutes long. The other faculty called me, "The Entertainer." They did not mean it as a compliment, but I sure took it as one. I'm more comfortable on a large stage speaking to people than I am at a meeting or most anything else. I was *in charge*, and that was a joke and a legend as to how mean I was to people who talked in class. I'd tell them that I have shot over the heads of more people than this. I'd say, "Hey, you in the bright yellow shirt. I'm working here. I don't come down to McDonald's and bother you while you work." Or to a couple, "Hey this is a college class, not a date. No foreplay, please." I got some of the highest teacher evaluations, and that meant a lot to me. I was as friendly and respectful as I could be to those young adults, not kids, adults. I learned all their names in a small class.

For many years, I taught seminar-size Honors classes with the brightest students, and that was a rich experience. I was also the Director of Petroleum Land Management, now called Energy Commerce, for fifteen years. The students were training for jobs in the oil business, mostly as land men and lease traders. I met some very wonderful students and we suffered through the usual booms and busts of the oil business. The program would have died when oil was $9 a barrel if it had not have been for Helen DeVitt Jones and our collective political influence. But luck is here for those students. Now oil is very high, and those great students can get high-paying jobs.

In 1988, Texas State Treasurer Ann Richards was the keynote speaker at the Democratic Convention. She said George H.W. Bush was "born with a silver foot in his mouth." The line drew great laughter and applause and became world-famous, quoted in every newspaper and magazine and on every T.V. show. I had originally written that line in a jokes column in Lubbock's underground newspaper, *The Catalyst*. A small item in *Texas Monthly Magazine* gave me credit as the author of the line. Ann Richards became identified with that line. George Bush sent her a "silver foot" necklace. She went on to be Governor of Texas. I talked with her about this once at Jerry Jeff's birthday party. This encouraged me to write more.

A salesman or a college teacher can make it on three hours work per day, maybe less. As a college teacher, I usually worked three days per week, and sometimes two. I'm proud of being lazy. It always gave me plenty of time to day dream about being a writer and what I was going to write. As a gambler and a band manager, I worked more hours than in my straight jobs. Smart people rent out their brains by the hour. I always had a way to minimize the hours I'd sell.

Poker Then and Poker Now: Praise for the Rio and Caesar's: Paradise Found

A t the World Series of Poker, they announce the event and coveted bracelet winners and then play the national anthem of the country they come from. Play stops at all the cash games and many players stand and remove their hats. When an American won, my table stood with their hands over their hearts and sang. I looked out over that vast sea of poker players and was overcome by emotion. The song always gives me tingles but there was also a love and astonishment at how wonderful the playing conditions have become for this sport. Yes, it is a sport.

I cannot sing enough praise for the poker management of Caesar's. I had long conversations with Bill Sattler, Director of Poker, and also Jake Reville, Cathy Klufer and Carrie Jacobs. For twenty years, I taught management subjects at Texas Tech University. The magnificent professionalism of Caesar's management makes me wish I could go lecture on how great they are. I've never lost at the Rio, but only played there nine times. I'm not trying to beat the best in the world anymore. I'm too old.

My first trip to the World Series was in 1975. I stayed in the old side of Binion's, in the world's worst room. I opened the window and there playing Texas music on a flat bed truck was my friend, Kenny Maines, Natalie's uncle. The World Series was a chance to get reacquainted with road gamblers I had not seen in a while. Early main event winners came from my area of West Texas: Amarillo, Odessa, Abilene, Lubbock, and San Angelo. Most of the gamblers in the pictures of the first two World Series were from Texas. There were "Outside Men" Amarillo Slim, Bryan "Sailor" Roberts, Doyle "Texas Dolly" Brunson, Jack "Treetop" Straus,

Crandell Addington, Aubrey Day, James "Tennessee Longgoodie" Roy, Pat Renfro, Puggy Pearson, Johnny Moss and Bill Smith. Outside men made their living from poker. These are not to be confused with the Mafia outside men. Inside men were bookies, loan sharks, casino workers, dice game and poker game owners. Chill Wills, the famous character actor from the movie *Giant*, was there. He had been a boyhood friend of Johnny Moss and Benny Binion in Dallas. There were several world-class con men, lead by Titanic Thompson, Joe Floyd, and two neighbors I won't mention.

The next year, I got big lucky again and won $4000 the first night or so. I was staying next door to Binion's in the old Mint, which Binion's later acquired. As I left the casino, I was approached by "working girls," whores: a white one, an African-American, an Asian, and a Hispanic. Two beefy security guards offered to walk me to the Mint, not because of the whores, but you are playing in public in downtown Las Vegas with the riff-raff of the world trying to see your hole cards and counting your stack. One year, a thief stole a woman's purse and ran. Two of Binion's extra-large sized security guards gave chase, knocking several old ladies from slot machines and quarters were everywhere on the floor. They tackled him by a dice table at the Mint after knocking over a few unlucky shooters. They escorted him to back to Binion's. Poker table gossip around Binion's was basically the grifters, cheaters, thieves and fools stay away or get the living hell beat out of them.

Jack Binion was the brains behind the World Series and its growth. You could hear the paging system constantly, "Telephone call for Mr. Binion, Mr. Jack Binion." He approved markers, selected the fantastic menu which included every type of seafood imaginable, and bear, elk, dove, quail and game animals. One always thanked both Jack and Benny Binion because they were our most gracious hosts.

One year, the culinary workers were on strike and picketers were attempting to block the casino entrances. The union, casino, and Las Vegas police all had their own video taping going. Jack Binion and his mother walked through the angry, shouting crowd, in a fearless, no care in the world way. There was a large parade of union people down Fremont Street in front of the casino. I'm normally pro-union, but the poker players all wore, "I BACK JACK" buttons. Around The Shop several including me wore Binion's hats and coats and we were loyal. When our homeboy, Bill Smith, won the World Series main event in 1985, we were cheering, and happy and so cohesive in our pride. Just like some of the other World champs, Sailor Roberts and Amarillo Slim, he couldn't beat The Shop.

Right before the start of the World Series, it was crazy. A few tables go by of "racehorse freezeout." The brokes and desperadoes that can't pump the ten dimes for the change in, pool their money and go for one-hand, one-table satellites. Put up a $1000 plus juice and you get a shot.

One year, the power failed for a moment or two. There was a poker only cage on the main floor to collect tournament entry money. This chip runner stole $200,000, got a big bag from the gift shop and successfully fled to the Philippines.

At the World Series, the Master of Ceremonies often was Gabe Kaplan, of *Welcome Back Kotter.* He was actually a great, big-time poker player. Chip Reese and Phil Hellmuth were both impressive on the mike and telephone interviews.

At the early World Series, and Binion's cash games, there seemed to be very regular squabbles, and the floor man was making constant, obvious rulings. We called them the "famous Binion's five-dollar squabble" because they were holding up the game. The Rio is almost void of that. One reason is that early players often blamed the dealer for bad luck and bad beats. No matter how tough the Binions were, and they were even tougher than you think, they allowed verbal and even physical abuse of the dealers. I have only played at the Rio nine or so times. I've just never seen any of this. The player's manners are terrific compared to the past. Johnny Moss was known for being abusive to dealers. Puggy Pearson was worse. He pissed on a dealer. Another Hall of Famer, Joe Bernstein, bit a dealer. Puggy wore costumes. Once he came as a Native American, with a full war bonnet with war paint and feathers to the floor. At the time of the first Gulf War, he came as Saddam Hussein. Puggy parked a motor home outside Binion's back door. On the side was painted, "I'll play any man from any land any game that he can name for any amount that he can count." He meant it. Puggy was a neighbor of my cousin's, Bill Stapp. Given poker's stigma, he told the neighborhood he was a school teacher.

Bad behavior included frequently tearing up the offensive bad beat cards, throwing cards, especially at the dealer.

The old regular retirees who came to Binion's in the early morning like shift workers would tip the dealer fifty cents. They might throw a dollar chip, and say, "Half back." Once at the Mirage, Bill Gates played the 3-6 limit. He'd throw a dollar and say, "Half back."

Late one night, back when I was damn fool enough to drink, I was ridiculing the half back crowd, and palming all the fifty cent pieces in the game and taking them off the table, which is technically rat holing, and against the rules. After a while, I looked behind me, and there was a plain clothes Binion's tough. He gave me a really scary look, and opened his jacket to expose a big semi-automatic pistol. My behavior improved in a heart beat, and the heart beats were coming fast.

One of the greatest things about the early World Series, were the stories I'd collect. For over fifty years, I've collected the stories and old gambling and West Texas sayings. At the Rio, I got on a really lucky rush, my best sequence of cards all year. I said, "I'm holding more hands than any manicurist in town. That hand was as big as a foot." After fifty years, the table still laughs.

I wore a hat with my novel title, and JohnnyHughes.com on it. After awhile, someone would ask if I was Johnny Hughes. I'd reply, "Do you think I'd wear this stupid hat if I wasn't?" At that World Series, I met Lance Bradley, editor of *Bluff Magazine*, and the legendary Kevin Mathers, another *Bluff Magazine* editor. I swapped stories with Toupee Jay at the Cardoza booth manned by a young man with the great name of Casagrande. I talked with Nolan Dalla who I remember a little as a loud and funny drunk at the poker table and the coffee shop, long ago. He was their press guy and he was with Benny Behan, the owner's son, which made it even funnier. He was that rarity, a charming drunk, like me. One thing that has not changed, but grown much richer, is the stories poker players share. Now there are top writers like Al Can't Hang, Dan Michalski, and Paul "Dr. Pauly" McGuire documenting poker's history as it happens.

Jack Binion was the real leader and major brain behind the growth of the World Series. When he left, his sister Becky Behen, oversaw a steady decline. Once there was a dealer walk out and she bad mouthed them in the newspaper. She didn't pay the floor staff the agreed on amount. The world class buffet went to plastic eating utensils.

When Binion's Horseshoe closed, I went to downtown Las Vegas and peeked in the front window. One lone lamp illuminated the ghost like dice tables, and slot machines. It reminded me of a dark theater, which it really was, with the lone work light. That was poker's darkest hour, and Harrah's rode to the rescue like John Wayne and the U.S. Cavalry. Hear the bugle?

I've been robbed and arrested several times because of poker. I'd have to move or the game would have to move. I've played poker many places. Once in the basement of a Catholic hospital, an angry nun broke up the game. In the dorms, the athletic trainer broke up the game. We played in a car lot with only four chairs. Late arrivals had to sit on a tire. Once we played above a cold storage facility. We wore coats, our teeth were rattling and we played seven-five low ball very fast to keep warm. I played regularly in a whore house. Poker was a lot of trouble.

In going to the World Series, I'd go watch the Lady's event, seven stud on Mother's Day. I was there when Poker Hall of Famer Barbara Enright was the first woman at the main event final table.

The contrast with the ideal playing conditions at the Rio is striking. There was very little waiting time for a seat in the cash games. The people from all over the world were friendly conversationalists. The dealer training and employee courtesy add to the enjoyment. Harrah's saved poker and made it what it is today. Their corporate culture produces skilled leaders like Bill Sattler, Jake Reville, Cathy Klufa and Carrie Jacobs. That culture can be felt on the green felt. Good vibes! Poker has come a long way. Caesar's deserves a lot of the credit. I stay at the centrally located and reasonable Imperial Palace, another

Caesar's property with a nice, small poker room. I'll be back!

POKERATI.COM

The Passing of Texas Culture

T he high stakes Texas hold 'em game that floats around West Texas was
always a cultural refuge for me where I could find home folks, hear
Texan spoken, eat the best home-cooked, native foods and enjoy the always
good natured joking and ribbing that are part of it. My dear poker friends
also represented the Texas culture a little better than everyone else. As time
passes, everything must keep changing. Poker has become more and more
universal and diverse. Last week, a barefoot twenty-one year old won three
dimes here. The best player is an Indian doctor's son who is great friends
with one of the Brownfield farmer/gamblers. There are Chinese, Yankees,
Frat Rats and women playing poker now.

It is so funny to hear the words "Texas Hold 'Em" over and over on
T.V. Poker is legal in all the neighboring states: New Mexico, Oklahoma,
Colorado and Louisiana. Not Texas. In the early days of the World Series
of Poker, Texans dominated and the crowd had many Texans. Texans are
not as special anymore.

In Lubbock, I can observe the passing of Texas culture as a constant
process of sad and unyielding change. As I leave the house, I can go west
to the Starbucks, university, medical district, chain restaurant, mall, and
newer parts of town with streets that look like any other medium-size city.
The older, family-owned businesses close and generic anywhere America
replaces it. The horse auction even closed.

I can go east to the blue-collar parts of town where the restaurant has
native Texas food, clothing, language and a certain laid back humorous
attitude. At the Ranch House, men eat with their hats on, most of which
are gimme or baseball hats, with cowboy hats now being in the minority.
The men have enormous amounts of stuff in their shirt pockets: pens,

papers, and contracts. Older ladies still have big, big hair. On the west side of town, people are ambitious, faster paced, more stressed, serious and road raged. Most are on cell phones or wishing they were. Folks leave each other alone.

At the Ranch House, the pace is slower and it is o.k., even expected, that you converse with strangers in certain comforting rituals, "You working hard or hardly working?" or "Is it hot enough for you?"

On the older side of town, a cheese omelet, whole wheat toast and coffee is four bucks. At Starbucks, most uptight yups drop four bucks or more for custom coffee.

It's like in the University/Medical area, the worker bees are all becoming something or writing a resume for the future. At the Ranch House or the Truck Stop, folks are already what they are. They appear happier. They don't appear as healthy. They don't appear as well off financially, but they have their life and it is all right with them.

I've always noticed that my heavily West Texas poker pals laugh and joke all through the day and like each other. We celebrate Texas, but all that is passing. My former academic colleagues were nearly all from the Midwest. A humorless, boring group that always badmouthed Texas. None ever leave, tenure being so easy and forgiving.

The small towns hold on to Texas food, language, and values in such a way that they are ten years behind if you call it behind.

I'll head for breakfast at the truck stop where I'll be observing the hats, and the "howdies" and the, "Can I hep' yew?" Folks will be reading the paper, taking their time and drinking too much coffee. I do so love Texas but I am afraid that much of what is so special about Texas culture is fading away. It is hard for the new folks to tell the fake Texas culture from the real. Whatever you do, don't wise up or wake up the Yankees that keep moving here.

Virtualubbock.Com

Remembering Jesse "Guitar" Taylor

When the Joe Ely Band first hit Nashville to record their album for MCA, after a bit of nipping, Jesse had them drive him to the Nashville Police Station, where he could piss on the door. By the time I arrived, they had stolen a giant, green Tanqueray sign, larger than a man, made of ply board. MCA put me up in a fancy joint, and the band in a $9 day motel in Murfeesboro, Tennessee run by a hillbilly woman who had been to prison for selling downers. When I asked how the band ended up in her joint, she said, "They couldn't find nobody to good deal them, so I good dealed them my own self." Jesse was a gentle man, and like Joe Ely, he was home on the highway. He always had a paperback book going, many which reminded me of the beatnik, hippy days. I was alone awhile yesterday with Jesse Taylor's art and my crystal-clear memories. He always got the dice wrong in his drawings, showing a six and an ace at the same time. Once in San Francisco, Jesse played lucky and won all my money shooting craps, and I had a terrifying walk through 4 a.m. China town back to my MCA-selected fancy joint which had a whirlpool and a real, but small, palm tree.

Last night, at the Underwood Center, and later at Tornado Gallery, Jesse was honored in Lubbock at an annual event, JesseFest. Pictures are available on Tony Greer, Jennifer Greer, and Larry Simmons pages on facebook, and on Tornado Gallery's page. Once, Jesse jumped off that main bridge in Austin. Long ago, circa 1977, Joey, Jesse, and some girl were arrested outside Sweetwater for a little bag of pot. As usual, I was called in the middle of the night, when I was higher than a hawk's nest, and drunker than Cooter Brown. Joe explained the deal, and he and I both knew Jesse had a handful of warrants out, and unresolved entanglements with Texas laws. The band was to play the Cotton Club that night. I got the Sheriff of Nolan County on the phone, and agreed that Joe would plead guilty, and I'd send Bo with $2500 cash. I knew it was Jesse's dope, and Joe did not smoke dope. One cannot describe the bond these two guys had, from teenage years to a million miles of world travel. Marijuana was still a minor felony in Texas, so Joe caught a year's probation. A dangerous year when he was traveling the high roads and back roads with all manner of outlaw. I went with Joe to Sweetwater to see the world's most boring probation officer. The only artifact on his desk, in his tiny cubicle, was a baseball he had purchased when he attended a big league baseball game. It sounded like the only time he ventured out of Sweetwater. Joe Ely showed a lot of love, to take a felony fall for his road partner and band mate.

At Jesse's funeral, John Reed and Bobbie Earl Smith were eloquent. The Texana Dames: Charlene Hancock, Conni Hancock, and Traci Lamar, played as beautiful as they are. Ponty Bone and John were also perfect with the music. At the graveside, Jimmie Dale Gilmore, Butch Hancock, and Terry Allen all spoke, and it was very moving. Jimmie Dale said, "Jesse was our bodyguard." Amen to that.

I knew Jesse was my backup in every joint I walked in, and no matter how awful I acted. I recall one great night when the Clash and the Joe Ely Band played Lubbock, and there was an after hours party. Along about dawn, this fellow had a choke hold on me. He had done some time in prison for killing some feller who probably needed killing. Jesse was there in a flash. A flash!

In a novel I am writing, the characters ponder luck, fortune, and those twists of fate that create a series of seeming unlikely coincidences. If this had not happened, this would not have happened. Jesse Taylor was hitchhiking down East Broadway in Lubbock when C.B. "Stubbs" Stubblefield picked him up. Together, they created the Sunday Night Jams at Stubbs. Joe and Sharon Ely became close friends of Stubbs. Sharon and singer/songwriter Kimmie Rhodes cooked up and bottled the first Stubbs' Bar-B-Que Sauce in the Ely's kitchen. They put it in old, sterilized whiskey bottles of varied shapes and sold it to get Stubbs a few coin, a noble, but eternal quest. Now, Stubbs' Bar-B-Que Sauce sells world wide. It is number six in the top ten bar-b-q sauces in America. Sharon Ely has created a new product, Holy Posole, which is selling on Amazon, and in H.E.B. Stores all over central Texas. Search it.

After the Joe Ely Band moved to Austin, Stubbs' Lubbock location really went down hill. Stubbs could spy me as a gambler, and a bit of a soft touch. He hit me up for money to open up rather often. Stubbs had some con about him. When Sasha was a toddler, we'd go down to Stubbs' when it was just him and a circle of old black men swapping stories. She'd play all over the joint, and we could always try to eat ourselves even.

Sasha and I were alone with Stubbs once when about a dozen gang-looking teenagers came in, two of them women. Stubbs was on his feet shouting, "I told y'all not to come in here! Get out of here."

"Now Stubbs," one of them said, "We just want to get a couple of pounds of meat to go."

"Y'all get out of here, now." Stubbs shouted. They beat a most hasty retreat. Sasha's eyes were as big as Cadillac hub cabs.

I was in Austin when Stubbs was closed by the health department. Stubbs was quoted in the newspaper as saying, "Cock roaches are God's doings." Stubbs told Jade, Sasha, and I about all the support, and donations. George Thorogood sent a big check. Stubbs said, "One man in Chicago has taken to his bed, and won't get up until Stubbs' is re-opened." Jesse Taylor showed up alone, and began a thorough and needed cleaning of the kitchen. Jesse had so much character. I almost helped. Jesse Taylor has been inducted into the West Texas Walk of Fame in Lubbock, Texas.

Truckin'

A SECOND VOLUME OF MY COLLECTED WRITINGS WILL
BE AVAILABLE ON ALL AMAZONS IN A FEW MONTHS.

Acknowledgements and Many Thanks To:

Michael Caselli, Chris Bradshaw, and Philip Conneller of *Bluff Europe*. Eric Morris and Lance Bradley of *Bluff Magazine*, the two biggest and most successful poker magazines in the world! Mason Malmuth and the *TwoPlusTwo Poker Forum*, and every single poster on there. Chris Ogelsby of *virtualubbock.com*, Anthony Kelly of *Player Ireland*, Joe Nick Patoski, Amarillo Slim, Casey Monahan, Director of the Texas Music Office, Paul "Dr. Pauly" McGuire, Iggy, Dan Michalski and Al Can't Hang of *Pokerati. com, Poker News, Hendon Mob, Poker Forum, Bet-the-Pot.com, Poker Pages*, Tommy Thomas, son of Titanic Thompson, Crandell Addington and Doyle Brunson, great sources for my history research, and my reviewers. To all my reviewers and the great radio hosts: Ashley Adams and Doug Weischadle, producer, of *House of Cards Radio*, Ryan Sayer, Big SC, and Robin and Pamela Jones of the *OnTilt Radio Network*, Lou Krieger of *Hold 'em Radio*, *Filthy Limper*, and John Hartness and Curtis Krumel of *Gambling Tales*, Ben Hudson and Jamie Mitchell of *iUniverse*, Dr. David Schwartz and Kelli Luchs of the University of Nevada, Las Vegas Gaming Research Center, Jeff and Sharon Hammond of Copy Outlet, Jon Holmes and the Southwest Collection at Texas Tech, Jim Douglass and Dave King of FoxTalk Radio, Jim Stewart, Wade Wilkes, and Kenny Ketner of KRFE, Tornado Gallery, Dr. Kim Boal, Dean Carl Stem, Dr. Carlton Whitehead, KCBD-TV, facebook and all my friends there, Marshall Trimble, Matthew Parvis, William Kerns, Chuck Blount, W.C. Stapp, and James Dodd. Thanks to English rocker Colin Gillman, who wrote and recorded a song about me.

Special thanks to my musical friends, Ponty Bone and Lloyd Maines, who produced, played several instruments on, and sang on demonstration tapes of songs I wrote with varied singers, recorded at the legendary Caldwell Studios. To the friends who co-wrote songs with me, and recorded them: Vic Jones, Joey Allen, Willie Redden, Chuck Barnes, Joel Hughes, and Jo Ann Park-Williams. Thanks also to Jane, Janie and Rosie, Teddy, and Leola.

If you do a search of Johnny Hughes, poker, and pod casts, you will find several radio interviews.

Sources, References, Highly Recommended Books

Subject...Author

Biographies

AMARILLO SLIM...Greg Dinkins, ARNOLD ROTHSTEIN... David Pietrusza, ARNOLD ROTHSTEIN...Leo Katcher, ARNOLD ROTHSTEIN...Nick Tosches, BAT MASTERSON...Robert DeArment, BEN THOMPSON...Floyd Streeter, BEN THOMPSON...G.R. Williamson, DOC HOLLIDAY...Bob Boze Bell, DOC HOLLIDAY...D.J. Herda, DOC HOLLIDAY...Gary Roberts, DOC HOLLIDAY...John Myers, DOC HOLLIDAY...Karen Tanner, JIMMY CHAGRA... Gary Cartwright, JOE HILL..William Adler, JOHNNY MOSS...Dan Jenkins, LOTTIE DENO...Cynthia Rose, LUKE SHORT..Wayne Short, MICKEY COHEN...John Nugent, MINNESOTA FATS...R.A. Dyer, MINNESOTA FATS...Tom Fox, MINNESOTA FATS...Walter Tevis, MOTHER JONES...Linda Atkinson, NICK THE GREEK...Cy Rice, OSCAR GOODMAN...John L. Smith, QUANAH PARKER...S.C. Gwynne, SOAPY SMITH...Jane Haigh, STU UNGAR...Nolan Dalla, Peter Alston, Mike Sexton, TITANIC THOMPSON...Carlton Stowers, TITANIC THOMPSON...Kevin Cook, TITANIC THOMPSON... Richard Cambell, TONY SPILOTRO...William Roemer, STEVE WYNN...John L. Smith, WILLIE NELSON...Joe Nick Patoski, WYATT EARP...Bob Bose Bell, WYATT EARP...Casey Tefertiller, WYATT EARP...Jeff Guinn, WYATT EARP...Stuart Lake

OTHER BOOKS

AMERICAN INDIANS...six books and authors: Frederick Drunner, Jan Reid, Jo Ella Exley, Lois Lensky, Paul Carlson, S.C. Gwynne, BIG DEAL...Anthony Holden, BODY LANGUAGE...Julius Fast, BODY LANGUAGE...Mike Caro, CHEATING...Eugene Villiod, CHEATING... Simon Lovell, CHEATING...John Maskelyne, CLASSIC...Herbert O. Yardley, GAMBLING HISTORY...Bob Boze Bell, GAMBLING HISTORY, ROLL THE BONES... Dr. David Schwartz, GAMBLING HISTORY...Des Wilson, GAMBLING HISTORY...James McManus, GAMBLING HISTORY...Robert DeArment, GUNFIGHTERS...Bat Masterson, GUNFIGHTERS...Bob Boze Bell, GUNFIGHTERS...Leon Metz, GUNFIGHTERS...Paula Marks, LAS VEGAS AND THE MOB, 5 books and authors,...Barney Vinson, Dennis Griffin, Norm Clarke, Steve Fischer, Suki Chung, POKER CULTURE...Tommy Angelo, POKER CULTURE...Tony Korfman, THE OLD WEST...*True West Magazine*, THE OLD WEST...*The Handbook of Texas History*.

PERIODICALS

Bluff Magazine, Bluff Europe Magazine, Card Player, Player Ireland, Texas Monthly, Texas Observer, True West, Old West, Las Vegas Review Journal, Psychology Today, Binion's World Series of Poker, annual brochures

INTERNET AND MEDIA

A special thanks to all of these! *Google* books, *Amazon* books, search inside, *Wikipedia, YouTube*, the *History Channel, Real West TV, National Public Radio, Pod Casts..Poker Radio Shows, TwoPlusTwo Poker Forum, Pokerati. com, Poker News, Wicked Chops Poker, Hendon Mob, Tao of Poker, Poker Forum, Bet-the-Pot.com, House of Cards Radio, Hold 'em Radio, Filthy Limper Radio, OnTilt Radio Network, Hartness and Krumel Radio, The Blogfather's Party Poker Blog.*

About the Author

Johnny Hughes, Ph.D., was a professional poker player. He ran poker games to put himself through college. He sold books for McGraw-Hill Book Company. His territory was half of Texas and all of New Mexico. He was an account executive at KCBD-TV, the NBC affiliate in Lubbock. Johnny was a professor and lecturer at Texas Tech University for twenty years. He taught a variety of management subjects to undergraduate, graduate, and Honors students. He was also the Director of Petroleum Land Management. Johnny was the original manager of the Joe Ely Band, securing contracts with MCA Records and the William Morris Agency for booking. The first three albums, all on MCA Records, were recorded during this time. Johnny is the author of the novel, *Texas Poker Wisdom*, available on all Amazons, and the upcoming novel, *The Darling of Two Plus Truth*. He has written for the many magazines and web sites listed in this book.